That You Can Believe

How John's Story of Jesus Has Impacted My Life

Dedication

The Tree of Palms —in 2018, on that Saturday after Good Friday and the day before Easter, our families united for our yearly tribute to the legacy of family and the resurrection of our Lord. We planted Papa's garden as usual, signifying the dying of seeds to produce plants and the dying of Jesus to produce a kingdom for God. For our art project that year, Nana and I wanted our grandchildren's painted handprints to be placed on our living room wall as a further reminder of the legacy we would leave to the next generation.

Our local artist and elderly saint from church, Sister Ruth Jackson, painted a bare tree in a grassy field on that wall a few days before our annual Easter weekend celebration. She painted our dog, Lucky, and a robin—Papa's alter ego—on either side of that tree. But even though all other indications were that the season should be spring, the tree was bare of its leaves.

With the help of several of the mothers, Joanna, Feydra, Holly, and Karyn, the palms of the grandkids' hands were painted different shades of green and carefully pressed onto the tree to become its leaves—kind of a palm tree—sorry for the pun. Although there were several hand prints, both right and left placed on the tree, only one of each grandchild's was signed and dated. Ten separate names were written that day on ten separate palm prints, which became important to that tree's survival. The roots represented those who had gone on before, those who were no longer with us. The trunk became the lives and faith of both Nana and Papa. The branches, which were many, signified the separate families and individuals—moms, dads, uncles, and aunts.

Like all trees, this tree cannot survive without the leaves of the tree absorbing energy from the light of the (Son) above. In what kind of soil is this tree growing? Are the branches and trunk strong enough to withstand the winds and rain, the ice and heavy snow of the seasons? Are the nutrients flowing freely through roots, up the trunk, and throughout the branches making a difference in those individual leaves?

This book is dedicated to real people, to grandchildren, whose names are written on those leaves—Josiah, Fisher, Ashlyn, London, Ethan, Avyn, Ella, Creed, Kendyl, Owen, and any other grandchildren that may be born after this book's publication. Each of them has a story, and some are written in this book.

Grandchildren, we have camped together, planted Papa's Garden together, drank Nana's coffee together, worshiped together, laughed and cried, sang and prayed, and done Christmas, Thanksgiving, and Easter, all together. Nana and I have watched you all grow in your faith in God. We have witnessed most of you claim Jesus as Lord and Savior, being baptized in His name. Interestingly, most of you were baptized, not by preachers, but by moms and dads. One was baptized by me.

The oldest of you will be 18 this year and will graduate from high school in 2023; the youngest will turn 12 and graduate in 2030. Some of you are driving or learning to drive and holding down summer or weekend jobs. You have excelled, — in academics, social and life skills, and how to live within your own family dynamics. You've played football, volleyball, basketball, soccer, softball, and baseball. You have been involved in cheer, powerlifting, track, cross country, karate, and showing animals for 4H and FFA. You have gone to Christian summer camps and, of course, yearly Nana camps. Some of you have played and mastered different kinds of instruments—percussion, saxophone, trombone, clarinet, and cello for school marching band, orchestra, and jazz band; bass guitar for church worship; or piano for your own pleasure at home; others have sung in school or church choirs;

some of you have awesome writing skills; several shine at art; many have mouthwatering cooking skills; others have excelled in church plays and musicals, and all of you have received awards at one time or another. And most of the time, Nana and I have been there to witness your accomplishments.

I am excited at the thought of where adulthood will take you, whether you go to college or find a job right out of high school. I know God will be with you whether you get married or stay single, have kids of your own, or remain childless.

I am excited, mostly though, for what God will have you doing in His kingdom. That tree and those leaves, mentioned above, need the firm and rich soil of the Father's love and the light of Jesus and His salvation to produce the fruit of the Spirit—love, joy, peace, patience, kindness, goodness, faithfulness, gentleness, and self-control.

There is a scripture I would like to share with you that is one of my favorites. Philippians 1:6: *I am sure that the good work God began in you will continue until he completes it on the day when Jesus Christ comes again.* I believe that for each of you. Go with God in all you do.

Be There! Papa

Forewords

Be There! Dad, Daddy, Pop! This is how my dad would sign his letters for a long time and still does to a certain extent. Yes, I did say letters. My dad—Darell Martin—the author of this book, loves to send good ol' typed and of course, handwritten letters. He only started typing the letters because none of the grandkids could read his cursive. Most of them can now. The letters always come, what seems like out of the blue. Then you read it and you realize it is actually about some incident that happened recently, a few years ago, or maybe even many years ago, and it brings you back to that event. Almost every time I receive one of these letters from Pop, I know some tears are not far away. They are happy tears, usually of something I remember happening, but with time had forgotten specific details. It's usually not a short letter because it's always filled with very specific things that happened surrounding the event, lots of details that I'm not sure how he remembers. There is always something thoughtful in these letters, and I always come away from reading them feeling a little bit wiser and in tune with the event and with God. Weird how he's able to spin those things together without giving any specific advice. You just "LISTEN" to the words and you understand.

This is also how I remember him raising my two brothers, sister, and me. He wasn't the type that gave you a lot of specific life instructions like change your oil or don't spit on your sister's head (although I do remember him saying both of those to me at least once). He was more of a, here's your Bible and here's the church, you know what you should do, type of guy. And when he did impart some specific wisdom on me it usually was pretty impactful and stuck with me to this day.

I remember my mom and I were loudly arguing—I don't even remember about what—but I do remember thinking that I was right in this case and my mom was very wrong. I usually conceded and apologized as my dad asked me to, but this time was different. I was right. I remember getting ready to walk out the door for a breather and my dad was standing there by the door saying nothing. As I walked by, I stopped and said, "Dad you know I'm right. Why don't you tell her?" He answered, "Jeremy, she's my wife. I love you but she's my wife." At the time that stung and it felt unfair. Many years later, though, when I was married with two kids of my own I realized what he meant. It was a lesson about marriage not about the rights and wrongs of that specific moment. That was wisdom.

A much softer lesson he taught all of us kids was when he would bring home silkworms every year. It was so cool having these fat worms that you could pick up and have crawl on you. And their feet would stick to your skin. We all looked forward to that each year. The lesson came from the things the silkworms would "silk over". We would put bookmarks in their box and they would completely silk over the bookmark. I kept wanting to put other things in the box because it was so cool. But Dad would explain that the silkworm only had so much silk in its body so if it used a lot of it on a bookmark, he wouldn't have very much left to build his cocoon for his transformation into a moth. And even if it did work, those moths would be weaker and die because their cocoon was so thin. Every year Dad would find a way to take this small event and turn it into many different lessons about being selfless or putting others first, or the thick cocoon being like trials in life that made you stronger. We learned a lot from those little silky caterpillars, or MAYBE it was the subtle lessons of my dad's words.

I hope that in reading this book you LISTEN to the words of God but also hear the stories of a wise Dad, Pop, and Papa that God has enlisted to help tell the story of Salvation and Love.

I'm proud of you Pop, and I love you!

Jeremy Martin

Market Leader – San Antonio

Often when visiting someone, the conversation will revolve around work, sports, or family. When I visit with Darell Martin, however, he immediately brings up Jesus, the Bible, and how that relates to our lives in this world. I first met Darell at Abilene Christian College in the late 1960s. He was my then-future wife's cousin and later sang at our wedding. His life has been filled with joy, but sorrow as well, having lost two wives to cancer. However, God has provided a third to bless him. Darell has preached for small churches, but by vocation, he is an elementary school teacher. He often taught at schools that contained students who would be considered underprivileged by society. But Darell liked it that way. He cares about people, and in doing so, his Christianity shows.

His Christianity also shows in this volume. One might take it to be a commentary, but it is not your ordinary academic type of commentary. To be sure, Darell comments on the text of the gospel of John with insights gathered both from the text and others' comments on it. But besides saying what the text means, he goes ahead to suggest ways that it needs to be applied. To further that application, he illustrates his points with stories from his life. In some of them, he comes off quite well. But in others, he exposes his faults, something we all share but often try to hide. The careful reader will realize that these stories not only illustrate how to apply the story of Jesus to Darell's life but to their own as well.

Darell often likes to share the prayer, "Abba, give us ears poised to hear your voice!" Hopefully, in this volume, you will hear the voice of God our Father.

Bruce Terry, Ph.D.

Former Professor of Bible and Humanities

Ohio Valley University

Preface

My oldest child, a son, turns 50 this year. There is something about the birth of that first child that is both strange and wonderful. **Strange**, in that I couldn't believe I was a father. Words escaped me, except, Wow! **Wonderful**, because for the first time, I loved someone unconditionally. It's like I finally understood. I understood my dad and mom's love for me, but more than that I think I have just an inkling of God's love for me. For that matter, the Father's love for the whole world.

Jeremy David Martin was born in September of 1973, in Abilene Texas to Carolyn and Darell Martin. He would be the first of three more siblings and three more step-siblings. He became a husband, a father, and perhaps someday, a grandfather.

Jeremy, as all children must, grew to be independent. I remember when I was teaching him to ride his bike at age five. I ran alongside as he rode and fell, got up again, and rode some more until he finally got the hang of balance. The conversation went something like this, "Don't let go, Daddy, don't let go." "I won't," I replied. And then he said the words that gave me pause, a prophecy of sorts of the way it would be, should be, "Let go, Daddy, let go." And I did let go, the first of many lettings go. Not only with him but with the rest of my children also. With tears of elation and a little sadness, I let go.

So, how could The Father, our Father do it? How could He let go of His firstborn? How could He allow His Son to come to a violent and unrepentant earth, a planet that would not understand Him, a world that would ridicule and kill Him? How could He allow that? John 3:16-17 answers that one: *"God loved the world so much that he gave his only Son, so that everyone who believes in him would not be lost but have eternal life. God sent his Son into the world. He* did not send him to judge the world guilty, but to save the world through him."

So, is this God a cruel Father who sends His unwilling Son to shepherd a people who will turn on Him? Listen to what the Son says in John 10:14-15 and 17-18: *"I am the shepherd who cares for the sheep. I know my sheep just as the Father knows me. And my sheep know me just as I know the Father. I give my life for these sheep...The Father loves me because I give my life. I give my life so that I can get it back again. <u>No one takes my life away from me. I give my own life freely.</u> I have the right to give my life, and I have the right to get it back again. This is what the Father told me."*

I sent my son, Jeremy, also, into a scary world. Unlike The Father, I wasn't a perfect dad, far from it. But I tried to raise him to become what God wanted him to become. Would I, like The Father, have sent him knowing he would die? I can't even imagine that thought. But Jesus came willingly. He came seeking sheep who would listen to His voice. He came to bring people to The Father, who would honor both Father and Son. He came to bring new sons and daughters to The Father.

The disciple John, the author of this gospel that bears his name, tells us this in 1:12-13: *But some people did accept him. They believed in Him, and he gave them the right to become children of God. They became God's children, but not in the way babies are usually born. It was not because of any human desire or plan. They were born from God himself.*

This book is for those of you who may not have been raised knowing a lot about the Bible. You may be a new Christian or someone interested but haven't decided to commit to Jesus. You may be someone who is just seeking a way to God and are giving Jesus a chance to make His case. Or, you may not be any of these and are reading this book because someone gave it to you and you didn't want to hurt their feelings.

I have written personal stories and comments after each section of scripture to make the Bible stories more understandable and with modern-day applications. I have also used the Easy-to-Read version of the Bible to help in understanding John's gospel (Good News) without all the old fashion language of other versions. All scripture in the main text and in the commentary sections are from the Easy-to-Read version unless otherwise indicated. Permission was given by Bible League International to use the entirety of John from the Easy-to Read version.

Introduction

to

That You Can Believe

All four of the gospel accounts of Jesus, the Son of God, begin differently. **Matthew** begins with the genealogy of Jesus starting with Abraham. Matthew, being a Jewish writer, wanted to show his Jewish audience that Jesus the Messiah's genealogy came from their patriarch (spiritual ancestor) Abraham and went through Isaac, Jacob, Judah, and King David. The gospel of **Mark** begins with the preaching of John the Baptist, his announcement of the coming of the Kingdom of God, and the long-awaited appearance of the Messiah. **Luke** begins at the birth of Jesus and includes the genealogy of Jesus going back to Adam. Luke, being the only Gentile (non-Jewish) writer of the Bible, wanted his Gentile audience to see that Christ (the Greek word for the Hebrew word, Messiah) came through Noah and before that, Adam, making Him related to all mankind.

John, on the other hand, begins before the beginning—before Genesis 1:1: *God created the sky and the earth.* John begins his gospel (Good News) with *Before the world began, the Word was there. The Word was with God, and the Word was God.*

John's intention is for his readers to understand that the Word named Jesus was present with God, before Genesis 1:1; that He has always existed with God and is, in fact, God Himself. In two other places in Scripture, John speaks of this "always existent Messiah." John 8:58: *Jesus answered, "The fact is, before Abraham was born, I* **Am***."* Revelation 22:13, also written by the disciple John: *"I am the Alpha and the Omega, the First and the Last, the Beginning and the End."* Alpha and Omega are the first and last letters of the Greek alphabet. The Book of John was originally written in Greek. The Message renders the text as: "I'm A to Z, the First and the Final, Beginning and Conclusion."

There are four distinct sections of the Book of John. **Part one— Prologue—** John 1:1-18. These 18 verses spell out the Apostle John's thesis (his premise, his conviction, his creed, his belief). **Part 2—Signs—** John 1:19-12:50, includes the ministry, teachings, and seven signs (miracles) of Jesus the Messiah. The disciple John is an eyewitness to all these events. He was first a disciple of John the Baptist until the Lamb who takes away the sin of the world came by. Then, with Andrew, the two became the first disciples of this new rabbi, Jesus. (Rabbi means my teacher.) The period for these chapters is about three years. **Part 3—Glory—** John 13:1-20:31 includes the passion of the Messiah, His death on the cross, and His resurrection. **Part 4—Epilogue—** John 21:1-25. This final chapter almost seems like an addendum (addition) to the Book of John. But it is an important addendum, not an afterthought, because it is what Jesus came to do, find all His lost sheep—in this case, Peter. This final story of John is about the reinstatement of Simon Peter after he denies his Lord. An interesting fact is the last nine chapters, almost half the book, deal with the last week of Jesus' life and the forty days after His resurrection.

The Purpose Statement of John—John 20:30-31: *Jesus did many other miraculous signs that his followers saw, which are not written in this book. But these are written so that you can believe that Jesus is the Messiah, the Son of God. Then, by believing, you can have life through his name.*

It seems odd to read the entirety of a book before discovering its purpose for being written, but that is what you find in the Book of John. The prologue, the first 18 verses of John, and these last two verses of chapter 20, verses 30 and 31, form bookends to the main narrative of the "Signs" and "Glory" sections.

The Apostle John never mentions his name in his gospel account of Jesus, but he is ever-present. He is with Jesus at every miracle (Sign), present at the Passover feast where Jesus washed the disciple's feet, in the garden where Jesus is betrayed, standing just outside at Jesus' trial, and is the only one of the 12 at the foot of the cross.

John lets you know what he believes in 1:1-18. He then gives you his eyewitness accounts of the three-year ministry in John 1:19-20:29 and finally lets you, his reader, decide whether this man is truly the Messiah, the Son of God. John 20:30-31 not only conveys the purpose for which John wrote this book, but it is the gospel (the Good News) of Messiah Jesus and the way to eternal life. **You can believe that Jesus** (Savior) **is the Messiah** (the anointed One, foretold by the prophets), **the Son of God** (Deity Himself). **Then by believing** (accepting by faith) **you can have life** (eternal life, by the grace of God, beginning the moment you believe) **through His name** (the <u>only</u> name in which there is salvation.)

In my writing, I have capitalized all pronouns of God (Father, Son, and Holy Spirit). On the other hand, I have begun the devil's name, satan, with a small "s." The only places that don't have these pronoun capitalizations are in the Biblical texts and the writing of other authors. I have italicized all scripture from the Bible. I have also used 1.5 line spacing for the text of John and single spacing for all other scriptures, comments, and stories about the text.

Abba, give us ears poised to hear your voice!

PART 1

Prologue/John 1:1-18

John 1:1-5

¹ Before the world began, the Word was there. The Word was with God, and the Word was God. ² He was there with God in the beginning. ³ Everything was made through him, and nothing was made without him. ⁴ In him there was life, and that life was a light for the people of the world. ⁵ The light shines in the darkness, and the darkness has not defeated it.

My Dad and His Word—My dad always kept his word. If he said it, you could "take it to the bank," as the saying goes. "His word was his bond," meaning, of course, he bound himself to what he said as true, and he would do whatever he told you he would do. Dad taught my two brothers and me many lessons about giving our word. It meant not lying, because if you were in the habit of telling untruths or exaggerations others wouldn't trust you. It meant following through with a promise. It meant being careful what others heard you say because it could either hurt or help your reputation.

God was no different when He spoke but since He was Spirit and not a human, He often spoke through humans called prophets. It was always in the plan of God, though, to one day speak to humans in person. How could He do that? Suppose, though, His Words could be spoken, not by some holy person but by God Himself in the form of a human.

The Trinity—We will discuss a difficult word in just a little while, called "Incarnation," which means God becoming human. But there is another word that you may or may not have heard that we must

1

define first—a religious word, "Trinity." We name girls Trinity, and there is a body of water in Texas called the Trinity River, a famous high school in Euless, Texas known for its football team, and there are churches in many cities called Trinity as a title before their denominational name, e.g., Trinity Lutheran or Trinity Baptist, etc.

So, what is the Trinity? Though the word, "Trinity" is not from the Bible, the concept and belief were. It was a word created to describe the complex idea of three separate but unified personalities within our One God. The disciple John believed in the Trinity. John calls Jesus the Word and tells us in verse 1: *The Word was with God, and the Word was God.* John also says, in verse 18: *No one has ever seen God. The only Son is the one who has shown us what God is like.* John calls Jesus, God, and goes on to say that Jesus *is at the Father's side.* It means Father, Son (Jesus), and Holy Spirit within one God. Now, I can explain the definition of the word, Trinity, but for the life of me, I can't understand its full meaning or impact. How can One God be three unique personalities with one goal, going in one direction with no dissension or disagreement?

The Trinity in the Life of Christians

"The Trinity represents the perfect example of how we are to live out community. From the beginning, the Trinity knew they needed each other and each had a specific purpose. Likewise, we as Christians are not designed to do Christianity alone. Not only do we need the Trinity to have abundant life, but we also need other people. Even Jesus needed relationships to encourage and to be encouraged. The body of Christ, directed by the Trinity, functions to serve each other and to be served until we are all united someday in heaven." (Paul Gorsline, 2022)

John 1:6-13

⁶ There was a man named John, who was sent by God. ⁷ He came to tell people about the light. Through him all people could hear about the light and believe. ⁸ John was not the light. But he came to tell people about the light. ⁹ The true light was coming into the world. This is the true light that gives light to all people.

¹⁰ The Word was already in the world. The world was made through him, but the world did not know him. ¹¹ He came to the world that was his own. And his own people did not accept him. ¹² But some people did accept him. They believed in him, and he gave them the right to become children of God. ¹³ They became God's children, but not in the way babies are usually born. It was not because of any human desire or plan. They were born from God himself.

Birdhouses—If you had visited our previous home before my wife's cancer had taken her life, you could have peeked out of the windows of our den, overlooking our backyard, and seen birdhouses of every shape and design. Maryanne loved birdhouses. She got started collecting them several years before when my parents were living with us, and my dad, then 89 and unable to maneuver at will, wanted to sit where he could watch the birds outside our home. Maryanne and our two youngest boys, Matt and Jonathan, constructed a birdhouse. After painting it, they set it up where their Papa would be able to watch through the window from his easy chair. From that birdhouse came many more over the years. Maryanne set up birdhouses, a decorative birdbath, and several bird feeders. It took a while but one year, birds began using those birdhouses for building nests and would come back every spring to reclaim their home.

One, nice spring day, a great deal of bustle was going on in our backyard, after Maryanne had scattered birdseed on the brick sidewalk very close to where the birds would congregate. Maryanne, who had gone back inside, heard the chatter of birds and thought she would return to her backyard for a peek. As she walked out to sit down on a wooden bench close to the commotion, she began to smile, looking at all the things she had constructed for these wonderful small creatures. But several birds thought she was getting too close to their babies and immediately proceeded to accost her. They began screeching and fluttering, flitting this way and that, until Maryanne retreated inside to watch from a safer vantage point. As I watched this take place from my already safe view I began to laugh. But then I was struck with a reminder from scripture, verses 10-11: *The Word was already in the world. The world was made through him, but the world did not know him. He came to the world that was his own. And his own people did not accept him.*

John 1:14-15

[14] The Word became a man and lived among us. We saw his divine greatness—the greatness that belongs to the only Son of the Father. The Word was full of grace and truth. [15] John told people about him. He said loudly, "This is the one I was talking about when I said, 'The one who is coming after me is greater than I am, because he was living before I was even born.'"

Growing Up in California—Mom, Dad, Bill, Bob, and I—I being the youngest by ten and thirteen years—spent Christmas with family. Sometimes we went to Texas and spent the holiday with grandparents, aunts, uncles, and cousins, all on Dad's side, but most of the time we spent it with my cousin, Barbara—a year older than me—and her family in either Long Beach, on the California coast or at our house in the Mojave Desert. It was, by far, my favorite time of the year.

There were several things that all these times and places had in common. There was the tree—with its decorations, food—especially desserts—and family. There was music—I loved the Christmas songs—there was laughter and there were presents—my favorites were a Lionel train I got at about age six or seven and a BB gun I received at age eight.

The one thing missing from my childhood memories of Christmas was the birth of Jesus. My church didn't celebrate Christmas as a religious holiday. I changed that with our children as they grew up. "We don't know the date Jesus was born," I was told. "The Bible never says anything about a Christmas celebration," our denomination demanded. But I was determined not to allow my children to miss what the true Christmas story was about. Whether or not December 25th was the actual date Jesus was born, it has always been a celebration of the Incarnation.

Incarnation! —Wow! Such a big word. What does it mean? The Bible tells us in Matthew 1:23: *All this happened to make clear the full meaning of what the Lord said through the prophet: "The virgin will be pregnant and will give birth to a son. They will name him **Immanuel**." (Immanuel means **"God with us.")***

According to Max Lucado: "Immanu means with us. El refers to Elohim, or with God. So, Immanuel does not mean 'above us God' or 'somewhere in the neighborhood God.'" "He meant 'God with us.'" (Max Lucado, 2020)

I mentioned earlier of Christmas songs I learned as a child, not so much in a church setting but in school music classes, at family times, and on the radio. I remember in the high school choir, learning, "Adeste Fideles," the Latin version of "O Come All Ye

Faithful." I still remember those Latin words to this day. Now the fourth verse of the song is what expresses the Incarnation of the Word, the Word becomes flesh. It takes the idea of The Word of God, the Father, and says that Word became flesh in the form of Jesus.

> "Yea, Lord, we greet Thee,
> Born this happy morning;
> Jesus, to Thee be glory given;
> Word of the Father,
> Now in flesh appearing."
> (John Frances Wade, 1744—composer and date uncertain)

There are some hints in the Old Testament that God Himself would come to earth as a man, born of woman. The Prophet Isaiah, who lived 700 years before Messiah, prophesied this in Isaiah 9:6-7:

> *...This will happen when the special child is born. God will give us a son who will be responsible for leading the people. His name will be "Wonderful Counselor, Powerful God, Father Who Lives Forever, Prince of Peace." His power will continue to grow, and there will be peace without end. This will establish him as the king sitting on David's throne and ruling his kingdom. He will rule with goodness and justice forever and ever. The strong love that the LORD All-Powerful has for his people will make this happen!*

John 1:16-18

[16] Yes, the Word was full of grace and truth, and from him we all received one blessing after another. [17] That is, the law was given to us through Moses, but grace and truth came through Jesus Christ. [18] No one has ever seen God. The only Son is the one who has

shown us what God is like. He is himself God and is very close to the Father.

Lady Justice—If you were to visit the Supreme Court you would see the figure of Lady Justice. The most recognizable form of her is one of her holding a sword, meaning justice is swift and final, a scale for weighing evidence, and wearing a blindfold over her eyes guaranteeing impartiality.

So, what is the law, that is, the law given through Moses? Remember hearing about the Ten Commandments?

1. You shall have no other Gods before me.
2. You shall not make for yourselves an idol.
3. You shall not misuse the name of the LORD your God.
4. Remember the Sabbath day by keeping it holy.
5. Honor your father and your mother.
6. You shall not murder.
7. You shall not commit adultery.
8. You shall not steal.
9. You shall not give false testimony.
10. You shall not covet.

The Law Given Through Moses—The law that Moses gave was more than just the ten given above. There were 613 commands altogether. The first ten formed the underpinning of Jewish moral principles, community regulations, and laws for religious sacrifices. Now, the Law was created by God and is therefore good. But the one thing the law could not do was save anyone. It could only point out sin.

When I once received a ticket for going too fast through a school zone, all the law of Texas could do is point out my wrongdoing. It couldn't pay the consequences of my indiscretion nor make me right with Texas law. The Law of Moses was good. But something was coming that was even better.

Grace and Truth—My first wife, Carolyn, left this world at age 28 due to cancer. She had a grandmother whom everyone called Waynie. Waynie was one of those old grandmothers who cooked lots of food, yelled at the grandkids for slamming the screen door, told you what you didn't want to hear, talked constantly, and complained about the government or taxes or the weather. But there was one thing everyone knew about Waynie, she loved family and would protect them to her dying breath. She would get mad at you one minute and cry or laugh with you the next. She was the epitome of *grace and truth*. She told you the truth but loved you and forgave you anyway.

If I were to ask you what kind of person you are, a grace person or a truth person, what would you say? I tend to be more of a grace person, probably because I care about what others think of me. I have those in my family who lean more toward the truth side. Waynie had the unique ability to be both, which Jesus, Himself was able to balance in His own life. Verses 16-17 above say this: *Yes, the Word was full of grace and truth…the law was given to us through Moses, but grace and truth came through Jesus Christ.* So, what do grace and truth mean?

Grace means "unmerited favor" or undeserved approval. It means, usually, in the New Testament, that you are receiving a gift that you didn't earn, nor do you deserve. It is given because God loves you and you accept His love. Grace means that even though you have broken every law in the book you can receive salvation by believing

Jesus took away the penalty of those sins at the cross and accepting His Lordship in your life.

Truth means many things, but I believe that John, in his book, was speaking about the truth that God the Father sent Jesus the Son into the world as a human to speak God's words to all people and to announce salvation to all who believe. Romans 10:9-10 says this: *If you openly say, "Jesus is Lord" and believe in your heart that God raised him from death, you will be saved. Yes, we believe in Jesus deep in our hearts, and so we are made right with God. And we openly say that we believe in him, and so we are saved.*

Ephesians 2:8 says this: *...you have been saved by grace because you believed. You did not save yourselves; it was a gift from God.*

Now, that's a double WOW!

PART 2

SIGNS/ John 1:19-12:50

John 1:19-36

[19] *The Jewish leaders in Jerusalem sent some priests and Levites to John to ask him, "Who are you?" He told them the truth.* [20] *Without any hesitation he said openly and plainly, "I am not the Messiah."*

[21] *They asked him, "Then who are you? Are you Elijah?"*

He answered, "No, I am not Elijah."

They asked, "Are you the Prophet?"

He answered, "No, I am not the Prophet."

[22] *Then they said, "Who are you? Tell us about yourself. Give us an answer to tell the people who sent us. What do you say about yourself?"*

[23] *John told them the words of the prophet Isaiah:*

"I am the voice of someone shouting in the desert:
  'Make a straight road ready for the Lord.'"

[24] *These Jews were sent from the Pharisees.* [25] *They said to John, "You say you are not the Messiah. You say you are not Elijah or the Prophet. Then why do you baptize people?"*

[26] *John answered, "I baptize people with water. But there is someone here with you that you don't know.* [27] *He is the one who is coming later. I am not good enough to be the slave who unties the strings on his sandals."*

[28] *These things all happened at Bethany on the other side of the Jordan River. This is where John was baptizing people.*

11

29 The next day John saw Jesus coming toward him and said, "Look, the Lamb of God. He takes away the sins of the world! 30 This is the one I was talking about when I said, 'There is a man coming after me who is greater than I am, because he was living even before I was born.' 31 I did not know who he was. But I came baptizing people with water so that Israel could know that he is the Messiah."

32-34 Then John said this for everyone to hear: "I also did not know who the Messiah was. But the one who sent me to baptize with water told me, 'You will see the Spirit come down and rest on a man. He is the one who will baptize with the Holy Spirit.' I have seen this happen. I saw the Spirit come down from heaven like a dove and rest on this man. So this is what I tell people: 'He is the Son of God.'"

35 The next day John was there again and had two of his followers with him. 36 He saw Jesus walking by and said, "Look, the Lamb of God!"

Introducing the President of the United States—My youngest son, Jonathan, and I went together on his eighth-grade trip to Washington D.C. One of the highlights of our trip was getting to visit the office of our, then, state representative, Congressman Charlie Stenholm. He took our group to the Capitol and allowed us to go inside the chamber of the House of Representatives. We got to see a lot of congressmen voting on a bill, which we thought was exciting. Someone asked him what he liked most about being a congressman. He told us that every year the President comes to the House to give the State of the Union speech. Because of the House's size both the House of Representatives and the Senate can be in the same room for the speech. Congressman Stenholm said he has heard and seen many presidents over the years from both parties give that once-a-year speech, and he always looked forward to it. But the one thing that still gives him goosebumps and brings tears to his eyes is the introduction of the President, "Mr. Speaker, the President of the United States."

Introducing the Lamb of God—John the Baptist was the prophet whom God sent to preach to Israel, getting them ready for the ministry of Jesus. Now just think about being in John the Baptist's place, as he sees Jesus walking toward him. He looked to the people gathered for baptism and announced that the Christ, the Messiah, the Son of God, the Creator of the Universe is about to come onto the world stage. His message was even more awesome than the introduction of the President of the United States. His declaration: "Planet Earth! *'Look, the Lamb of God. He takes away the sins of the world!'*"

Passover—Why did John the Baptist refer to Jesus as the Lamb of God? Passover was a yearly, Jewish religious holiday celebrating Israel leaving slavery in Egypt during the terrible night of the death of the firstborn of Egypt by the death angel. The firstborn of the Jews was saved from death by a substitute lamb offered in their place.

The people, from that time, until Jesus came on the scene, offered the best of their flocks, or had to buy one when they came to the Passover celebration in Jerusalem. Jesus was God's Passover Lamb, offered by God Himself so God's creation, humans, would not have to die eternally. The blood of the Passover lamb, on the doorposts of the Israelites' houses, saved the people inside from the death angel. Jesus, who is our Passover Lamb, shed His blood on the Roman crossbeams of death, so death would not have a hold on His disciples.

Also, a contract, or in Bible terms, "covenant," was formed with the people inside these homes that they were God's people. In the same way, we who stand under the protection of the cross of the

Messiah, have made that same contract—"we are the people of God."

John 1:37-48

37 The two followers heard him say this, so they followed Jesus. 38 Jesus turned and saw the two men following him. He asked, "What do you want?"

They said, "Rabbi, where are you staying?" ("Rabbi" means "Teacher.")

39 He answered, "Come with me and you will see." So the two men went with him. They saw the place where he was staying, and they stayed there with him that day. It was about four o'clock.

40 These men followed Jesus after they had heard about him from John. One of them was Andrew, the brother of Simon Peter. 41 The first thing Andrew did was to go and find his brother Simon. Andrew said to him, "We have found the Messiah." ("Messiah" means "Christ.")

42 Then Andrew brought Simon to Jesus. Jesus looked at him and said, "You are Simon, the son of John. You will be called Cephas." ("Cephas" means "Peter.")

43 The next day Jesus decided to go to Galilee. He met Philip and said to him, "Follow me." 44 Philip was from the town of Bethsaida, the same as Andrew and Peter. 45 Philip found Nathanael and told him, "We have found the man that Moses wrote about in the law. The prophets wrote about him too. He is Jesus, the son of Joseph. He is from Nazareth."

46 But Nathanael said to Philip, "Nazareth! Can anything good come from Nazareth?"

Philip answered, "Come and see."

47 *Jesus saw Nathanael coming toward him and said, "This man coming is a true Israelite, one you can trust."*

48 *Nathanael asked, "How do you know me?"*

Jesus answered, "I saw you when you were under the fig tree, before Philip told you about me."

Listening to Bands with My Buds in College—When I was a college student and went, with my friends, to watch a band play, we paid our money and entered the coliseum at our university. There was usually a leadup band for the night, which began the concert, but that wasn't the headliner we came to see, nor was it the one whom we paid to hear. After the crowd had been warmed up, the band all the hype was about came onto the stage. The announcement was made, and the crowd began to cheer. This is the difference between the comings of John the Baptist and Jesus.

After John the Baptist made that announcement to his followers, his mission was pretty much over. Like the announcer of the President at the State of the Union address or the minister at a wedding, John voiced his proclamation, and quietly walked off the stage. All attention immediately became directed to where it belonged, on the Messiah. And John's disciples began following this new voice, which was from heaven itself. John had prepared his followers for this moment, so it was only natural for them to go to Jesus.

One of the two disciples was named, Andrew. Most scholars believe the other disciple is John (not the Baptist) but the author of the Book of John. (John never mentions himself by name in his gospel.)

John and his brother James are friends and partners in the fishing business with two other brothers, Peter and Andrew, according to Luke 5:1-11. And it seems from the accounts in Matthew 4:18-22 and Mark 1:16-20, along with Luke's and John's accounts, already mentioned, that Jesus had several encounters with these men before they left their boats and followed Him. These men, also, had been listening to John the Baptist and were ready to follow Jesus when He said, *"Follow Me."*

John 1:49-51

49 Then Nathanael said, "Teacher, you are the Son of God. You are the King of Israel."

50 Jesus said to him, "Do you believe this just because I said I saw you under the fig tree? You will see much greater things than that!" 51 Then he said, "Believe me when I say that you will all see heaven open. You will see 'angels of God going up and coming down' on the Son of Man."

Jacob's Dream at ACU—There is a small area, a park, on the campus of Abilene Christian University, in Abilene, Texas that has special meaning for our children and grandchildren. Every year, on the Saturday before Easter Sunday, we gather at Nana and Papa's house for the Planting and Easter egg hunt. For more than a decade—some of the grandkids were not yet even born—the family planted Papa's Garden and worked on some kind of grandkid art project—making gourd birdhouses, painting small crosses, writing Scripture on stones, etc. Afterward, we would go to Jacob's Dream to have an Easter egg hunt and take family pictures. One year, three of our grandchildren, Kendyl, Ethan, and Ella, were baptized in a small pool in that park, confessing their loyalty to their Savior Jesus.

Jacob's Dream was created by Jack Maxwell, in 2006, to commemorate the 100th anniversary of the University. It has various stone structures made from Lueders' limestone, featuring many Scripture references carved into the soft rock. The central part of the entire structure is a metal sculpture of four, larger than life, angels ascending a stairway or ladder to heaven. There is a plaque not far from the four angels that refer to the story in Genesis. Jacob, son of Isaac and grandson of Abraham, is running away from his twin brother, Esau, after duping him into giving up his inheritance and blessing as the firstborn son. His brother is so angry he is ready to kill Jacob. Genesis 28:10-17 gives us the story of Jacob's journey to a place he names Bethel:

> *Jacob left Beersheba and went to Haran. The sun had already set when he came to a good place to spend the night. He took a rock there and laid his head on it to sleep. Jacob had a dream. He dreamed there was a ladder that was on the ground and reached up into heaven. He saw the angels of God going up and down the ladder. And then Jacob saw the* LORD *standing by the ladder. He said, "I am the* LORD, *the God of your grandfather Abraham. I am the God of Isaac. I will give you the land that you are lying on now. I will give this land to you and to your children. You will have as many descendants as there are particles of dust on the earth. They will spread east and west, north and south. All the families on earth will be blessed because of you and your descendants.*
>
> *"I am with you, and I will protect you everywhere you go. I will bring you back to this land. I will not leave you until I have done what I have promised."*
>
> *Then Jacob woke up and said, "I know that the* LORD *is in this place, but I did not know he was here until I slept."*

Jacob was afraid and said, "This is a very great place.
This is the house of God. This is the gate to heaven."

Now, why is this story so important to the verses we just read in John? Read John 1:51, once again, for Jesus said: *"Believe me when I say that you will all see heaven open. You will see 'angels of God going up and coming down' on the Son of Man."*

The Son of Man in this passage is Jesus' reference to Himself. The ladder in the story of Jacob leading up to heaven is the Son of Man or Jesus, Himself. The meaning is undeniable, that through this Son of Man, the way to God is found. Jesus will later say in John 14:6: *"I am the way, the truth, and the life. The only way to the Father is through me."*

The term "son of man" is used many times in the Old and New Testaments. Jews believed they were the sons of man or humans, but they also believed that there was a special significance to a "Son of Man" from the book of Daniel. That, they believed, was a title for Messiah. When Jesus used the term, Son of Man, He was referring to Himself as Messiah. Daniel 7:13-14:

> *"In my vision at night I looked, and there in front of me was someone who looked like a <u>human being</u>* (**Son of Man—NIV**). *He was coming on the clouds in the sky. He came up to the Ancient King, and the King's servants brought him before the King.*

> *"The one who looked like a <u>human being</u>* (**Son of Man—NIV**) *was given authority, glory, and complete ruling power. People from every nation and language group will serve him. His rule will last forever. His kingdom will continue forever. It will never be destroyed.*

When Jesus uses "Son of Man" in the four gospel accounts it is a code word for Messiah (Christ) without really saying it. The term is never used by others about Jesus but always by Jesus about Himself. "The term Son of man appears 81 times in the four Gospel accounts—30 times in Matthew, 14 times in Mark, 25 times in Luke, and 12 times in John." (Son of Man Christianity, Wikipedia)

John 2:1-2

¹ Two days later there was a wedding in the town of Cana in Galilee, and Jesus' mother was there. ² Jesus and his followers were also invited.

"Loose Lips Sink Ships"—This phrase was employed by our government during the Second World War as a short phrase to warn sailors and others to be careful what they said to people or what they wrote home about. Those words might fall into enemy hands and could be used for disastrous results. My mom tells the story about my dad writing home from aboard his navy ship. "There sure are a lot of goats where we are." She had no idea what he meant until he got home and told her that the ship had been docked at Goat Island somewhere near Australia.

The True Bridegroom—The author, John, never has a story without a bigger picture in mind. It wasn't so much "code" as in the account of my dad and the whereabouts of his ship during wartime, but more a representation of spiritual things. Since this story of the wedding in Cana is only found in John, what could be the bigger picture he has in mind? We will see in the next chapter that John the Baptist (not the author) is portrayed as the best friend (best man) of the bridegroom. He is introducing Jesus as the true Groom (Bridegroom), but he also introduced Him as the Lamb of God. Who, then is the bride? The theme of a wedding, a Lamb, a Bridegroom, a bride, and a city is also found in another book, in which John is the author, Revelation. In Revelation 19:6-8, we find this:

Then I heard something that sounded like a large crowd of people. It was as loud as crashing waves or claps of thunder. The people were saying,

"Hallelujah!
 Our Lord God rules.
 He is the All-Powerful.
 Let us rejoice and be happy
  and give God glory!
Give God glory, because the wedding of the Lamb has come.
 And the Lamb's bride has made herself ready.
Fine linen was given to the bride for her to wear.
 The linen was bright and clean."

(The fine linen means the good things that God's holy people did.)

In chapter 21 of Revelation, verses 1-5, we find this:

Then I saw a new heaven and a new earth. The first heaven and the first earth had disappeared. Now there was no sea. And I saw the holy city, the new Jerusalem, coming down out of heaven from God. It was prepared like a bride dressed for her husband.

I heard a loud voice from the throne. It said, "Now God's home is with people. He will live with them. They will be his people. God himself will be with them and will be their God. He will wipe away every tear from their eyes. There will be no more death, sadness, crying, or pain. All the old ways are gone."

The one who was sitting on the throne said, "Look, I am making everything new!"

The Bridegroom, Jesus, is here portrayed as the Lamb. The bride in chapter 19 is identified as the holy people of God. The bride's dress is represented by *the good things that God's holy people did.* The bride in chapter 21 is described as the New Jerusalem. A city is not the buildings and land so much as the people who live there. As such, the New Jerusalem is, yet again, the holy people of God.

John 2:3-5

³ At the wedding there was not enough wine, so Jesus' mother said to him, "They have no more wine."

⁴ Jesus answered, "Dear woman, why are you telling me this? It is not yet time for me to begin my work."

⁵ His mother said to the servants, "Do what he tells you."

It Is Not Yet Time—Two of our grandchildren, brother and sister, shovel in hand, walked toward our turtle pen. Years ago, we received several box turtles from my niece, Melody Martin. She found them in her west Texas town of Snyder and kept them for years as a learning tool for her young son. Now, it was my turn. Although I hadn't raised box turtles with my children, I thought it would be a good thing to try with Annette's and my grandkids.

We quickly found out that having male and female turtles together, and their obedience to God's directive in Genesis 1:28, to *"Have many children. Fill the earth..."* baby turtles were going to be the result. We had seen the female lay her eggs in a hole she had dug, and then she quickly covered them with dirt. I had told Ethan and his younger sister, Kendyl that they could have a baby or two, once they hatched. They were excited, to say the least. But when I discovered that they were headed to the turtle pen to begin digging, to help the babies along, I, their Papa intervened. "I know you two are excited, but you can't hurry them along by digging up the eggs. You must wait. They will hatch at the right time."

Jesus and Time—In his book, John uses the words "time" or "hour" depending on which version you are reading. There are instances when the words are used in relationship to the time of Jesus' death and glorification on the cross. Here, though, in John 4, Jesus is not referring to that. I have quoted from several versions that, I believe, express what Jesus meant in this passage:

> Easy to Read Version (This is the version we are using)—*"It is not yet time for me to begin my work."*

> New Life Version—*"It is not time for Me to work yet."*

> New International Reader's Version—*"The time for me to show who I really am isn't here yet."*

> Living Bible—*"It isn't yet my time for miracles."*

> Amplified Bible—*"My time [to act and to be revealed] has not yet come."*

(First Sign)

Water Turned into Wine

John 2:6-11

⁶ There were six large stone waterpots there that were used by the Jews in their washing ceremonies. Each one held about 20 or 30 gallons.

⁷ Jesus said to the servants, "Fill the waterpots with water." So they filled them to the top.

⁸ Then he said to them, "Now dip out some water and take it to the man in charge of the feast."

So they did what he said. ⁹ Then the man in charge tasted it, but the water had become wine. He did not know where the wine had come from, but the servants who brought the water knew. He called the bridegroom ¹⁰ and said to him, "People always serve the best wine first. Later, when the guests are drunk, they serve the cheaper wine. But you have saved the best wine until now."

¹¹ This was the first of all the miraculous signs Jesus did. He did it in the town of Cana in Galilee. By this he showed his divine greatness, and his followers believed in him.

Honeymoon in the Caribbean—Annette and I spent our delayed honeymoon on a New Year's cruise in the western Caribbean. Our stateroom was small but had a balcony and an ocean view of the Gulf of Mexico. Every morning we would arise and go to one of the many restaurants for breakfast where we could order anything from cereal to Eggs Benedict. We made ports of call in the island paradises of the Grand Caymans, Cozumel, and Montego Bay, enjoying their beautiful beaches and unique island cuisines. Each evening found my new wife and me at a dinner table, being served multiple-course meals by waiters dressed in tuxedos. For that week, Annette and I felt like we were visitors in a fairy tale. No matter where future treks would take us, that first vacation together would always be the standard by which all vacations would be judged.

I wonder if the bride and groom at the wedding feast in Cana had a similar memory as they looked back years later. The Lord had prevented embarrassment when they ran out of wine at their marriage feast by changing water into wine, that would surely rival any California, French, Italian, or Texas wines of the present. I can just hear them saying to someone when tasting wine after that incident, "This wine is good, but you should have tasted the wine at our wedding." And it was the best, not just because it was their wedding, but because the Creator was a guest, and He had made it. Once we have tasted of the Lord, nothing else in life that use to fill us quite tastes the same. Psalm 34:8, in the NIV, says this, *"Taste and see that the LORD is good; blessed is the one who takes refuge in him."*

John is the only gospel writer to include this story and this miracle. So why is it here? At first reading, this incident seems straightforward. Jesus performs a miracle because His mom asks Him to, and people put their faith in Him.

The Deeper Message—But there is something about the way John writes his gospel account that tells us that there is an even deeper meaning. There is a reason why John puts this miracle in this spot at this time. The miracle becomes a statement at the beginning of Jesus' ministry. He did not come, to just renew the old, but to usher in a brand-new system—the Kingdom of God.

The first wine represented the old order of things—old law and old worship. It tasted good and the people seemed to be satisfied with its taste. The writer of Psalm 119:97 said, *"Oh, how I love your law! I meditate on it all day long."* (NIV) And Psalm 19:10 says this of these laws, *"…They are sweeter than honey, even the finest honey."* (NCV) But the law was written on stone and not on the hearts of the people. The worship was based on ritual and the people's sacrifice of possessions. The stone jars themselves represented the religion of the day, which had become cold and hard. The water in the jars, for ceremonial hand cleansing, purified the flesh for a short time but had to be repeated at each gathering. Although the hands were clean, the water could not reach the hand washer's heart or more importantly the individual's soul. It is interesting what the master of the banquet said in verse 10: *"People always serve the best wine first. Later, when the guests are drunk, they serve the cheaper wine..."*

Even the religion of the day had become a cheaper and more watered-down version of the original and had only dulled the senses of the people. Jesus didn't come to bring back the good old wine; He came to bring new wine. The fact that He used the ceremonial washing jars for the new wine is no accident. The jars also represented the old, but the new would take the place of the old. The Kingdom of God, or the rule of God, would take the place of the old religion. The physical kingdom would be replaced by a spiritual one. The ritual water used for cleaning the flesh had itself been transformed into wine from heaven—the saving blood of Jesus, which alone could truly cleanse the heart and the soul of an individual.

The stale and monotonous ceremony of the old order would give way to true praise in the Kingdom of God. The sacrifices of the people would be replaced by the great sacrifice of God's own Son. The law would no longer be written on cold, hard stone but on the hearts of human beings. And God would no longer be confined to a temple made with hands but would come to live inside people. So, we, like the master of the banquet, can also say to God, *"But you have saved the best... until now."*

Over the past twenty centuries in Christendom, many of the disciples of Jesus, have lost the taste of that new wine—that spiritual Kingdom of God. Some have become accustomed to, and satisfied with, a watered-down version of the kingdom that Jesus proclaimed. Hopefully, as kingdom people, all sons and daughters of the Father will be able to taste once again the new wine that only Jesus can create. And may He continue to use all of us in bringing that new wine of the Kingdom of God, to a lost and dying world—to those who know only the stale and putrid taste of dead and dying religion. Christ, the Messiah Jesus, is the only answer for a lost world, and His people are the ones He has assigned to spread His kingdom throughout the ends of the earth.

Signs—Once a year or so, my mom and dad would travel, with us three boys, from our home in the California, Mohave Desert community of Ridgecrest to our Mommie and Bompa's home in Refugio, Texas near Corpus Christi. When my brothers, who were ten and thirteen years older than I, left home, it was just me and my parents. I would see aunts and uncles and especially cousins at, what would seem, like a yearly family reunion. My cousins and I would play, and the adults would talk about family stories, discuss politics, or play a domino game called 42.

I was always fascinated, every time we made that trek to Texas and back, how my dad seemed to know the way. This was back in the nineteen fifties, before freeways. I often thought, "I could never find my way, all the way from California to Texas." How did he do it? I asked him one time that very question. He said, "I have a map, and I follow the signs."

When Jeremy and Joanna, my oldest two children were young, I gave them, each, an assignment on one of our long trips. Jeremy had to keep track of how much gas we used, the cost, and the miles per gallon. This was, of course, before cars were smart enough to do it themselves. I gave Joanna a book of maps, an atlas, and asked her to keep track of where we were going and how we were going to get there by following the signs. And another "of course"—this was before GPS. They both did their jobs well. Now, while I had given them their assignment, I didn't leave the results of the trip just up to them. I helped them by showing them "signs" along the way.

There are seven signs in the book of John that lead you from the beginning of Jesus' ministry to His death on the cross and His resurrection from the dead. If you follow these signs, they not only confirm, plainly and undeniably, that Jesus is truly Lord over nature, illness, and especially death, but He is God come in the flesh. (Remember the word, incarnation?) There is nothing that can defeat Him. The signposts on this journey through John's gospel are:

1. Water turned into wine—2:1-11

2. Royal official's son is healed—4:46-54

3. Paralyzed man healed after 38 years—5:1-15

4. Feeding of the 5,000—6:1-14

5. Jesus, walking on the water—6:16-21

6. Healing of the man born blind—9:1-41

7. Lazarus was raised from the dead after four days—11:1-44

Follow them with me as we travel this "Good News" journey of Jesus the Messiah, the Son of God.

John 2:12-25

12 Then Jesus went to the town of Capernaum. His mother and brothers and his followers went with him. They all stayed there a few days.

13 It was almost time for the Jewish Passover, so Jesus went to Jerusalem. 14 There in the Temple area he saw men selling cattle, sheep, and doves. He saw others sitting at tables, exchanging and trading people's money. 15 Jesus made a whip with some pieces of rope. Then he forced all these men and the sheep and cattle to leave the Temple area. He turned over the tables of the money traders and scattered their money. 16 Then he said to those who were selling pigeons, "Take these things out of here! Don't make my Father's house a place for buying and selling!"

¹⁷ When this happened, his followers remembered what was written in the Scriptures:

"My strong devotion to your Temple will destroy me."

¹⁸ Some Jews said to Jesus, "Show us a miracle as a sign from God. Prove that you have the right to do these things."

¹⁹ Jesus answered, "Destroy this temple and I will build it again in three days."

²⁰ They answered, "People worked 46 years to build this Temple! Do you really believe you can build it again in three days?"

²¹ But the temple Jesus meant was his own body. ²² After he was raised from death, his followers remembered that he had said this. So they believed the Scriptures, and they believed the words Jesus said.

²³ Jesus was in Jerusalem for the Passover festival. Many people believed in him because they saw the miraculous signs he did. ²⁴ But Jesus did not trust them, because he knew how all people think. ²⁵ He did not need anyone to tell him what a person was like. He already knew.

Cleaning Day—"Darell, I'm tired of finding your shoes and your toys all over the house," my mom called out, not too gently. It was cleaning day and she was trying to set the house in order. And this certainly was not the order she had been thinking of. On cleaning day, I often found my shoes and my scattered toys outside on the back porch. Usually, she would place everything in a nice pile on the porch, but I knew she had enough, one day when I witnessed her sweeping my "prized possessions" out the back door. I had turned her ordered home into a den of childish clutter once too often, and she let me know with a swish of her broom that changes were coming.

Why did Jesus clean out the Temple? The Temple represented where God resided in the Jewish nation. That is why Jesus called it His Father's house. But the people were making a mockery of God's house by buying and selling, generally turning it into a market. In Matthew, Mark, and Luke, Jesus says they are turning the house of prayer into a den of robbers, indicating that crookedness was also going on within its walls. The people had forgotten about true worship and the real purpose and meaning of Passover. They had turned it into a moneymaking business and like the wedding party at Cana had become drunk on watered-down religion. They had dishonored God by dishonoring His house.

Later, in John 4 when Jesus speaks to the woman at the well, He tells her that a time is coming when worship won't be done just in Jerusalem at the Temple. Worship will become what God has always desired it to be, *"...in spirit and in truth."* (NIV) And it will take place wherever Messiah's followers gather. Jesus said in Matthew 18:20: *"... if two or three people are together believing in me, I am there with them."* What was the point Jesus was making by throwing out these people who were making money in the Temple? First, Jesus was showing His authority at the beginning of His ministry. Second, John placed the story of the Temple fracas (brawl) right after turning the water into wine. There was a change in the air—a change from the old to the new, a change from good to the best, a change from an earthly kingdom to a spiritual one (the Kingdom of God). In John 18:36: *Jesus said, "My kingdom does not belong to this world. If it did, my servants would fight so that I would not be handed over to the Jewish leaders. No, my kingdom is not an earthly one."*

After being confronted by the Jews about His authority in purging the temple of bad actors, Jesus said in verse 19: *"Destroy this temple and I will build it again in three days."* He was deemphasizing the temple of stone and emphasizing the temple of His body. The temple itself was destroyed in AD 70 by the Romans, and it has never been rebuilt, to this day. But the body of Jesus, which both Romans and Jews thought they had destroyed was raised on the third day as Jesus predicted. After the Resurrection, His body would symbolically be identified as the church.

John 3:1-3

¹ There was a man named Nicodemus, one of the Pharisees. He was an important Jewish leader. ² One night he came to Jesus and said, "Teacher, we know that you are a teacher sent from God. No one can do these miraculous signs that you do unless they have God's help."

³ Jesus answered, "I assure you, everyone must be born again. Anyone who is not born again cannot be in God's kingdom."

The Queen Is Dead—At this writing, Queen Elizabeth has just died and is lying in State before her burial. When the Queen died, her son, Prince Charles became King. With a Constitutional Monarchy, the king or queen has very limited powers. The Kingdom of God though is much different. When the Messiah Jesus died, no one took His place, for, three days later He rose from the dead and became victorious over death. He is the undisputed King of Kings and Lord of Lords. He has all power, and His Kingdom will last forever. His subjects, unlike the British, are under the King and submit to Him in all things. Fortunately, He is a completely loving and benevolent monarch, and His subjects will live forever in His wonderful city, the New Jerusalem.

What Is the Kingdom of God?

"The kingdom of God is the rule and reign of God— announced and promoted in both testaments. It is his sovereign rule and the existence that corresponds to his will and being.

So . . . the church is the clearest manifestation of the kingdom. But it's not the full expression. Not by any means. Maybe the visible manifestation of the kingdom on the earth. But even there—when one looks at the church in the West today, it hardly brings to mind an existence where God's way is the lived experience.

So, we pray. We ask God to bring His kingdom on earth as it is in heaven—which I take to, first of all, be a confession (that we haven't yet fully embodied God's life) and an enlistment (to be radically transformed by the Spirit for the sake of the world)." (Mike Cope 2022)

John 3:4-13

4 Nicodemus said, "How can a man who is already old be born again? Can he go back into his mother's womb and be born a second time?"

5 Jesus answered, "Believe me when I say that everyone must be born from water and the Spirit. Anyone who is not born from water and the Spirit cannot enter God's kingdom. 6 The only life people get from their human parents is physical. But the new life that the Spirit gives a person is spiritual. 7 Don't be surprised that I told you, 'You must be born again.' 8 The wind blows wherever it wants to. You hear it, but you don't know where it is coming from or where it is going. It is the same with everyone who is born from the Spirit."

9 Nicodemus asked, "How is all this possible?

10 Jesus said, "You are an important teacher of Israel, and you still don't understand these things? 11 The truth is, we talk about what we know. We tell about what we have seen. But you people don't accept what we tell you. 12 I have told you about things here on earth, but you do not believe me. So I'm sure you will not believe me if I tell you about heavenly things! 13 The only one who has ever gone up to heaven is the one who came down from heaven—the Son of Man.

Matt and the New Birth—Matt's cry was the most beautiful sound my ears had heard in almost fourteen hours. It meant he was fine and so was Maryanne. Maryanne's labor had been very difficult. Matt's head was just too big for the birth canal and a C-section was ordered. I got to be in the room when Matt was pulled from his mother's womb. Head, arms, chest, legs, and feet, almost eleven pounds of baby, all wet and chalky white was delivered in front of my ever-widening eyes. And boy did he scream. But he was my son from the womb of my wife, and I fell instantly in love with him. I knew I would fight to the death to protect him even though he didn't have an inkling of who I was. I loved him even though all he could do was eat, cry, and wet his diaper. I loved him because he was my son, and I held him proudly in public so all could see.

Just think, now, of our Father watching one of his children being born, not from the womb of a woman but the womb of heaven; born again, born from above, born spiritually. The angels of heaven are even cheering the birth. And the Father looks at that new child still dripping wet as the most beautiful thing He's ever seen because that child is His child, born of His Spirit, born because of His love.

What is this being *born again* Jesus tells Nicodemus he must undergo? Baptism? I agree that being *born from the water* in verse 5 is speaking of baptism. But this rebirth, Jesus is speaking to

Nicodemus about, is bigger than baptism. Being **born a second time**, being **born again,** and being **born of the Spirit** all mean, essentially, the same thing. The word translated **"again"** literally means **"from above."** It is speaking of spiritual birth, not physical birth. You are being born into the family of God, yes! But you are also starting over. The believer who agrees to water baptism is symbolically going through what is taking place in the spiritual realm. Since water baptism is a very public action, and Nicodemus came at night, Jesus may be telling him that he cannot be a secret disciple. Jesus seems to be telling him, "You must be born from above spiritually, and you must acknowledge Me publicly." Remember above, when we spoke of the apostle Paul's statement in Romans 10:9: *If you openly say, "Jesus is Lord" and believe in your heart that God raised him from death, you will be saved.*

An Hour and a Half in a Mexican Jail—We arrived promptly at 10:00 AM, Saturday at the front of the city jail—the time the warden had told us to be there. "I will give you fifteen minutes," he had said, and we wanted every minute."

We were on a mission to Arcelia, Mexico. Joe and Bill had walked by the jail yesterday; I, as usual, was following close behind—I have short legs. Joe had this awareness in his spirit that someone from inside those walls was crying out to God. Praying as he walked up to the door, Joe was reminded that no religious group had been allowed in that jail for several years. Even so, there he stood thinking aloud, 'Unless I speak to the warden, no one else will let me in, but what are the chances of talking to him?'"

At that improbable moment, the warden walked out of the door on his way home and almost bumped into Joe. Not missing a beat, this never-timid evangelist began asking the warden if our small company could come back on Saturday to speak to the prisoners about Jesus. They chatted for a few moments, and though I couldn't understand the language they were speaking, I knew by the nod of his head that the warden had agreed to allow us in.

The following morning Joe, Augustine—a local Christian—and I were escorted into a foyer and patted down for contraband. Bill, Robert, and Jim had not come with us, opting instead to work on other pressing projects at the church. But I, as Joe's scribe, tagged along, with pen and notebook, to record the event. I also knew from experience that if God and Joe Almanza were together, something big was going to happen, and I wanted to be there to witness it.

God was definitely in charge, even arranging for a Christian trustee to be in that jail. This brother prayed with us and then led us to a woodshop where we could hold a service. A large cluster of suspicious but intrigued inmates gathered in that small, covered space at Joe's invitation. Those fifteen minutes we were originally allowed turned into an hour and a half as Augustine began leading our small congregation in several songs. When he opened with "Sweet By and By," I could almost see in my mind's eye, my dad swinging his hand, leading that same song, in English, at a fifth-Sunday singing from my boyhood church.

Augustine began to speak first. I couldn't understand his language, but I sure could feel his heart. I kept looking over at one young man in the corner. His face seemed so intense and callous that I wondered how long he would last; he seemed ready to bolt at any moment. He walked out twice but came back each time.

When Augustine concluded his thoughts, he asked Brother Joe to speak. As Joe began his witness to the men, all their nervous movements ceased. Joe told of his own time in prison and being part of a gang before Jesus entered and changed his heart. The young man with the hard face looked intently in Joe's direction. As

Joe began to tell his story in that beautiful Spanish, all ears perked up; the young man's face began to soften, and my spirit began to soar. The Holy Spirit was working His limitless and mighty power, and I was standing right there getting to participate in the event.

Joe then asked this throng of lost but searching men if there was anyone present who wanted to come and make Jesus his Lord and Savior. Nine expectant souls answered the call, and the formerly calloused, young man was among the cluster. I stood with those men as first Joe and then Brother Augustine prayed. And then I watched as these same nine men acknowledged their sins and confessed Jesus Christ as the Son of God."

Joe disappeared for a few minutes to ask the warden if he would allow him to baptize these men. The Christian trustee was also at work, suggesting to the warden where the men could be baptized. How could the warden say no to the Holy Spirit?

We were then led to a large cement tank of water, which we converted into a baptistery. Joe asked the men which of them wanted to go first. As in an unspoken answer, the young man, with the previously calloused face, sprinted to the head of the line and dove into the water. He was followed by eight others who were baptized and added to the Kingdom of God that very day.

As he left, Joe called together the trustee and some others who claimed Christ. He urged this jail church family to make sure that these new brothers were encouraged in their new faith.

Public water baptism is anything but secret. It is confession in action. Early Christians all went through water baptism as a confession to all others of what they believed in their heart. Peter in 1 Peter 3:21 calls baptism *asking God for a clean conscience. It saves you because Jesus Christ was raised from death.* In other words, it was a disciple's way of saying "yes" to God.

I have asked two Bible professors at Abilene Christian University to give us their thoughts on **Being Born Again**:

What Is Being Born Again? (1)

"The conversation that Jesus has with Nicodemus is similar to those that he has with a variety of people throughout the book of John. Jesus is always talking at one level and people are hearing at a different level. So, when he says to Nicodemus "you must be born again", Nicodemus thinks, "it is going to be hard to get back in that womb". And when Jesus says, "I am the bread of life," people think "do you really want us to be cannibals," and when Jesus says, "I am the living water," the Samaritan woman says, "Great, I won't have to come to the well anymore."

In this particular instance, Nicodemus is a high official in the synagogue. He has an impeccable religious pedigree. He is like the bird that got pushed from the highest branch of the tree. He has all of the spiritual and social advantages that a person could have.

When Jesus tells him he must be born again he is telling him that none of that matters. The only way to come into the kingdom of God is as a helpless baby. None of his spiritual privileges account for anything. He must be willing to let all of that go and be dependent on Jesus Christ. Interestingly, the next story of the Samaritan woman involves someone who is born with no privilege and no spiritual pedigree. But Jesus teaches her in the same way he does Nicodemus. Your past, whether good or bad, does not matter.

We all come into a relationship with God as little dependent babies." (Randy Harris, 2022)

What Is Being Born Again? (2)

"...John is full...of symbolism...That is certainly the case with the references to water. Here in John 3, it is wind and water, because the Greek, Hebrew, and Aramaic word that means "spirit" also means "wind" and "breath." So, we remember that we have the spirit/breath and water mentioned at the Creation (Genesis 1:2), as well as the wind over the waters bringing forth a new creation after the Flood (Genesis 8:1). Wind/Spirit and creation or new births go together. The early Christians (with John the Baptist and the Apostles) not only connected water Baptism and the Holy Spirit, but they saw the ceremony of Christian baptism as a rebirth— reminding us that birth is another thing that involves water and fluids, and you can think of the breathy wind of the Spirit as a kind of airy fluid that blows through us so that the work of Spirit-imparting and cleansing and rebirthing gets vividly depicted by this rich imagery of being born of water and the Spirit. Some interpreters have ignored the water symbolism throughout John, just wanting to talk about the water Jesus mentions In John 3 on its own terms, saying that we should read it as referring to the waters of your first, natural birth. Nicodemus talks about that birth from his mother's womb, so it is easy to see why someone would go that way. But most interpreters today agree with those of the early centuries of Christianity: this water means more than that, it connects with the Spirit and means the water of Christian Baptism.

Or, to put it differently, nobody in the first century could possibly read this chapter and not think of Baptism, since there weren't any Christians at that time who didn't have water Baptism as a crucial part of their Christian journey. And the imagery of water and Spirit and rebirth and baptism were all tied together in their practices and their preaching... (Jeff Childers, 2022)

John 3:14-21

[14] "Moses lifted up the snake in the desert. It is the same with the Son of Man. He must be lifted up too. [15] Then everyone who believes in him can have eternal life."

[16] Yes, God loved the world so much that he gave his only Son, so that everyone who believes in him would not be lost but have eternal life. [17] God sent his Son into the world. He did not send him to judge the world guilty, but to save the world through him. [18] People who believe in God's Son are not judged guilty. But people who do not believe are already judged, because they have not believed in God's only Son. [19] They are judged by this fact: The light has come into the world. But they did not want light. They wanted darkness, because they were doing evil things. [20] Everyone who does evil hates the light. They will not come to the light, because the light will show all the bad things they have done. [21] But anyone who follows the true way comes to the light. Then the light will show that whatever they have done was done through God.

Rattlesnakes—In the early 1990s, I was preaching on Sundays at a church of about 50 members in the small town of Woodson, in west Texas. Our family would get up early on Sundays and drive about

65 miles from Abilene, where we lived, to Woodson each Sunday for about nine years. I worked as a teacher in the Abilene schools during the week and a preacher on Sundays.

There was a young family of five, a husband, a wife, and three young children who were members of our congregation who lived not far from town. One Sunday, in the fall of the year, they told our church family of a harrowing experience when they got ready to leave the house one morning. As they walked out on their porch, they saw about a hundred rattlesnakes slithering in their driveway toward their house. Really, they were moving underneath their house. The couple had parked outside their home, so they gathered their children in their arms and did some high-stepping to reach the safety of their car.

Rattlesnakes in Texas den up during the fall, usually in small rock caves, but sometimes they find the space under a pier and beam house to hibernate for the winter. These venomous reptiles will then reemerge and leave their dens in April to hunt for food during the warm months of the year.

The story ends well, and they called a person whose job it is to retrieve these venomous creatures from the crawl space of homes like theirs. How would you like that job?

Venomous Snakes—There is a strange story in Numbers 21:4-9:

> *The Israelites…began complaining against God and Moses. The people said, "Why did you bring us out of Egypt? We will die here in the desert! There is no bread and no water! And we hate this terrible food!"*
>
> *So the LORD sent poisonous snakes among the people. The snakes bit the people, and many of the Israelites died. The people came to Moses and said, "We know that we sinned when we spoke against*

39

the LORD and against you. Pray to the LORD. Ask him to take away these snakes." So Moses prayed for them.

The LORD said to Moses, "Make a bronze snake and put it on a pole. If anyone is bitten by a snake, that person should look at the bronze snake on the pole. Then that person will not die." So Moses made a bronze snake and put it on a pole. Then when a snake bit anyone, that person looked at the bronze snake on the pole and lived.

Wait a minute. The second commandment says in Exodus 20:4: *"You must not make any idols. Don't make any statues or pictures of anything up in the sky or of anything on the earth or of anything down in the water.* And now God is telling Moses to make a bronze snake and have the people look at it and be healed.

I'm sure Moses had questions in his mind about this. What could all of this mean? Jesus answers this in verses 14-15 above. Jesus compares the bronze snake being lifted up on the standard to Him being lifted up on the cross. The snake reminded the people that they had sinned, but by looking at the snake they could be healed of the snake's deadly bite.

Paul tells us in 2 Corinthians 5:21: *Christ had no sin, but God made him become sin so that in Christ we could be right with God.* The snake reminded the people of their sin against God and therefore became a sin offering to heal them physically. Christ on the cross reminds us of our sins against God and becomes the sin offering to heal us spiritually. That then leads us back to the conversation between Nicodemus and Jesus. Snakes in the desert, being born again—this was a lot even for the intellectual Nicodemus.

Nic at Night—What did Nicodemus bring to Jesus that night? He brought his credentials: his position in the community, his religion, his standing on the Jewish ruling council, his pride in being a Pharisee, his degrees, his heritage as a Jew and a descendant of Abraham, his knowledge of scripture, and even his manhood. Jesus' first statement to him in verse 3 is: *"I assure you, everyone must be born again. Anyone who is not born again cannot be in God's kingdom."* The Apostle Paul, years later, made this statement about his credentials in Philippians 3:8: *I lost all these things, and now I know that they are all worthless trash. All I want now is Christ.*

With Nicodemus, *all these things* were getting in the way of knowing God. God's kingdom wasn't about things; it was about being born from above. The interesting thing was that Nicodemus couldn't **do** anything. Being *born again* was something the Spirit did. All that was needed was his acceptance. The big problem, even though Nicodemus was, himself, a teacher, he did not understand the spiritual. Jesus had to tell him, "Nicodemus, physical birth is one thing, but I'm talking about spiritual birth."

It's all about belief. Look, again at verse 16: *"Yes, God loved the world so much that he gave his only Son, so that everyone who believes in him would not be lost but have eternal life."*

And it's all about grace. Nicodemus was told that he had nothing to offer God that made him acceptable to God. The Apostle Paul said in Ephesians 2:8-9: *You have been saved by grace because you believed. You did not save yourselves; it was a gift from God. You are not saved by the things you have done, so there is nothing to boast about.*

Nicodemus had to come to God and let God begin again with him. Nothing before mattered, not his sins and not his credentials. Being *born again* meant, just as a baby is both pure and without credentials, so in the same manner Nicodemus must come to be born from above. And so, in the same way, we must all come to God. *"Everyone must be born again."*

John 3:22-30

²² After this, Jesus and his followers went into the area of Judea. There he stayed with his followers and baptized people. ²³ John was also baptizing people in Aenon, a place near Salim with plenty of water. People were going there to be baptized. ²⁴ This was before John was put in prison.

²⁵ Some of John's followers had an argument with another Jew about religious washing. ²⁶ Then they came to John and said, "Teacher, remember the man who was with you on the other side of the Jordan River? He is the one you were telling everyone about. He is also baptizing people, and many are going to him."

²⁷ John answered, "A person can receive only what God gives. ²⁸ You yourselves heard me say, 'I am not the Messiah. I am only the one God sent to prepare the way for him.' ²⁹ The bride always belongs to the bridegroom. The friend who helps the bridegroom just waits and listens. He is happy just to hear the bridegroom talk. That's how I feel now. I am so happy that he is here. ³⁰ He must become more and more important, and I must become less important.

A Marriage That Unites Two Families—When Annette and I married in 2007 we had, between us, seven grown children and three grandchildren. The entirety of this large brood made up our wedding party as we vowed our undying love for one another. Since both Annette and I had lost our mates in death, having our family surround us at this touching observance was moving, to say the least. Our two eldest sons, Jeremy and Paul, performed this unusual ceremony with laughter and tears but also with dignity and respect. Although our sons did most of the speaking, when the final introduction of husband and wife was made, all eyes turned from the speakers to the bride and groom. The ministers were never the most important people in the ceremony even though, at first you heard only their voices. The marriage of the bride and groom was the reason the people were present.

There seemed to be some competition between the followers of John the Baptist and the followers of Jesus. John's disciples were jealous for him, but John set them straight. He told them, "I'm doing exactly what God sent me to do, no more and no less." John had earlier quoted from Isaiah applying it to himself in 1:23: *"I am the voice of someone shouting in the desert: 'Make a straight road ready for the Lord.'"*

This was fulfilled when John came baptizing telling the people to repent of their sins for the Kingdom of God was near. The Kingdom of God is the rule of God. May his rule on earth become like it already is in heaven!

John knew his place in God's plans. He had already stated that he was not the Messiah but said of Jesus, in 1:29: *"Look, the Lamb of God. He takes away the sins of the world!* The phrase that John used, in verse 30, is one we must all remember when we are trying to talk to someone about the Messiah, *"He must become more and more important, and I must become less important."* It helps me remember to get out of God's way. I am not indispensable; I am not on center stage; Christ is. That is His place, not mine. Verse 27: *"A person can receive only what God gives."* We might do well to remember that when we become envious of another's ministries and accomplishments.

John 3:31-36

[31] *"The one who comes from above is greater than all others. The one who is from the earth belongs to the earth. He talks about*

things that are on the earth. But the one who comes from heaven is greater than all others. ³² He tells what he has seen and heard, but people don't accept what he says. ³³ Whoever accepts what he says has given proof that God speaks the truth. ³⁴ God sent him, and he tells people what God says. God gives him the Spirit fully. ³⁵ The Father loves the Son and has given him power over everything. ³⁶ Whoever believes in the Son has eternal life. But those who do not obey the Son will never have that life. They cannot get away from God's anger."

The Heart of My Daughter—I watched my daughter, Joanna step into the baptistery and gracefully walk toward me. Her mom was standing on the step Joanna had just left. I had baptized Jeremy several years before as I would baptize Matt and then, Jonathan, several years later. But this was my only daughter and at this moment I was going to baptize her. She was eleven years old and had that usual smile on her face as she glided toward me through the water, though the smile seemed more radiant at this moment. I thought ahead a few years to a day when another would be taking her hand as it slipped from mine. She would be giving her heart to another, and I would step aside, cheering her on. And today her hand slipped from her mother's hand to mine and from mine to her Lord's. She was giving her life to the One who came from heaven to the One who is greater than all. Her mother and I would, now, watch from the sidelines cheering her on.

John the Baptist calls Jesus the Son of God who knows, hears, and speaks the words of God. In John 1, Jesus is called the Word of God. Everything He says, every word He utters is from the Father. He is not a prophet who is just a mouthpiece for God. He is God. The Son also has the Spirit without limit. In other words, the Son has all power on earth, even over death itself.

Verse 36: *"Whoever believes in the Son has eternal life."* Eternal life is only in Messiah Jesus. The sin of the world separates humans from God. *"But those who do not obey the Son will never have that life"* (Eternal life). God will not forgive sin apart from belief in His Son who died for humankind. *"They cannot get away from God's anger."*

John 4:1-4

¹ Jesus learned that the Pharisees had heard the report that he was making and baptizing more followers than John. ² (But really, Jesus himself did not baptize anyone; his followers baptized people for him.) ³ So he left Judea and went back to Galilee. ⁴ On the way to Galilee, he had to go through the country of Samaria.

My Daughter's Children Baptized in the Llano River—I remember, clearly, the two different occasions when Nana and I were invited to witness the baptisms of our grandchildren, Ashlyn and Creed Crabtree. Both wanted their dad, Kyle, to baptize them. Both wanted to be baptized in the Llano River near their home in Junction, Texas, and near the land where their paternal grandparents, Jo and Marvin Crabtree, lived.

The first, Ashlyn, was baptized one very cold November, the Saturday after Thanksgiving. Creed, her younger brother, picked a hot, July 4th. Ashlyn's baptism made us all feel full of "Thanksgiving" for this, newest disciple of the Messiah. Creed's baptism generated thoughts of his new-found "Freedom" in his Savior Jesus.

Not Out of Rivalry—Jesus was making a name for Himself, not out of rivalry with John nor like that of a politician trying to sway people to His side. His name was becoming known because of His teaching. The flocking of people trying to listen to Him brought, also, the ever-suspicious Pharisees. They were the "hall monitors" of the Jewish faith and wanted to be sure this new teacher was not twisting the Scripture. Jesus knew that this unwanted interference of the Pharisees, and others like them, would finally bring about His death, but "that time," "His hour," was not now. It was best to go somewhere else, for today.

John 4:5-18

5 In Samaria Jesus came to the town called Sychar, which is near the field that Jacob gave to his son Joseph. 6 Jacob's well was there. Jesus was tired from his long trip, so he sat down beside the well. It was about noon. 7 A Samaritan woman came to the well to get some water, and Jesus said to her, "Please give me a drink." 8 This happened while his followers were in town buying some food.

9 The woman answered, "I am surprised that you ask me for a drink! You are a Jew and I am a Samaritan woman!" (Jews have nothing to do with Samaritans.)

10 Jesus answered, "You don't know what God can give you. And you don't know who I am, the one who asked you for a drink. If you knew, you would have asked me, and I would have given you living water."

11 The woman said, "Sir, where will you get that living water? The well is very deep, and you have nothing to get water with. 12 Are you greater than our ancestor Jacob? He is the one who gave us this well. He drank from it himself, and his sons and all his animals drank from it too."

13 Jesus answered, "Everyone who drinks this water will be thirsty again. 14 But anyone who drinks the water I give will never be thirsty again. The water I give people will be like a spring flowing inside them. It will bring them eternal life."

15 *The woman said to Jesus, "Sir, give me this water. Then I will never be thirsty again and won't have to come back here to get more water."*

16 *Jesus told her, "Go get your husband and come back."*

17 *The woman answered, "But I have no husband."*

Jesus said to her, "You are right to say you have no husband. **18** *That's because, although you have had five husbands, the man you live with now is not your husband. That much was the truth."*

Growing Up in the Mojave Desert—When I was growing up in the Mojave Desert of California back in the 1950s and 1960s, I used to go out looking for lizards and horned toads. I even caught a few snakes, to my mom's annoyance. It got hot out in the desert in the summer. I would finally come home with my trusty dog, Frisky beside me. With her tongue hanging out, my pockets full of wild animals, and the cuffs of my blue jeans full of sand, I had a body so thirsty I could drink a gallon of water on the spot, and drink I would. I would then lie down on the living room floor with a bellyache and listen to my stomach slosh from side to side.

Meeting the Woman at the Well—In John chapter 4, Jesus met the unimpressive "woman at the well." I wonder if synagogue was somewhat different in Sychar than it was in Jerusalem. I can't help but think that this "rough around the edges" sort of woman would have looked "out of place" sitting in the same place of worship as the pious Nicodemus. Nicodemus was everything that the woman was not. He was a righteous Pharisee; she was a woman living in sin. He was well-schooled, and she was ignorant. He was a child of Abraham, and she was a Samaritan, a half-Jew. He, of course, was a man and she was a woman. He was well respected and on the Jewish Council, and she was an outcast having to come in the middle of the day to get water when no one else was around. He brought abundance to Christ and was told he would have to start all over—to be "born again". She brought an empty water pot and was told she could be filled. Finally, I noticed how each left his or her audience with the Master. I assume that Nicodemus exited the same way he entered—by stealth, so as not to be seen. But the woman, we are told, whom we don't even know by name, ran back to her village shouting, "I have found the Messiah!"

The conversation began with Jesus asking the woman for a drink, a simple request, except that, as the woman knew, *Jews have nothing to do with Samaritans.* Jesus seemed to break all the social rules of the day. But then Jesus wasn't much for traditions that made one group more privileged anyway. In verse 10, Jesus told the woman that God had a gift and that He, Jesus, was the giver of that gift. The gift was *"living water."* The woman, of course, misunderstood. Look at verse 12: *"Are you greater than our ancestor Jacob? He is the one who gave us this well. He drank from it himself, and his sons and all his animals drank from it too."*

She is thinking physically and He is speaking of the spiritual. We are much like the woman and much like Nicodemus. We are physical beings who have a hard time thinking in the spiritual. *"Born again?" "Living water?"* What are you saying, Jesus?

The woman came thirsty bringing her water pot. Upon leaving she left her water pot behind. She had been relieved of the real thirst in her life. Each of us, also, can have our spiritual thirst quenched. Jesus says in verses 13-14: *"…anyone who drinks the water I give will never be thirsty again. The water I give people will be like a spring flowing inside them. It will bring them eternal life."*

Some Bible scholars say that this *"living water"* is eternal life, using verse 14: *"The water I give people will be like a spring flowing inside them. **It will bring them eternal life."***

But other scholars point out that Jesus uses the *"living water"* phrase again in John 7:37-39, which says this: *"Whoever is thirsty may come to me and drink. If anyone believes in me, rivers of living water will flow out from their heart. That is what the Scriptures say." **Jesus was talking about the Spirit.***

John 4:19-24

[19] *The woman said, "Sir, I can see that you are a prophet.* [20] *Our fathers worshiped on this mountain. But you Jews say that Jerusalem is the place where people must worship."*

[21] *Jesus said, "Believe me, woman! The time is coming when you will not have to be in Jerusalem or on this mountain to worship the Father.* [22] *You Samaritans worship something you don't understand. We Jews understand what we worship, since salvation comes from the Jews.* [23] *But the time is coming when the true worshipers will worship the Father in spirit and truth. In fact, that time is now here. And these are the kind of people the Father wants to be his worshipers.* [24] *God is spirit. So the people who worship him must worship in spirit and truth."*

Two Churches, Two Styles of Worship—I love coming to Highland Church for worship. The song service is encouraging and uplifting; the band and praise team are gifted and always on key. The sermons are inspiring and convicting, but always short and to the point. And I am awed at the way we do communion. We allow families to bring to the table their own unique experiences of life, which moves us to a thought-provoking breaking of bread and a reflective drinking of the cup of Messiah. The prayers are reverent in their praises and humble in their requests. Everything is precisely planned and is always neat and tidy. Truth is, I am never hesitant in asking my friends to visit one of our services and am proud when they comment on the worshipful and inspirational atmosphere they have just encountered. I would wager that Nicodemus, in the third chapter of John, went to a synagogue that was much like Highland. And I'll bet the people who worshiped there really knew how to do church.

Every Wednesday night, some friends of mine and I worship at Freedom Fellowship. Dubbed "Freedom" for short, this ministry of Highland Church is an outreach by the Holy Spirit into one of the economically depressed areas of Abilene. In 2005, a small cluster of Highland members began meeting on Wednesday nights, on the corner of South Ninth and Chestnut Street, for a Bible study and prayer service, dreaming of a full building, sometime in the future, and praying that God's Spirit would whisper His love into the hearts of our neighbors. On Sunday afternoons several of us began walking through the surrounding neighborhood, where poverty was widespread and satan had bound so many of our fellow sufferers of sin with addiction and abuse. Our small army would walk up to houses and, as several doors would crack open slightly at our knock, we would ask, "Do you or anyone in your home have prayer needs?" As the Sundays came and went, many of these, the "disregarded of the world's political and financial power," would seem to enjoy our weekly visits, even inviting us to come inside.

One Saturday evening in the fall of the year, Freedom Fellowship opened its doors to a hamburger fry, followed by an awesome worship service, in our small auditorium, led by our very own praise band. With guitars, drums, keyboard, and an occasional tambourine we would act out David's 150th Psalm, verse 6: *Everything that breathes, praise the LORD!* Those Saturdays became monthly affairs, even adding communion and inviting everyone present to come to the Table of the Lord, where the Master Himself welcomes all. Wednesdays became a teaching time as both adults and children began filling this once-empty building with voices and bodies. Two summers of Vacation Bible Schools, umpteen Saturday guest speakers, and Wednesday evenings have brought a whole lot of children and adults to our weekly Bible classes and once-a-month praise nights.

Sometimes, I must admit, I squirm a little when we do church in that setting. When we have testimonies, I never know what I am going to hear, and I have been known to cringe, thinking, "Is what's being said even scriptural?" Communion is usually a grand experience, but I also remember the occasion when two men became involved in a heated discussion as they were waiting together in line coming to our Lord's Table. The praise time is typically inspiring, although sometimes we use someone from the community to change the song transparencies on the overhead who may be so involved in the music that we may be singing the third verse while the first verse or even the previous song is still showing on the screen. And some of our voices might, in a different setting, be the first casualties of America's Got Talent.

Both Highland Church and Freedom Fellowship share the Table of Messiah regularly with the Master. Jesus equally loves the worship where His people seem practiced in how to do church and the praises of His children where "church" can be somewhat less tidy. I'm sure He was just as comfortable in Sychar's brush arbor as He was in Jerusalem's Temple. He is just as pleased or displeased in either setting today. Jesus is not concerned with the label on my clothes, the way I blend my voice in song with others, or the credentials I bring or lack. His concern is with the condition of my heart. I can't help but think of His words from Matthew 5:3: *"Great blessings belong to those who know they are spiritually in need. God's kingdom belongs to them."*

You and I are siblings born of the same Father, and, just as I didn't get to choose my earthly family, I also wasn't able to pick my spiritual one either. I must stop behaving as though the citizens of Sychar are somehow less deserving of dignity and love than the people of Jerusalem. The same God who created the cultured Nicodemus also created the uncouth woman at the well. And as God witnessed each of their births, I'm sure His heart was just as proud of both of His creations. Thank God that when I stand before Him, He will not ask me about my social standing, my education, or how much money was in my bank account. And I have my doubts that He will care whether I was in a group who knew how to do church well. He may ask me, though, "Darell, what did you do when you saw your brother hungry or thirsty or naked or sick or a stranger or in prison? Did you see in them, Jesus?" I sure hope I have a good answer to that one.

As Jesus continued speaking to the woman the conversation seemed to take another turn. The woman changed the subject from something she thought was very uncomfortable, her marital status. They had been discussing "living water." Now she asks about worship, and Jesus answers in verses 23-24: *"...the time is coming when the true worshipers will worship the Father in spirit and truth. In fact, that time is now here. And these are the kind of people the Father wants to be his worshipers. God is spirit. So the people who worship him must worship in spirit and truth."*

We are both physical beings and spiritual beings. Though we worship with our physical bodies, true worship comes from the spiritual part of us. The place of worship is unimportant, whether in Jerusalem, at the Temple, in a church building, or under a tree. The style of worship is unimportant, whether solemn quietness, loud shouting, or somewhere in between. Even the position of worship is unimportant, hands raised, knees bent, standing, sitting, or prostrate. We are each a temple of the Holy Spirit. All believers are part of the spiritual House of God. Our spiritual hands are raised in praise, our spiritual knees are bent in reverence, our spiritual eyes are on the One who died for our sins and our spiritual hearts sing to the King of Kings.

True worship is also done in truth. The Samaritans were half Jews, who, many years before, worshiped Jehovah as just another god among many. Even though they learned over the years about the One true God, they only accepted the first five books of the Old Testament and were ignorant of a true knowledge of God.

Where the Samaritan woman worshipped what she didn't know, we believe in and know the Father, through His Son and our Lord and Savior Jesus. True worshipers are believers in God's Messiah. The woman didn't understand all that Jesus had told her. She says in verse 25: *"I know that the Messiah is coming...When he comes, he will explain everything to us."* When Jesus revealed whom, He was to the woman by saying, *"I am the Messiah."* the woman ran back to her village and told everyone she could find that the Messiah had come to visit them. She, now, can not only worship in spirit, but also in truth, because she has met, talked to, and believed in God's Messiah, Jesus.

John 4:25-33

[25] *The woman said, "I know that the Messiah is coming." (He is the one called Christ.) "When he comes, he will explain everything to us."*

[26] *Then Jesus said, "He is talking to you now—I am the Messiah."*

[27] *Just then Jesus' followers came back from town. They were surprised because they saw Jesus talking with a woman. But none*

of them asked, "What do you want?" or "Why are you talking with her?"

²⁸ Then the woman left her water jar and went back to town. She told the people there, ²⁹ "A man told me everything I have ever done. Come see him. Maybe he is the Messiah." ³⁰ So the people left the town and went to see Jesus.

³¹ While the woman was in town, Jesus' followers were begging him, "Teacher, eat something!"

³² But Jesus answered, "I have food to eat that you know nothing about."

³³ So the followers asked themselves, "Did someone already bring him some food?"

"It's Supposed to Be a Secret, for Now"—That's what Andrea and Clyde told each person in the immediate family. Andrea, exclaimed, "Clyde asked me to marry him at the fireworks show in Anson on July 3rd!" They kept it off Facebook for a while until they told the important people in their lives. "We're engaged," they excitedly exclaimed to Annette and me! And, of course, we were thrilled.

I Am the Messiah—Usually, people who want to make an important announcement tell family and friends first; then they tell the world. The unnamed woman answers Jesus in verse 23: *"I know that the Messiah is coming. When he comes, he will explain everything to us."* Jesus had hinted to some and used code language—**Son of Man**— to others. But here, in Samaria, to a person He had just met, to an uneducated, immoral woman who is avoided even among her people, Jesus announces for the first time, *"I am the Messiah."* Why would He make such a declaration to a person the world would see as foolish? The Apostle Paul answers this about the "so-called" wise of the world in 1 Corinthians 1:18-31:

The teaching about the cross seems foolish to those who are lost. But to us who are being saved it is the power of God. As the Scriptures say,

"I will destroy the wisdom of the wise

I will confuse the understanding of the intelligent."

So what does this say about the philosopher, the law expert, or anyone in this world who is skilled in making clever arguments? God has made the wisdom of the world look foolish. This is what God in his wisdom decided: Since the world did not find him through its own wisdom, he used the message that sounds foolish to save those who believe it.

The Jews ask for miraculous signs, and the Greeks want wisdom. But this is the message we tell everyone: Christ was killed on a cross. This message is a problem for Jews, and to other people it is nonsense. But Christ is God's power and wisdom to the people God has chosen, both Jews and Greeks. Even the foolishness of God is wiser than human wisdom. Even the weakness of God is stronger than human strength.

Brothers and sisters, God chose you to be his. Think about that! Not many of you were wise in the way the world judges wisdom. Not many of you had great influence, and not many of you came from important families. But God chose the foolish things of the world to shame the wise. He chose the weak things of the world to shame the strong. And God chose what the world thinks is not important—what the world hates and thinks is nothing. He chose these to destroy what the world thinks is important. God did this so that no one can stand before him and boast about anything. It is God who has made you part of Christ Jesus. And Christ has become for us wisdom from God. He is the reason we are right with God and pure enough to be in his presence. Christ is the one who set us free from sin. So, as the Scriptures say, "Whoever boasts should boast only about the Lord."

John 4:34-42

[34] Jesus said, "My food is to do what the one who sent me wants me to do. My food is to finish the work that he gave me to do. [35] When you plant, you always say, 'Four more months to wait before we gather the grain.' But I tell you, open your eyes, and look at the fields. They are ready for harvesting now. [36] Even now, the people who harvest the crop are being paid. They are gathering crops for eternal life. So now the people who plant can be happy together with those who harvest. [37] It is true when we say, 'One person plants, but another person harvests the crop.' [38] I sent you to harvest a crop that you did not work for. Others did the work, and you get the profit from their work."

[39] Many of the Samaritan people in that town believed in Jesus. They believed because of what the woman had told them about him. She had told them, "He told me everything I have ever done." [40] The Samaritans went to Jesus. They begged him to stay with them. So he stayed there two days. [41] Many more people became believers because of the things he said.

[42] The people said to the woman, "First we believed in Jesus because of what you told us. But now we believe because we heard him ourselves. We know now that he really is the one who will save the world."

Peach Picking Time—Two of our granddaughters, Avyn and Ella have gone, with their Nana, to a small farm outside of Abilene to pick peaches as a part of "Nana Camp." Nana looks forward to this yearly harvest, but it only comes in the summer. Sometimes, because of a late winter frost, the harvest is a week late. At other times it is a week early. There is great excitement as Nana takes each granddaughter to that peach orchard. After the peaches are picked and paid for, these harvesters hurry home to peel, cut up, bag, and freeze those peaches. The fruit will, one day soon, turn into peach cobbler or peach dumplings.

Harvesting Time—As his disciples come back to Jesus, He tells them in verse 35, to look at the people coming: *"...open your eyes, and look at the fields. They are ready for harvesting now."* These true worshipers are coming to hear the good news that the Father sent the Son to die for the world. And the statement the Samaritan people make to the woman who first witnessed to them is the same that we now make. Verse 42: *The people said to the woman, "First we believed in Jesus because of what you told us. But now we believe because we heard him ourselves. We know now that he really is the one who will save the world."*

(Second Sign)

John 4:43-54

Royal Official's Son Healed

[43] Two days later Jesus left and went to Galilee. [44] (Jesus had said before that a prophet is not respected in his own country.) [45] When he arrived in Galilee, the people there welcomed him. They had been at the Passover festival in Jerusalem and had seen everything he did there.

[46] Jesus went to visit Cana in Galilee again. Cana is where he had changed the water into wine. One of the king's important officials

lived in the city of Capernaum. This man's son was sick. ⁴⁷ The man heard that Jesus had come from Judea and was now in Galilee. So he went to Jesus and begged him to come to Capernaum and heal his son, who was almost dead. ⁴⁸ Jesus said to him, "You people must see miraculous signs and wonders before you will believe in me."

⁴⁹ The king's official said, "Sir, come before my little son dies."

⁵⁰ Jesus answered, "Go. Your son will live."

The man believed what Jesus told him and went home. ⁵¹ On the way home, the man's servants came and met him. They said, "Your son is well."

⁵² The man asked, "What time did my son begin to get well?"

They answered, "It was about one o'clock yesterday when the fever left him."

⁵³ The father knew that one o'clock was the same time that Jesus had said, "Your son will live." So the man and everyone in his house believed in Jesus.

⁵⁴ That was the second miraculous sign that Jesus did after coming from Judea to Galilee.

My Cousin Barbara, Healed! —I came home on the bus from school as usual. My dad was in the backyard, but his face told me something was wrong. "Your cousin, Barbara, is not expected to live," he told me. The words went into my brain but didn't make sense. I heard them, but I knew this couldn't be happening. He had been over to her parents' house when she suddenly started screaming and clawing at the front window. "Your Uncle Duane and I were outside when it happened. We saw her in the window and rushed to her. She's at the hospital. The doctors think she had a brain aneurysm."

Barbara was like my sister. She and I had grown up almost always together. She was fourteen, and I was a year younger. I fell to the ground crying. I couldn't accept the words. Barbara was dying. I prayed harder than I'd ever prayed in my life. I begged God and pleaded with God not to take her away. There were lots of prayers prayed, more than just mine, and lots of tears shed, and lots of begging. "Please God, let her live."

We were told she had one chance in a thousand to live, and even if she did, the hemorrhage may have caused a lot of brain damage. But live she did. God answered those prayers. With no brain damage, Barbara went on to graduate from college and become a teacher. She got married and raised three daughters. God healed her completely. I did notice one thing different about Barbara, though. She was more serious about God and life. Oh, she was still fun to be around, and we still laughed a lot together, but she was definitely different.

The Son Is Healed—This miracle in John 4, was also performed in Galilee. Jesus was not even with the sick boy when He healed him, proving that the Messiah could heal at a distance.

Verse 45 tells us that the Galileans welcomed Jesus because they had seen all the things He had done in Jerusalem. This, most likely, is speaking of the miracles and the clearing of the Temple in 2:12-25. Many of the people were seeing Jesus as either a political figure or a miracle worker which is probably why Jesus made the statement in 4:48: *Jesus said to him, "You people must see miraculous signs and wonders before you will believe in me."*

The comment was most likely directed more toward the Galileans than the royal official himself. I like the attitude of this man. The Bible said he begged Jesus to heal his son. Having children, I know the feeling that you would do anything for your child, even begging someone to heal them.

The man also took Jesus at His word, because we are told he left and didn't insist that Jesus follow him home. I'm sure if he was like most of us, there would still be that lingering doubt in his mind, for when his servants met him with the good news, he asked what time the boy got better. Because the boy was healed, the father and his whole family put their faith in Jesus.

(Third Sign)

John 5:1-15

Paralyzed Man Healed after 38 Years

¹ Later, Jesus went to Jerusalem for a special Jewish festival. ² In Jerusalem there is a pool with five covered porches. In Aramaic it is called Bethzatha. This pool is near the Sheep Gate. ³ Many sick people were lying on the porches beside the pool. Some of them were blind, some were crippled, and some were paralyzed. ⁵ One of the men lying there had been sick for 38 years. ⁶ Jesus saw him lying there and knew that he had been sick for a very long time. So he asked him, "Do you want to be well?"

⁷ The sick man answered, "Sir, there is no one to help me get into the water when it starts moving. I try to be the first one into the water. But when I try, someone else always goes in before I can."

⁸ Then Jesus said, "Stand up! Pick up your mat and walk." ⁹ Immediately the man was well. He picked up his mat and started walking.

The day all this happened was a Sabbath day. ¹⁰ So some Jews said to the man who had been healed, "Today is the Sabbath. It is against our law for you to carry your mat on the Sabbath day."

¹¹ But he answered, "The man who made me well told me, 'Pick up your mat and walk.'"

¹² They asked him, "Who is the man who told you to pick up your mat and walk?"

¹³ But the man who had been healed did not know who it was. There were many people there, and Jesus had left.

¹⁴ Later, Jesus found the man at the Temple and said to him, "See, you are well now. But stop sinning or something worse may happen to you!"

¹⁵ Then the man left and went back to the Jews who questioned him. He told them that Jesus was the one who made him well.

Robert Reid—I have a friend whom I've known for quite some time who has an interesting story. Robert was born with cerebral palsy. It affected his speech, produced lameness in his arms and legs, and affected his body movements. It, however, did not affect his mind. After graduating from high school, he went on to enter a Christian college in Abilene, Texas. There were no laws in the 1960s that helped the disabled, and there were no computers that helped them navigate the academic world. Robert was on his own. Now, that's not to say he didn't have friends, family members, fellow students, and professors to help; he did.

Robert graduated from college and became a missionary to Portugal, where he had to, again, navigate a different culture and language. He established several churches while there. He met and married his wife, Rosa, who became his hands and feet. They even had a daughter, born to them. After years in that country, Robert came back to the United States and Rosa became a citizen. Now Robert, in his 80s, and Rosa, visit a Texas prison each week teaching the men life skills and the Bible.

Healing the Paralyzed Man—Jesus is looking for belief in all individuals, but belief and gratitude are not necessarily prerequisites for healing. This man didn't know who Jesus was before he was healed and didn't know Him after he was healed. I'm not even sure he wanted to be healed. When asked that question, the man made an excuse for not being able to get into the pool when the water "starts moving," verse 7. This man had a different reaction than another man who was healed of lameness, begging Peter and John for some money. In Acts 3: 6-8:

> But Peter said, "I don't have any silver or gold, but I do have something else I can give you. By the power of Jesus Christ from Nazareth—stand up and walk!"

> Then Peter took the man's right hand and lifted him up. Immediately his feet and legs became strong. He jumped up, stood on his feet, and began to walk. He went into the Temple area with them. He was walking and jumping and praising God.

The man Jesus healed wasn't even grateful. When he found out who Jesus was, he went and told the authorities about Him. It reminds us of when Jesus healed the ten men who had leprosy in Luke 17, and only one of them returns to thank Him.

I often wonder about the others who were present that day at the pool, also needing healing. Why didn't Jesus heal them? Why didn't He heal someone who would have been more grateful? I guess the same thing can be said today when we praise God for someone who is healed of an illness and yet we're left to wonder why another doesn't get well. Why did God choose that one and not the other? Why does He heal some who are not grateful, and leave others unhealed who would surely have been grateful?

In my case, my first wife, Carolyn died of adrenal cancer at the age of 28, leaving behind a son, age four, and a daughter age one. I married again to have my second wife die of ovarian cancer, leaving a son of twenty and another still in high school at age sixteen. Many prayers were lifted up for both of these women of faith, but God did not intervene in sparing their lives.

Job says this after losing all his children, possessions, and health in Job 1:21:

> *"When I was born into this world,*
> *I was naked and had nothing.*
> *When I die and leave this world,*
> *I will be naked and have nothing.*
> *The LORD gives,*
> *and the LORD takes away.*
> *Praise the name of the LORD!"*

Isaiah 55:8: *The LORD says, "My thoughts are not like yours. Your ways are not like mine."*

I don't have an answer to the mysteries of God in matters like these. He is God and I trust that He knows what He is doing, even if I don't. But I will make a few observations that help me understand this healing of the lame man a little better and may help me trust God more in other circumstances. God sent His Son to a world that neither loved Him nor cared about Him.

In Romans 3:10-18, Paul says this:

> *... "There is no one doing what is right,*
> *not even one.*
> *There is no one who understands.*
> *There is no one who is trying to be with God.*
> *They have all turned away from him,*
> *and now they are of no use to anyone.*

There is no one who does good,
  not even one."

"Their words come from mouths that are like open graves.
  They use their lying tongues to deceive others."

"Their words are like the poison of snakes."

"Their mouths are full of cursing and angry words."

"They are always ready to kill someone.
Everywhere they go they cause trouble and ruin.
They don't know how to live in peace."

"They have no fear or respect for God."

It's not a very complementary picture of humankind, is it? Paul goes on to say this about Jesus Christ in Romans 5:6-8:

Christ died for us when we were unable to help
ourselves. We were living against God, but at just
the right time Christ died for us. Very few people will
die to save the life of someone else, even if it is for a
good person. Someone might be willing to die for an
especially good person. But Christ died for us while
we were still sinners, and by this God showed how
much he loves us.

Jesus even died between two thieves and for them, as well. Luke 23 tells us that one of the thieves hurled insults at Jesus and taunted Him, while the other asked Jesus to remember him when He comes into His kingdom. Jesus died for both. One accepted the offer of salvation; the other rejected it. The same is true with those Jesus healed. He healed both the grateful and the ungrateful, both those who would believe in Him and those who would not. In Matthew 5:45 Jesus said: *...He lets the sun rise for all people,* *whether they are good or bad. He sends rain to those who do right and to those who do wrong.*

John 3:16-17 doesn't say, "For God so loved the grateful or the educated or the righteous or the rich or the ones who will believe..." It says: *"God loved the world so much that he gave his only Son, so that everyone who believes in him would not be lost but have eternal life. God sent his Son into the world. He did not send him to judge the world guilty, but to save the world through him.*

Ok, I can understand that none of us deserve any of the good things He does for us, but still, I wonder why did Jesus not heal the others at the pool that day. Maybe part of our problem is what we see as normal. Should God make us all smart or beautiful or athletic or tall or skinny? Is being crippled a curse or could it ever be a blessing? And what about cancer? Could the healing of one show glory to God and the death of another also show glory to God? Remember the story above about Robert Reid who has cerebral palsy and has been in a wheelchair his entire life. Robert never felt sorry for himself. His infirmity has shown glory to God in a way that his complete health may not have. When Paul had a painful problem, he wrote in 2 Corinthians 12:8-10:

> *I begged the Lord three times to take this problem away from me. But the Lord said, "My grace is all you need. Only when you are weak can everything be done completely by my power." So I will gladly boast about my weaknesses. Then Christ's power can stay in me. Yes, I am glad to have weaknesses if they are for Christ. I am glad to be insulted and have hard times. I am glad when I am persecuted and have problems, because it is when I am weak that I am really strong.*

What did Christ do for the man He healed? One thing He did was to take away his dependence on begging for a living. Notice, Jesus asked him, *"Do you want to be well?"* That wasn't just a silly question someone might ask to begin a conversation. Jesus was asking him if he wanted to have the means to work like others, or did he want to beg for the rest of his life. The man was reluctant and never did agree to be healed, but Jesus healed him anyway. Healing may not be all that it is cracked up to be. "Now that I'm healed," the man may have thought, "I no longer have an excuse for begging." Sometimes the gift Jesus may give us is the very thing we least want but in the scheme of things it may be what we most need. I remember when the school where I was teaching was shut down and I was going to be transferred somewhere else. I asked God, "What are you doing? Everything was going well here." But then I was placed in a setting much better than what I had before. God had blessed me; I just hadn't given God a chance to work it all out before I began complaining.

Members of Alcoholics Anonymous use this phrase from Jesus, *"**Do you want to be well?**"* when confronting a fellow alcoholic. The new person must decide whether or not they have the desire to get well and if they can handle the responsibility that goes with it.

FaithWorks—I worked as a teacher for seven years for a wonderful program called FaithWorks. Joyce Dalzell began this program to teach life skills, work skills, and spiritual skills to people who were at a point in their life where they were having a difficult time navigating their world.

The first class graduated in 2003. Some had come from difficult situations due to the death of a spouse, a breakup in a marriage, or another rough life circumstance. Others just wanted to begin a new career and weren't sure how to do it. Two-thirds of these students graduated, and most went on to be successful, finding the job of their dreams. Others did not. Some quit early on because life circumstances wouldn't allow them to work the program only to come back later and finish with a different class. Others needed to work and couldn't juggle both work and school. But others quit just before graduation. "Why?" I would wonder. "Why would these last individuals quit when success was only a week away?" The answer, though unspoken, was difficult to fathom. "If I succeed in this program, I will be expected to produce something, and I'm afraid I can't."

Was the lame man afraid of what others would now expect? We don't know about his early home life. We don't know even what made him lame. But we do know the question Jesus asked him from the beginning: *"**Do you want to be well?**"*

One final question on this healed lame man. What does Jesus mean when he says, *"See, you are well now. But stop sinning or something worse may happen to you!"*

I see several possibilities for this statement of Jesus. First, the man may have wanted to continue his life of begging because it was easier for him. Another possibility may be that it was a self-inflicted injury much like that of an intoxicated individual who wrecks his car and injures himself. Or Jesus could be speaking of the eternal consequences of sin.

John 5:16-29

[16] Jesus was doing all this on the Sabbath day. So these Jews began trying to make him stop. [17] But he said to them, "My Father never stops working, and so I work too."

[18] This made them even more determined to kill him. They thought it was bad enough that he was breaking the law about the Sabbath day. And now he was saying that God is his Father, making himself equal with God!

[19] But Jesus answered, "I assure you that the Son can do nothing alone. He does only what he sees his Father doing. The Son does the same things that the Father does. [20] The Father loves the Son and shows him everything he does. This man was healed. But the Father will show the Son greater things than this to do. Then you will all be amazed. [21] The Father raises the dead and gives them life. In the same way, the Son gives life to those he wants to.

[22] "Also, the Father judges no one. He has given the Son power to do all the judging. [23] God did this so that all people will respect the Son the same as they respect the Father. Anyone who does not respect the Son does not respect the Father. He is the one who sent the Son.

[24] "I assure you, anyone who hears what I say and believes in the one who sent me has eternal life. They will not be judged guilty. They have already left death and have entered into life. [25] Believe me, an important time is coming. That time is already here. People who are dead will hear the voice of the Son of God. And those who listen will live. [26] Life comes from the Father himself. So the Father has also allowed the Son to give life. [27] And the Father has given him the power to judge all people because he is the Son of Man.

[28] "Don't be surprised at this. A time is coming when all people who are dead and in their graves will hear his voice. [29] Then they will come out of their graves. Those who did good in this life will rise and have eternal life. But those who did evil will rise to be judged guilty.

Working on Sunday—Mike was my friend. I knew him in college. He never completed college and became a cook. He was a good cook, although he didn't make a whole lot of money doing it. But it was something he knew how to do well. He married a girl and raised several kids. They lived in a small trailer for a time, and he would always provide the best he could. The family went to church, but he couldn't always make it because he had to work most Sundays. Oh, he loved the Lord and knew the Bible well; he would teach his kids about his Lord but come Sunday the boss needed him to work. And, because the family needed the money, he worked. I don't know why the preacher said what he did. I'm sure he meant well, but he told Mike, God didn't want him working on Sundays. "Ought to be in church," he told him. Mike wanted to be in church. More than anything he wanted to be there with his family, worshipping together, but someone had to put food on the table. So, he felt guilty, and he worried a lot.

I always wondered why the preacher didn't help Mike a little more, seeing as he wanted him to be at church. I wondered why he didn't help him find a better job, one where he didn't have to work on Sundays. I also wondered why the preacher was working on Sunday, seeing how he was so against it. But maybe he didn't think about those things.

Healing on the Sabbath—Jesus does a lot of healing on the Sabbath in the book of John. Verse 17, above says: *In his defense Jesus said to them*, *"My Father never stops working…"* (Even on the Sabbath) *"and so I work too."* (Even on the Sabbath) Matthew 12:8 says: **"***The Son of Man* (Messiah) *is Lord over the Sabbath day."*

There is a Christian worship song titled "Way Maker," Part of the chorus speaks of Father and Son always at work in Their children's lives with this refrain:

> "… Even when I don't see it, You're working
> Even when I don't feel it, You're working
> You never stop, You never stop working
> You never stop, You never stop working" (Leeland, 2019)

John is also affirming, in no uncertain terms, that Jesus is Divine (God in human form). He is continuing his thoughts on John 1:1, *Before the world began, the Word was there. The Word was with God, and the Word was God.* Now John is quoting Jesus, calling God *"my Father"* which the Jewish leaders know was making Jesus equal to God.

Jesus goes on to speak of the relationship between the Father and the Son, both being One God in **agreement**, for example, look at verse 19: *I assure you that the Son can do nothing alone. He does only what he sees his Father doing. The Son does the same things that the Father does."*

They are one in **honor**. For instance, look again at verse 23: *"…God did this so that all people will respect the Son the same as they respect the Father. Anyone who does not respect the Son does not respect the Father. He is the one who sent the Son."*

They are **separate in the work They do**, such as judgment (the Father), being in human form (the Son), and the raising of the dead (the Son).

The Jew was taught from his childhood that there is One God. Now a part of God has been revealed that up till now had not been. How does the Triune God (Father, Son, and Holy Spirit) become part of the belief system of the Jew? It was difficult for the Jew, but it is also a mystery to us who believe in the Son of God. But John makes the doctrine of the Trinity very plain in one respect. If you accept Jesus as Master and Lord, you must also accept Him as the divine God and Creator. You can't have one without the other. *"People* (must) *respect the Son the same as they respect the Father."*

Jesus is also very plain here about eternal life. He tells His disciples that He will raise them. Verses 28-29: *"Don't be surprised at this. A time is coming when all people who are dead and in their graves will hear his voice. Then they will come out of their graves. Those who did good in this life will rise and have eternal life. But those who did evil will rise to be judged guilty."*

Matthew, in his gospel, chapter 24 verses 30-31 quotes Jesus with these words: *"Then there will be something in the sky that shows the Son of Man is coming. All the people of the world will cry. Everyone will see the Son of Man coming on the clouds in the sky. He will come with power and great glory. He will use a loud trumpet to send his angels all around the earth. They will gather his chosen people from every part of the earth."*

The Apostle Paul in his letter to the Gentile Christians of Thessalonica quotes Jesus with these words in 1 Thessalonians 4:15-17:

> *What we tell you now is the Lord's own message. Those of us who are still living when the Lord comes again will join him, but not before those who have already died. The Lord himself will come down from heaven with a loud command, with the voice of the archangel, and with the trumpet call of God. And the people who have died and were in Christ will rise first. After that we who are still alive at that time will be gathered up with those who have died. We will be taken up in the clouds and meet the Lord in the air. And we will be with the Lord forever.*

John 5:30-47

[30] "I can do nothing alone. I judge only the way I am told. And my judgment is right, because I am not trying to please myself. I want only to please the one who sent me.

31 "If I tell people about myself, they cannot be sure that what I say is true. **32** But there is someone else who tells people about me, and I know that what he says about me is true.

33 "You sent men to John, and he told you what is true. **34** I don't need anyone to tell people about me, but I remind you of what John said so that you can be saved. **35** John was like a lamp that burned and gave light, and you were happy to enjoy his light for a while.

36 "But I have a proof about myself that is greater than anything John said. The things I do are my proof. These are what my Father gave me to do. They show that the Father sent me. **37** And the Father who sent me has given proof about me himself. But you have never heard his voice. You have never seen what he looks like. **38** The Father's teaching does not live in you, because you don't believe in the one the Father sent. **39** You carefully study the Scriptures. You think that they give you eternal life. These same Scriptures tell about me! **40** But you refuse to come to me to have that life.

41 "I don't want praise from you or any other human. **42** But I know you—I know that you have no love for God. **43** I have come from my Father and speak for him, but you don't accept me. But when other people come speaking only for themselves, you accept them. **44** You like to have praise from each other. But you never try to get the praise that comes from the only God. So how can you believe? **45** Don't think that I will be the one to stand before the Father and accuse you. Moses is the one to accuse you. And he is the one you hoped would save you. **46** If you really believed Moses, you would believe me, because he wrote about me. **47** But you don't believe what he wrote, so you can't believe what I say."

Matt and His Reputation—When my son, Matt was growing up, I use to tell him how important a reputation was. "A reputation," I would tell him, "is what others think about you. In a sense, it is evidence about who you are and how you act." When Matt was in the sixth grade, a boy, a bully, would come up behind the smaller boys and pull on their backpacks, making the boys fall backward to the ground. When that same boy pulled Matt down, one day, Matt fell in such a way that he broke his leg. When the principal found out the identity of the two boys involved, he immediately began to conclude what had taken place. The other boy was known as a troublemaker and fortunately, Matt was not. Other teachers and students were quick to tell the principal about Matt and the other boy, and Matt learned a valuable lesson. Your reputation precedes you and gives testimony to who you are.

Some versions of the book of John use the word testimony. The NIV uses "testimony" and "testify." They are very much words you may hear today in a court of law. Read verses 31-32 above again in that version: *"If I testify about myself, my testimony is not true. There is another who testifies in my favor, and I know that his testimony about me is true.*

Testimony and testify were also important to the Jews. The ninth commandment was *"Do not give false testimony."* A testimony that involved the death penalty had to be given by more than one witness. If a Jew was selling a piece of property usually it was done with several witnesses present. Jesus gives five examples of testimonies about who He is.

The First Witness Is the Father—Verses 32 and 37 say: *"But there is someone else who tells people about me, and I know that what he says about me is true..." "But I have a proof about myself that is greater than anything John said. The things I do are my proof. These are what my Father gave me to do. They show that the Father sent me."*

The Father's voice at the baptism of Jesus should have been enough proof. Read with me Matthew 3:16-17: *So Jesus was baptized. As soon as he came up out of the water, the sky opened, and he saw God's Spirit coming down on him like a dove. A voice from heaven said, "This is my Son, the one I love. I am very pleased with him."*

The Second Witness Is John the Baptist—Verse 33 says: *"You sent men to John, and he told you what is true."*

Read the word of John the Baptist in John 1:32-34: *Then John said this for everyone to hear: "I also did not know who the Messiah was. But the one who sent me to baptize with water told me, 'You will see the Spirit come down and rest on a man. He is the one who will baptize with the Holy Spirit.' I have seen this happen. I saw the Spirit come down from heaven like a dove and rest on this man. So this is what I tell people: 'He is the Son of God.'"*

The Third Witness Is the Miracles Themselves—Verse 36 says: *"But I have a proof about myself that is greater than anything John said. The things I do are my proof. These are what my Father gave me to do. They show that the Father sent me."*

The book of John calls these miracles, signs. There are seven, leading up to the resurrection. Matthew, Mark, and Luke record even more. There were about 38 separate miracles recorded in all four gospel accounts plus others implied.

The Fourth Witness Is Scripture—Verse 39 says: *"You carefully study the Scriptures. You think that they give you eternal life. These same Scriptures tell about me!"*

The Old Testament Scriptures about Jesus are too numerous to recount here, but a story from Luke's gospel tells of two disciples who met Jesus after His resurrection on a road to the town of Emmaus. Here is a portion of that discussion from Luke 24:25-27:

Then Jesus said to the two men, "You are foolish and slow to realize what is true. You should believe everything the prophets said. The prophets said the Messiah must suffer these things before he begins his time of glory." Then he began to explain everything that had been written about himself in the Scriptures. He started with the books of Moses and then he talked about what the prophets had said about him.

The Fifth Witness Is Moses—Verses 46 and 47 say: *"If you really believed Moses, you would believe me, because he wrote about me. But you don't believe what he wrote, so you can't believe what I say."*

You may ask, "How is Moses a witness?" Moses is a witness because of what he wrote. Moses is the author of the first five books of the Bible.

Moses wrote in Genesis 49:10:

> *"Men from Judah's family will be kings.*
> *The sign that his family rules*
> *will not leave his family before the **real king comes.***
> ***Then many people will obey and serve him.***"

Again, he wrote in Numbers 24:17:

> *"I see him coming, but not now.*
> *I see him coming, but not soon.*
> ***A star will come from the family of Jacob.***
> ***A new ruler will come from the Israelites.***
> *He will smash the heads of the Moabites*
> *and crush the heads of all the sons of Sheth"*.

And, Finally, in Deuteronomy 18:15: *"The LORD your God will send to you **a prophet**. This prophet will come from among your own people, and he will be like me. You must listen to him."*

I would venture to say that if this much evidence would be given before the court that condemned Jesus to death, a positive identity of Son of God and Messiahship would have been established. How much more proof would I, personally, need to proclaim and claim Him, to trust and obey Him and to love and worship Him? (Paraphrased from the NIV Study Bible notes, 1995)

(Fourth Sign)

John 6:1-15

Feeding the 5,000

¹ Later, Jesus went across Lake Galilee (also known as Lake Tiberias). ² A great crowd of people followed him because they saw the miraculous signs he did in healing the sick. ³ Jesus went up on the side of the hill and sat there with his followers. ⁴ It was almost the time for the Jewish Passover festival.

⁵ Jesus looked up and saw a crowd of people coming toward him. He said to Philip, "Where can we buy enough bread for all these people to eat?" ⁶ He asked Philip this question to test him. Jesus already knew what he planned to do.

⁷ Philip answered, "We would all have to work a month to buy enough bread for each person here to have only a little piece!"

⁸ Another follower there was Andrew, the brother of Simon Peter. Andrew said, ⁹ "Here is a boy with five loaves of barley bread and two little fish. But that is not enough for so many people."

¹⁰ Jesus said, "Tell everyone to sit down." This was a place with a lot of grass, and about 5000 men sat down there. ¹¹ Jesus took the loaves of bread and gave thanks for them. Then he gave them to the people who were waiting to eat. He did the same with the fish. He gave them as much as they wanted.

¹² They all had plenty to eat. When they finished, Jesus said to his followers, "Gather the pieces of fish and bread that were not eaten. Don't waste anything." ¹³ So they gathered up the pieces that were left. The people had started eating with only five loaves of barley bread. But the followers filled twelve large baskets with the pieces of food that were left.

¹⁴ The people saw this miraculous sign that Jesus did and said, "He must be the Prophet who is coming into the world."

¹⁵ Jesus knew that the people planned to come get him and make him their king. So he left and went into the hills alone.

Food Miracle for a Family—We were living for a time in Salinas, California. It was about 1985 and Jeremy and Joanna were twelve and eight, and Matt was a year old. Times were hard financially; I was working three jobs, and Maryanne was babysitting and cutting people's hair in our home, along with taking care of our three children. Things were unusually difficult one month; we ran out of money and food before we ran out of month. Maryanne said, "We need to pray." And we did. We gathered our children, and the five of us prayed for food for the next week. It wasn't long after that prayer, maybe fifteen or twenty minutes, there was a knock on our door. One of our elders, at the congregation where we worshipped, was standing there with several bags of food. He said his daughter had just gotten married, and they had a lot of food left over from the reception. Would we like to have it? You could hear Maryanne, as usual, whispering a prayer of thanksgiving. We had been blessed; God had provided. I wish I could tell you I learned from that day forward to trust God, but I'm afraid fear and worry are two sins I have a difficult time giving up.

Food Miracle for 5000 Plus—I believe there was a reason why Jesus withdrew to this lonely place by the sea, other than just trying to get away from the crowds. The book of John tells us about the death of John the Baptist. But in Matthew 14:13-14, that author fills in some details. Matthew tells us that John the Baptist had been put into prison and had just been beheaded. Part of the reason, too, is that Jesus needed some time to process His upcoming martyrdom.

> *When Jesus heard what happened to John, he left in a boat. He went alone to a place where no one lived. But the people heard that Jesus had left. So they left their towns and followed him. They went by land to the same place he went. When Jesus got out of the boat, he saw a large crowd of people. He felt sorry for them, and he healed the ones who were sick.*

The other gospel writers don't say anything about the motives of the people, but John does. John 6:2 says: *A great crowd of people followed him because they saw the miraculous signs he did in healing the sick.*

At first glance, this seems like people following Jesus because He can heal them but something else changed after the miracle that Matthew, Mark, and Luke don't seem to take up in their narratives. Verses 14 and 15 of John: *The people saw this miraculous sign that Jesus did and said, "He must be the Prophet who is coming into the world." Jesus knew that the people planned to come get him and make him their king. So he left and went into the hills alone.*

Looking for the Wrong Kind of Messiah—The people not only saw Jesus as a miracle worker but as a powerful force to deliver them from Roman domination. The Romans had conquered most of the known world by this time, including the land of Jesus and His fellow Jews. Most Jews were looking for a savior, a messiah, who would lead them and save them from the Romans. They were looking for a physical kingdom like the one their forefather, David, led. Even His closest disciples did not fully understand. Jesus was not that kind of savior or messiah. Jesus came to save us from the power of bigger enemies than the Romans. He came the save us from satan, sin, and death. He was truly the Savior (Capital S) and Messiah (capital M). So, I will ask you. Do you see Jesus as a political solution to your needs and wants? Do you see Him as the leader of a political party or movement of violent people wanting to right all the wrongs of our nation? Do you see Him as a savior and messiah, or do you see Him as your Savior and your Messiah?

Jesus heals the physically sick people and feeds the physically hungry people who have impure motives. That is very God-like and reminds us that Jesus tells us to pray for our enemies and to do good to those who persecute us. That concept seems so foreign to us humans, but Jesus calls the people of His kingdom to be different from those of the world.

Thinking Out of the Box—In verses 5-6, Jesus tests His disciples with: *When Jesus looked up and saw a large crowd coming toward him, he said to Philip, "Where can we buy enough bread for all these people to eat?" He asked Philip this question to test him. Jesus already knew what he planned to do.*

Philip sees this problem as impossible, thinking only of the amount of money it would cost. Andrew, at least, goes a little farther in his thinking and says that there is a boy with five small barley loaves and two small fish. But even Andrew sees the whole thing as irresolvable. Jesus, of course, thinks out of the box; He knows the power of God and uses it to feed the people. Jesus does what only God can do. Now, if you think about it, you know if God could create all that exists out of nothing, and if He fed Israel in the desert for forty years, surely, He can provide food to feed these people. And He does.

John tells us there were five thousand men. Matthew tells us that the number five thousand does not include the women and children present. So, there were a lot of people. There was also a lot of food left over. Jesus doesn't waste a thing. He and the disciples gathered up the leftovers.

(Fifth Sign)

John 6:16-21

Jesus, Walking on the Water

16 That evening Jesus' followers went down to the lake. 17 It was dark now, and Jesus had not yet come back to them. They got into a boat and started going across the lake to Capernaum. 18 The wind was blowing very hard. The waves on the lake were becoming bigger. 19 They rowed the boat about three or four miles. Then they saw Jesus. He was walking on the water, coming to the boat. They were afraid. 20 But he said to them, "Don't be afraid. It's me." 21 When he said this, they were glad to take him into the boat. And then the boat reached the shore at the place they wanted to go.

Don't Be Afraid—When our younger two kids were growing up, we had an elderly dog we named Frisky that stayed in our backyard, protecting our property from squirrels. Usually, they were faster than she, and almost always they got to the tree ahead of her, but she had done her duty and would bark until we told her she had done a great job. She then went back and lay down waiting for the next one. One day, a squirrel didn't quite make the tree, and Frisky was right on its tail.

The squirrel did the only thing it could do to save its life. It ran up inside one of the gutters attached to our house, which allows the rain to drain through onto the grass. There, the squirrel discovered what others had found out over the years. There is no outlet big enough at the top to allow it to escape. The second problem is the gutter was too skinny to allow the squirrel to turn around. So here was the squirrel holding on to something inside for dear life and screeching at the top of its lungs while the jaws of death are at the other end barking and just waiting for that squirrel to let go.

The kids' mother decided that I needed to rescue the squirrel, so, I proceeded to draw up a plan. First, I put Frisky in her kennel and shut the door. Next, I tried to coax the squirrel out, but it was just as scared of its rescuer as it was of its tormenter. That's when my wife came up with the next idea. She told me I should get the water hose, climb up on a ladder, and squirt water down the top of the gutter. This, she thought, would wash the squirrel out to safety. The water did make the squirrel slide down to the bottom but all I could see was its tail. So, I jumped down and grabbed the tail, and began to pull. Now the squirrel was screeching. Our other inside dog was barking, and the kids and their mom were yelling, "Don't let it bite you!" I managed to get a hold of the squirrel's back legs, and slowly it loosened its grip, probably from exhaustion, and slipped to the ground. It was soaking wet and looked like a drowned rat. It hobbled over to the tree and finally got up enough energy to disappear in the foliage.

I often think of the times in my life when I'm not sure where God is. Everything seems to be going wrong, or I may be sinning and not know how to stop. Out of the mess I seem to be in, Jesus says to me through a song, a person, a scripture, a sermon, or even a seemingly insignificant event, *"Don't be afraid. It's me. Let go."* God doesn't always take us out of the storm, but He does tell us He'll get in the boat and ride through the storm with us.

The disciples in the story were also fearful. They still didn't realize that the Creator of storms and waves was coming toward them. Matthew 14:26 gives this addition to the story: *When they saw him walking on the water, it scared them. "It's a ghost!" they said, screaming in fear.*

I wonder sometimes if we become more fearful of God, who is trying to rescue us than we are of everyone and everything else in our lives that means to do us harm?

John 6:22-27

²² The next day came. Some people had stayed on the other side of the lake. They knew that Jesus did not go with his followers in the boat. They knew that the followers had left in the boat alone. And they knew it was the only boat that was there. ²³ But then some boats from Tiberias came and landed near the place where the people had eaten the day before. This was where they had eaten the bread after the Lord gave thanks. ²⁴ The people saw that Jesus and his followers were not there now. So they got into the boats and went to Capernaum to find Jesus.

²⁵ The people found Jesus on the other side of the lake. They asked him, "Teacher, when did you come here?"

²⁶ He answered, "Why are you looking for me? Is it because you saw miraculous signs? The truth is, you are looking for me because you ate the bread and were satisfied. ²⁷ But earthly food spoils and ruins. So don't work to get that kind of food. But work to get the food that stays good and gives you eternal life. The Son of Man will give you that food. He is the only one qualified by God the Father to give it to you."

If You Feed Them, They Will Come—I noticed, when I began preaching, that we had the biggest crowds at church on potluck Sundays. Oh, we would always have plenty of food, but we also had plenty of people. And, of course, I thought they came to hear me. I always thought about preaching on fasting on potluck Sundays, but I didn't think that would go over well. Everybody would jokingly say, "Preacher, you may need to shorten your sermon today, since it's potluck Sunday," which may be another way of saying, "Preacher, don't talk so much about Jesus; let's get on with the eating." I always wondered why they never asked the song leader to sing fewer songs. Or maybe asked for shorter prayers or possibly do away with the announcements for one Sunday. But we wouldn't change those things, so, as usual, I preached shorter sermons on potluck Sundays.

Jesus, in referring to Himself said in the second part of verse 27: *"The Son of Man will give you that food."* What is the *"food"* Jesus is telling them about? The *"food"* is Jesus, Himself. You will see this in verse 35 where Jesus refers to Himself as the *"bread that gives life."* The problem, as Jesus sees it, is that the people are looking for what Jesus can provide rather than who He is.

John 6:28-34

28 The people asked Jesus, "What does God want us to do?"

29 Jesus answered, "The work God wants you to do is this: to believe in the one he sent."

30 So the people asked, "What miraculous sign will you do for us? If we can see you do a miracle, then we will believe you. What will you do? 31 Our ancestors were given manna to eat in the desert. As the Scriptures say, 'He gave them bread from heaven to eat.'"

32 Jesus said, "I can assure you that Moses was not the one who gave your people bread from heaven. But my Father gives you the true bread from heaven. ³³ *God's bread is the one who comes down from heaven and gives life to the world."*

³⁴ *The people said, "Sir, from now on give us bread like that."*

Sing Along with Ray and Eat Along with Kay—To a freshman in college, food is always important. I remember attending a church, which on Sunday nights after worship, a middle-aged couple we called Ray and Kay would invite the college group to their house to eat. Now, there was a catch. We had to stay and sing along with Ray before we could eat along with Kay.

I always enjoyed singing church songs as a child and that carried over to my college days, but what I enjoyed more than singing was eating. I hate to admit it, but I'm not sure that if the eating part didn't follow the singing part, I, and possibly several others, would not have stayed.

Free Lunch—The crowds didn't fool Jesus. He knew what they were seeking. They wanted a free lunch. They had seen the miracle and yet somehow, they had missed the point. Just who was this man? He was someone who could lead them in their fight against the Romans, someone to feed them, someone who could heal them, and yet Jesus tells them they are seeking the wrong thing.

They are thinking about the physical and He is speaking about the spiritual. Physical food spoils or is eaten, digested and the person is hungry again. But the spiritual food Jesus is offering is Himself. He will never spoil. Once digested, He will give them *"life."* In verse 28 *"The people asked Jesus, "What does God want us to do?"* The NIV translates verse 28 this way, *"What must we do to do the works God requires?"* Jesus answers them in the next verse, *Jesus answered, "The work God wants you to do is this: to believe in the one he sent."*

The people ask Jesus for manna from heaven like Moses gave the children of Israel during their forty years of wandering in the desert. Jesus tells them that He is the true bread from heaven. The people who ate manna still died, but He offers Himself, and those who believe in Him will never die. Of course, Jesus is speaking of spiritual death when He says that they will never die. The people still don't understand. Like the woman at the well who misunderstood Jesus and thought He could give her physical water so that she would never thirst again, or even the intelligent and very religious, Nicodemus who wondered how he could be born again, these people wanted physical bread that would prevent them from dying.

(First, I Am Statement)

John 6:35-51

"I Am the Bread that Gives Life"

35 Then Jesus said, "I am the bread that gives life. No one who comes to me will ever be hungry. No one who believes in me will ever be thirsty. 36 I told you before that you have seen me, and still you don't believe. 37 The Father gives me my people. Every one of them will come to me. I will always accept them. 38 I came down from heaven to do what God wants, not what I want. 39 I must not lose anyone God has given me. But I must raise them up on the last day. This is what the one who sent me wants me to do. 40 Everyone who sees the Son and believes in him has eternal life. I will raise them up on the last day. This is what my Father wants."

41 Some Jews began to complain about Jesus because he said, "I am the bread that comes down from heaven." 42 They said, "This is Jesus. We know his father and mother. He is only Joseph's son. How can he say, 'I came down from heaven'?"

43 But Jesus said, "Stop complaining to each other. 44 The Father is the one who sent me, and he is the one who brings people to me. I will raise them up on the last day. Anyone the Father does not bring to me cannot come to me. 45 It is written in the prophets: 'God will teach them all.' People listen to the Father and learn from him. They are the ones who come to me. 46 I don't mean that there is anyone who has seen the Father. The only one who has ever seen the Father is the one who came from God. He has seen the Father.

47 "I can assure you that anyone who believes has eternal life. 48 I am the bread that gives life. 49 Your ancestors ate the manna God gave them in the desert, but it didn't keep them from dying. 50 Here is the bread that comes down from heaven. Whoever eats this bread will never die. 51 I am the living bread that came down from heaven. Whoever eats this bread will live forever. This bread is my body. I will give my body so that the people in the world can have life."

Live to Eat or Eat to Live—Mom had read something in a magazine that stirred her interest. I was a teenager and not paying much attention. We were sitting in our living room, and she turned to me and asked. "Darell, do you live to eat or eat to live?"

Not being very good at questions which made me think too hard, I didn't know what she meant. So, I said the first thing that came to mind. "I live to eat." Wrong answer!

She tried to explain the concept to me, and I sort of understood—not really—but I acted as if I did. The strange thing about that question was that I remembered it over the years and finally "got it." Being someone who was always hungry and not having seen poverty, I had a very naive, white American concept of food. I guess, truth be told, I did "live to eat."

Jesus says, "Eat to Live." *"I am the bread that gives life,"* says verse 35. John's gospel will have seven I am statements.

1. **"I am the bread that gives life"** (John 6:35, 41, 48, 51)

2. **"I am the light of the world"** (John 8:12)

3. **"I am the gate for the sheep"** (John 10:7,9)

4. **"I am the good shepherd"** (John 10:11, 14)

5. **"I am the resurrection! I am life!"** (John 11:25)

6. **"I am the way, the truth, and the life"** (John 14:6)

7. **"I am the vine, and you are the branches"** (John 15:5)

Jesus will make in each of these I am statements a description of Himself. In the current description, Jesus is declaring that to believe in Him is not to just believe His words but to believe in Him—consume Him. He is the true spiritual bread from heaven.

Now, let's read, again, verses 28-29: *The people asked Jesus, "What does God want us to do?" Jesus answered, "The work God wants you to do is this: to believe in the one he sent."*

Verses 37-39: *"The Father gives me my people. Every one of them will come to me. I will always accept them. I came down from heaven to do what God wants, not what I want. I must not lose anyone God has given me. But I must raise them up on the last day. This is what the one who sent me wants me to do."*

And verse 44: *"The Father is the one who sent me, and he is the one who brings people to me. I will raise them up on the last day. Anyone the Father does not bring to me cannot come to me."*

This dialog is so important we must spend a little time here. Firstly, there seems to be a paradox, that is, the work of God is faith or belief. And secondly, verses 37-39 seem to be implying that we don't even come to God in the first place, but God gives the people to His Son. Verse 44 then makes it even plainer. The NIV translates it this way: *"No one can come to me unless the Father who sent me **draws them"** (that is, pulls or attracts like a magnet). Do you feel the pull of God in your own life?

John 6:52-63

52 Then the Jews began to argue among themselves. They said, "How can this man give us his body to eat?"

53 Jesus said, "Believe me when I say that you must eat the body of the Son of Man, and you must drink his blood. If you don't do this, you have no real life. 54 Those who eat my body and drink my blood have eternal life. I will raise them up on the last day. 55 My body is true food, and my blood is true drink. 56 Those who eat my body and drink my blood live in me, and I live in them.

57 "The Father sent me. He lives, and I live because of him. So everyone who eats me will live because of me. 58 I am not like the bread that your ancestors ate. They ate that bread, but they still died. I am the bread that came down from heaven. Whoever eats this bread will live forever."

59 Jesus said all this while he was teaching in the synagogue in the city of Capernaum.

60 When Jesus' followers heard this, many of them said, "This teaching is hard. Who can accept it?"

61 Jesus already knew that his followers were complaining about this. So he said, "Is this teaching a problem for you? 62 Then what will you think when you see the Son of Man going up to where he came from? 63 It is the Spirit that gives life. The body is of no value for that. But the things I have told you are from the Spirit, so they give life.

My Brother Bill and the Last Supper—Bill was thirteen when I was born and left home to join the Air Force by the time I was five. I don't remember Bill much as a brother at home, but I remember many things about him as a grown-up brother. He had become an adult, married a girl from North Carolina, and had children of his own.

Bill was the quiet brother. He wasn't out in front, much, but was a gentle servant. He was a strong believer but had a soft but passionate voice for his Lord. He was my ideal of what I wanted to be like, especially in his maturity.

Bill learned, in 2007, he was going to die of mesothelioma. He had been exposed to asbestos years earlier and it was now raising its ugly head in Bill's body. Annette and I visited him early in the disease's progression but when I found out from his wife, Eloise, he would be dying soon, I made a trip to his home in south Texas, by myself, to see him one more time. It was almost fall in 2008, but the weather, in that part of Texas, was always warm to hot.

When I entered the living room, Bill was sitting in a recliner and next to him was his youngest son, Jeff, and his wife, Eloise. He was frail for his 72 years, as the disease was ravaging his body. His voice was barely a whisper as he greeted me with a hug.

We talked for some time, but I wanted to share something with him that was more important than the conversation. I brought grape juice and crackers so the four of us could share in this last communion, this final supper of the Lord, together. With tears streaming down our cheeks, we shared the bread, intoning, "This is the body of Christ, broken for you." And when we then drank from the cup, speaking, "This is the blood of Christ, shed for your sins." That solemn moment is etched in my mind to this day.

Afterward, not wanting to break the sacred moment, I asked each of the others, "What communion moment in your past do you feel was the most significant? I don't remember what I said or that of my brother or sister-in-law, but I will always remember the answer my nephew, Jeff gave. "I will always remember this moment with my dad."

Although this discourse in John 6 is not speaking of the Lord's Supper, we can't but think of it while we read it. The bread of communion reminds us of the body of Christ given for us all. And the wine we drink reminds us of the blood Jesus shed on the cross for our sins.

Jesus is not a politician running for office. He isn't telling the people what they want to hear but what they need to hear. Jesus wants to make His point perfectly clear. Beginning in verse 53 He said:

> ... "Believe me when I say that you must eat the body of the Son of Man, and you must drink his blood. If you don't do this, you have no real life. Those who eat my body and drink my blood have eternal life. I will raise them up on the last day. My body is true food, and my blood is true drink. Those who eat my body and drink my blood live in me, and I live in them…Whoever eats this bread will live forever."

They Didn't Get It—Why are the people not getting it? Do they believe Jesus wants them to become cannibals? What was the problem with Nicodemus when Jesus spoke of being born again? He was thinking of physical birth, and Jesus was speaking of spiritual birth. "You must be born from above, Nicodemus." Here Jesus is telling the people and us, "The spiritual food and drink you need for eternal life is Me. You must believe in Me. You must believe that I am the Messiah God has sent to die as a Savior for your sins and to shed My blood for you. Take Me in as you would food and drink. Eat Me and drink Me. Consume Me, every spiritual part of Me, every spiritual cell, every spiritual thought. Come to Me and believe that I am food and drink. Live for Me and live in Me. If you believe this, then I will resurrect you on the Day I come back."

The people don't understand and so in verse 63 Jesus said: *"It is the Spirit that gives life. The body is of no value for that. But the things I have told you are from the Spirit, so they give life.* In other words, "I have been speaking of spiritual things not physical."

John 6:64-71

[64] *But some of you don't believe." (Jesus knew the people who did not believe. He knew this from the beginning. And he knew the one who would hand him over to his enemies.)* [65] *Jesus said, "That is why I said, 'Anyone the Father does not help to come to me cannot come.'"*

[66] *After Jesus said these things, many of his followers left and stopped following him.*

[67] *Jesus asked the twelve apostles, "Do you want to leave too?"*

[68] *Simon Peter answered him, "Lord, where would we go? You have the words that give eternal life.* [69] *We believe in you. We know that you are the Holy One from God."*

[70] *Then Jesus answered, "I chose all twelve of you. But one of you is a devil."* [71] *He was talking about Judas, the son of Simon Iscariot. Judas was one of the twelve apostles, but later he would hand Jesus over to his enemies.*

The Atheist and Me—I Know the last place you would expect to find an atheist is at a Christian college, but there was this guy, this student a year or two older than me, that claimed to be one. I was in a group with him, at one point, and was frightened he would speak to me about his faith or lack of it. I purposely avoided him out of fear. What if he said something that convinced me that there was no God, after all? Years later, I did meet and talked to several people who believed that way, but I had grown in my faith enough that I no longer feared their words. Even when I was asked a question by one of them, I couldn't answer, I always thought, who else offers eternal life, and something deep down inside me knew that I was created for eternity.

Many of the people who had been following Jesus now turned back and stopped following Him. They wanted the miracles, they wanted the bread, but they didn't want the truth. They were afraid of this man's words. Several people I went to college with had a crisis of belief and also lost faith.

I'm not sure the Twelve understood all that He had been saying either. Sometimes we may have a hard time understanding God. Some of the things He says in Scripture are difficult. Some of the things that He allows to happen to us don't seem fair. Some of the circumstances we may find ourselves in, whether from our sins or just the trials of life, leave us wondering whether He is watching over us. I love the statement Peter makes that I hope will always be my statement of faith. Jesus asks in verses 67-69: *"Do you want to leave too?" Simon Peter answered him, "Lord, where would we go? You have the words that give eternal life. We believe in you. We know that you are the Holy One from God."*

John 7:1-9

¹ After this, Jesus traveled around the country of Galilee. He did not want to travel in Judea, because the Jewish leaders there wanted to kill him. ² It was time for the Jewish Festival of Shelters. ³ So his brothers said to him, "You should leave here and go to the festival in Judea. Then your followers there can see the miracles you do. ⁴ If

92

you want to be well known, you must not hide what you do. So, if you can do such amazing things, let the whole world see you do them." ⁵ Jesus' brothers said this because even they did not believe in him.

⁶ Jesus said to them, "The right time for me has not yet come, but any time is right for you to go. ⁷ The world cannot hate you. But the world hates me, because I tell the people in the world that they do evil things. ⁸ So you go to the festival. I will not go now, because the right time for me has not yet come." ⁹ After Jesus said this, he stayed in Galilee.

We Found You on the Side of the Road—Since Bill and Bob were much older than me, I got a lot of attention from them. But I was also told a lot of stories I didn't know whether or not to believe. There was one story that could always ruin my day, and my brothers knew it. They would tell me, "We found you on the side of the road and felt sorry for you, so we took you in." I was 99% sure they were just making it up, but it was that 1% that bugged me.

One day when someone commented about how much I resembled my middle brother, Bob, I looked at both and said, "Ha! I look like Bob, so you couldn't have found me on the side of the road."

Bill was quick to answer, "We found him on the side of the road, too."

Unbelieving Brothers—Jesus' brothers didn't believe in Him as the Messiah. I guess it would be odd to admit that your own brother was the Messiah. They ridiculed Him when they said in verses 4-5: *"If you want to be well known, you must not hide what you do. So, if you can do such amazing things, let the whole world see you do them."*

Public figures show themselves to the world for their recognition and gain. Jesus was doing His teachings and miracles to show the Father's glory, who in turn glorified His Son. In the same way, it is not our job to glorify ourselves. We glorify God, who in turn, will glorify us.

As we know from later writings, Jesus' brothers came to believe in Him after His resurrection. James became one of the main church leaders in the Jerusalem church and the writer of the Book of James. Jude, who wrote the book that bears his name, is also thought to be a brother of Jesus.

What does Jesus mean when He tells His brothers in verse 7: *"The world cannot hate you. But the world hates me, because I tell the people in the world that they do evil things."* The fact that God in the form of man has come to earth is a testimony that the world is evil. Now we can no longer compare ourselves to ourselves; we must compare ourselves to God as a man. It would be like seeing a dirty room in a dim light. It might not look too dirty but shine a bright light into that room and the dirt is no longer hidden. Remember John 1:9? *The true light was coming into the world. This is the true light that gives light to all people.* So, we see that Jesus, as the light, not only shines to mark the way but to show the world what it's really like.

John 7:10-13

10 So his brothers left to go to the festival. After they left, Jesus went too, but he did not let people see him. 11 At the festival the Jewish leaders were looking for him. They said, "Where is that man?"

12 There was a large group of people there. Many of them were talking secretly to each other about Jesus. Some people said, "He is a good man." But others said, "No, he fools the people." 13 But no one was brave enough to talk about him openly. They were afraid of the Jewish leaders.

Camping with London—I remember, not long ago, my grandson London was going to have his birthday. He wanted all his family, including Nana and Papa to go camping. "Make sure you pack the right kinds of food. Where will we go to the bathroom? What if it rains? Who knows how to put up a tent?" All those questions and a thousand more were asked.

I was thinking, "I sure hope the air mattress keeps its air. I hate sleeping on a bed that wobbles from side to side and makes noise every time you move." "By the way," I said aloud, "I hope someone remembered to pack the pump for the air mattresses."

We did get the tent set up, and in the middle of the night, it did begin to rain. "Didn't I tell everyone not to touch the sides of the tent if it rains?" But someone did and, well, you know what happened next. There was water everywhere—the blankets, the sheets, and our clothes were all soaked. We were all sleepy, wet, and grumpy. But then someone, I can't remember who began to laugh at the situation. Pretty soon all of us were laughing. Tents, fortunately, are temporary shelters. Well, maybe the homeless among us would argue that point. But tents are not constructed to be lasting dwellings.

The Festival of Shelters—When Israel was in the desert for 40 years, between their harrowing escape from Egypt and their entrance into the Promise Land, they lived in shelters. This annual festival was a week-long re-enactment of that time, which the Jewish people used as a remembrance for themselves and a teaching tool for their children.

The people were looking for Jesus to show up. Where can He be? Jesus does go to the festival but not in the open. Some were whispering good things, and others were quietly saying the opposite. Verse 13: *But no one was brave enough to talk about him* openly. *They were afraid of the Jewish leaders.* Everyone seemed to be afraid of these men, these leaders. Who were they? They were men who held a lot of authority, as we will see throughout the book of John. They had the power to kick a person out of the synagogue (Jewish church community), as we will see in the story of the man born blind in chapter 9. And they wielded enough influence over the Roman governor Pilate, to get him to crucify the Messiah.

John 7:14-24

14 When the festival was about half finished, Jesus went to the Temple area and began to teach. 15 The Jewish leaders were amazed and said, "How did this man learn so much? He never had the kind of teaching we had!"

16 Jesus answered, "What I teach is not my own. My teaching comes from the one who sent me. 17 People who really want to do what God wants will know that my teaching comes from God. They will know that this teaching is not my own. 18 If I taught my own ideas, I would just be trying to get honor for myself. But if I am trying to bring honor to the one who sent me, I can be trusted. Anyone doing that is not going to lie. 19 Moses gave you the law, right? But you don't obey that law. If you do, then why are you trying to kill me?"

20 The people answered, "A demon is making you crazy! We are not trying to kill you."

21 Jesus said to them, "I did one miracle on a Sabbath day, and you were all surprised. 22 But you obey the law Moses gave you about circumcision—and sometimes you do it on a Sabbath day. (Really, Moses is not the one who gave you circumcision. It came from our ancestors who lived before Moses.) Yes, you often circumcise baby boys on a Sabbath day. 23 This shows that someone can be circumcised on a Sabbath day to obey the Law of Moses. So why are you angry with me for healing a person's whole body on the Sabbath day? ²⁴ *Stop judging by the way things look. Be fair and judge by what is really right."*

A Dancing Mom—My brother Bob, then 15 or 16, was good at playing the accordion; he and the other band members were playing a Polka. Everyone else was dancing and having a good time. I was 5 or 6 and remember getting to dance with my mom. We won a box of chocolate-covered cherries for being the best dancers. By the way, I hate chocolate-covered cherries.

A lot changed in the next few years. A new preacher moved to town, and we had to give up our dancing. I couldn't play cards anymore, and I couldn't go to the movies on Sundays.

Years later, after my dad passed away, my mom was living at a retirement home. She decided to take up line dancing as an exercise but asked my brothers and me what we thought about it. We all told her she should go right ahead and enjoy herself. We even came to watch her a few times, and she was pretty good.

One day, a few months later, I asked her if she was still enjoying line dancing and she said she had stopped. When I asked her why, she told me that a lady she knew complained to her that a preacher's wife should not be dancing. It's strange how we can make so many rules for other people, rules that God never made, and bind them on others.

What is this miracle Jesus is referring to in verse 21? Back in Chapter 5, Jesus heals the man who had been lame for 38 years, at the pool of Bethzatha. If you will remember, there was a back-and-forth discussion between the man and the Jewish leaders. Finally, the leaders even confront Jesus. Here is the climax of that discussion in 5:16-17: *Jesus was doing all this on the Sabbath day.*

So these Jews began trying to make him stop. But he said to them, "My Father never stops working, and so I work too."

The Sabbath day will come up quite a few times in the four gospels. So, let's look back in Exodus 20:8-11 to see what is being referred to:

> *"You must remember to keep the Sabbath a special day. You may work six days a week to do your job. But the seventh day is a day of rest in honor of the LORD your God. So on that day no one should work—not you, your sons and daughters, or your men and women slaves. Even your animals and the foreigners living in your cities must not work! That is because the LORD worked six days and made the sky, the earth, the sea, and everything in them. And on the seventh day, he rested. In this way the LORD blessed the Sabbath—the day of rest. He made that a very special day.*

Keeping the Sabbath is the fourth of the Ten Commandments. Throughout the 1500 years from Moses to Jesus, the Jewish leaders wrote many of their ideas about how others should keep this special day. What was considered work? Circumcision was commanded by God to Abraham and his descendants in Genesis 17:12: *When the baby boy is eight days old, you will circumcise him. Every boy born among your people and every boy who is a slave of your people must be circumcised.* But if the eighth day came on the Sabbath, then circumcision took precedence over the Sabbath.

What if some emergency came up on the Sabbath? Jesus brings up several situations in Luke. Jesus is indignant because the Jewish leaders hound Him for healing a crippled woman on the Sabbath in Luke 13:13-16:

He laid his hands on her, and immediately she was able to stand up straight. She began praising God.

The synagogue leader was angry because Jesus healed on the Sabbath day. He said to the people, "There are six days for work. So come to be healed on one of those days. Don't come for healing on the Sabbath day."

The Lord answered, "You people are hypocrites! All of you untie your work animals and lead them to drink water every day—even on the Sabbath day. This woman that I healed is a true descendant of Abraham. But Satan has held her for 18 years. Surely it is not wrong for her to be made free from her sickness on a Sabbath day!"

In Luke 14:5, Jesus healed a man right in a Jewish leader's home where He had been a guest. Again, it happened to be the Sabbath Day. *Jesus said to the Pharisees and teachers of the law, "If your son or work animal falls into a well on the Sabbath day, you know you would pull him out immediately."*

Jesus was a Sabbath keeper, but He also understood that a loving act, an emergency, or even giving water to your thirsty animals, on the Sabbath, was not what God meant when He commanded keeping the Sabbath. Men had come up with their own rules about Sabbath keeping, and they were binding these rules of men on others.

John 7:25-36

25 Then some of the people who lived in Jerusalem said, "This is the man they are trying to kill. 26 But he is teaching where everyone can see and hear him. And no one is trying to stop him from teaching. Maybe the leaders have decided that he really is the Messiah. 27 But when the real Messiah comes, no one will know where he comes from. And we know where this man's home is."

28 Jesus was still teaching in the Temple area when he said loudly, "Do you really know me and where I am from? I am here, but not by my own decision. I was sent by one who is very real. But you don't know him. 29 I know him because I am from him. He is the one who sent me."

30 When Jesus said this, the people tried to grab him. But no one was able even to touch him, because the right time for him had not yet come. 31 But many of the people believed in Jesus. They said, "We are waiting for the Messiah to come. When he comes, will he do more miraculous signs than this man has done?"

32 The Pharisees heard what the people were saying about Jesus. So the leading priests and the Pharisees sent some Temple police to arrest him. 33 Then Jesus said, "I will be with you a little while longer. Then I will go back to the one who sent me. 34 You will look for me, but you will not find me. 'You cannot come where I am.' What does this mean?"

35 These Jews said to each other, "Where will this man go that we cannot find him? Will he go to the Greek cities where our people live? Will he teach the Greek people there? 36 He says, 'You will look for me, but you will not find me.' He also says, 'You cannot come where I am.' What does this mean?"

According to Rachel—I remember watching the Dallas Cowboys play when my wife and I were visiting my brother, Bob, and his wife, Rachel, after church one Sunday. This was when Roger Staubach was the quarterback, the greatest, according to Rachel. She said he could run around in the backfield forever and no defender could catch him. Rachel always thought about Roger Staubach when she would read about Jesus in verse 30: ...*the people tried to grab him.*

100

But no one was able even to touch him, because the right time for him had not yet come.

Here is that phrase again, *The right time…* He escapes the people who were after Him: *no one was able even to touch him.* The Temple police come to arrest Him. We will find out more about them in the next section. God is sovereign (supreme, superior, and absolute); His will is going to be done when He wants it done. Humans may have self-determination, but it never takes precedence (priority) over God's will.

"Where will this man go," the people ask in verse 35, *that we cannot find him?"* Jesus is good at speaking in figurative language. Even His true disciples have a difficult time following His train of thought. In chapter 16, Jesus' disciples, will again, find the symbolic language difficult to understand when He tells them He is going away. But finally, He tells them plainly in John 16:*28: "I came from the Father into the world. Now I am leaving the world and going back to the Father."* And the disciples "do" understand. Verses 29-30 continue: *Then his followers said, "You are already speaking plainly to us. You are not using words that hide the meaning. We can see now that you know all things. You answer our questions even before we ask them. This makes us believe that you came from God."*

The other people, though, receive a rebuke, *"You cannot come where I am."* Back in chapter 6 verse 44, Jesus, speaking to another crowd, states it this way: *"The Father is the one who sent me, and he is the one who brings people to me. I will raise them up on the last day. Anyone the Father does not bring to me cannot come to me."* God will not send these people to Jesus because their hearts are not right.

Jesus will, at another time, comfort His true disciples with these words in John14:1-3: … *"Don't be troubled. Trust in God, and trust in me. There are many rooms in my Father's house. I would not tell you this if it were not true. I am going there to prepare a place for you. After I go and prepare a place for you, I will come back. Then I will take you with me so that you can be where I am.*

John 7:37-53

37 *The last day of the festival came. It was the most important day. On that day Jesus stood up and said loudly, "Whoever is thirsty may come to me and drink.* **38** *If anyone believes in me, rivers of living water will flow out from their heart. That is what the Scriptures say."* **39** *Jesus was talking about the Spirit. The Spirit had not yet been given to people, because Jesus had not yet been raised to glory. But later, those who believed in Jesus would receive the Spirit.*

40 *When the people heard the things that Jesus said, some of them said, "This man really is the Prophet."*

41 *Other people said, "He is the Messiah."*

And others said, "The Messiah will not come from Galilee. **42** *The Scriptures say that the Messiah will come from the family of David. And they say that he will come from Bethlehem, the town where David lived."* **43** *So the people did not agree with each other about Jesus.* **44** *Some of the people wanted to arrest him. But no one tried to do it.*

45 *The Temple police went back to the leading priests and the Pharisees. The priests and the Pharisees asked, "Why didn't you bring Jesus?"*

46 *The Temple police answered, "We have never heard anyone say such amazing things!"*

47 The Pharisees answered, "So he has fooled you too! *48* You don't see any of the leaders or any of us Pharisees believing in him, do you? *49* But those people out there know nothing about the law. They are under God's curse!"

50 But Nicodemus was there in that group. He was the one who had gone to see Jesus before. He said, *51* "Our law will not let us judge anyone without first hearing them and finding out what they have done."

52 The Jewish leaders answered, "You must be from Galilee too! Study the Scriptures. You will find nothing about a prophet coming from Galilee."

53 Then they all left and went home.

Accused but not Arrested—I was a junior in college and a group of us students would visit the Taylor County jail on Sunday afternoons to teach, worship and pray with inmates. We visited with a threesome from Connecticut who had been arrested for marijuana possession while traveling down Interstate 20. Dubbed the "Connecticut Three" after the infamous "Chicago Seven", they were coming to trial and were going to be tried together. We told them that we would come to their trial.

On the day of the trial, we were seated, waiting for the trio to be led in. As they were being escorted in, I looked at all three and motioned with my hand, "We will be praying for you." Not five minutes later the court had to be cleared because someone had called in a bomb threat. We went outside, and I remember saying to the rest of my friends, "Wouldn't it be crazy if they tried to blame us for the bomb threat?"

The words were barely out of my mouth when the sheriff pointed at me to follow him into his office. He then began accusing me of the offense, by putting his hands in a "T" formation and saying what is this a sign for? Does it mean, "It is time?"

I told him, "No, I made a praying sign to those men. And anyway, why would I do something to harm their case?

He either believed me or thought he didn't have enough evidence to hold me, so he let me go. One lesson I learned was that coded messages can be misunderstood.

Now I know who my law enforcement people are, firsthand, almost being arrested, but who are these temple police? Although the nation of Israel, at this time, is under Roman rule and authority in secular government, the Romans allowed the Jews religious freedom. The Jewish leadership had its own police force, the temple guard, and the use of Roman soldiers, if needed, to help keep the Jews in line. The Romans did not want a repeat of the Jewish rebellions of the past. The Roman governor, Pilate, had a ready army to put down any rebellion but allowed the Jews to keep their people in line before he got involved. Whenever there was talk of a Messiah among the people, the Jewish religious leaders would get nervous. That was the reason they questioned John the Baptist so carefully. Jesus made the leaders very nervous because there was not only talk of a Messiah, which led them to think of rebellion but there was talk of a kingdom and a king, which would make the Romans think the Jews were trying to usurp the rule of Caesar. Jesus would, one day, be arrested at night, by these temple police, at the bidding of the Jewish leaders.

When Jesus tells the people in verses 37-39: *If anyone believes in me, rivers of living water will flow out from their heart. That is what the Scriptures say." Jesus was talking about the Spirit.* It sounds much like what he said to the woman at the well back in chapter 4.

Later in chapter 16:4-10, Jesus will be more open about the Holy Spirit whom He will call the Helper:

> "I did not tell you these things at the beginning, because I was with you then. Now I am going back to the one who sent me...Let me assure you, it is better for you that I go away. I say this because when I go away I will send the Helper to you. But if I did not go, the Helper would not come.

> "When the Helper comes, he will show the people of the world how wrong they are about sin, about being right with God, and about judgment. He will prove that they are guilty of sin, because they don't believe in me. He will show them how wrong they are about how to be right with God. The Helper will do this, because I am going to the Father.

After the resurrection, Jesus will tell His disciples once more to stay in Jerusalem until the Holy Spirit comes to them, as promised. In the second chapter of Acts the Holy Spirit baptizes or floods the new church. And Peter tells the people listening that they can now, for the first time, be baptized in the name of Jesus, and they, too, can receive the Holy Spirit Jesus promised to all those who believe in Him.

The crowd is divided. The Jewish leaders don't know what to do so they decide to arrest Him. They send the temple guard to apprehend Jesus, but they cannot arrest Him. They come back empty-handed. I wonder if John smiled as he wrote the reason Jesus was not arrested in verses 45-47:

> The Temple police went back to the leading priests and the Pharisees. The priests and the Pharisees asked, "Why didn't you bring Jesus?"

The Temple police answered, "We have never heard anyone say such amazing things!"

The Pharisees answered, "So he has fooled you too!

Nicodemus is mentioned in the latter part of this narrative. He is the man who earlier came to Jesus by night to speak with Him. This passage seems to indicate that Nicodemus' friends didn't know about his rendezvous with Jesus, or if they did, he kept quiet about his feelings toward Jesus. It seemed that Nicodemus was still fence-sitting. My question to all who are reading this commentary is, when it comes to really expressing your faith in Jesus as the Savior of the world, are you like Nicodemus, still sitting on the fence?

John 8:1-11

¹ Jesus went to the Mount of Olives. ² Early in the morning he went back to the Temple area. The people all came to him, and he sat and taught them.

³ The teachers of the law and the Pharisees brought a woman they had caught in bed with a man who was not her husband. They forced her to stand in front of the people. ⁴ They said to Jesus, "Teacher, this woman was caught in the act of adultery. ⁵ The Law of Moses commands us to stone to death any such woman. What do you say we should do?"

⁶ They were saying this to trick Jesus. They wanted to catch him saying something wrong so that they could have a charge against him. But Jesus stooped down and started writing on the ground with his finger. ⁷ The Jewish leaders continued to ask him their question. So he stood up and said, "Anyone here who has never sinned should throw the first stone at her." ⁸ Then Jesus stooped down again and wrote on the ground.

106

⁹ When they heard this, they began to leave one by one. The older men left first, and then the others. Jesus was left alone with the woman standing there in front of him. ¹⁰ He looked up again and said to her, "Where did they all go? Did no one judge you guilty?"

¹¹ She answered, "No one, sir."

Then Jesus said, "I don't judge you either. You can go now, but don't sin again."

Don't Be a Turkey—Turkeys are really stupid animals. I love to eat them, but I hate to raise them. That is what I got to do during the summer of 1967, days after I graduated from Victor Valley High School and not long before entering college life in Abilene, Texas.

I worked that summer for a friend of my dad's, who was also an elder of our church. He hired me as his right-hand man. Of course, I was his only employee. My job was to take care of feeding and watering 40,000 turkeys, searching for hurt or deformed ones, and once a week collecting the dead ones, which I had to dispose of in a large covered pit.

Remember earlier when I said that turkeys were stupid animals? I wore on my right hand my senior ring, which had a large green stone in the middle. The turkeys were fascinated with that stone. Every time I would reach down to their level to fix something that they had broken, several turkeys would gather around me and peck at that green stone. I would shoo them away only to have them gather right back pecking at it again.

A green stone was not the only thing they would peck at. If another turkey had a small injury or a sore spot the other turkeys would begin pecking at that turkey's defect until they would get it on the ground. Other turkeys would then surround that injured turkey and begin pecking at that same sore spot until they would peck that turkey to death.

It's strange how much some people are like these birds. They find a spot they don't like, and instead of offering to heal, they peck that person to death, all the while covering their own spots lest they become the next victim.

The law was plain; the woman had broken the seventh commandment. The penalty was harsh and quick. Leviticus 20:10 said: *"If a man has sexual relations with his neighbor's wife, both the man and the woman are guilty of adultery and must be put to death!*

But wait, where is the man? Why is just the woman brought before Jesus? This whole situation is a setup, of course. John had just told us in verse 6: *"They were saying this to trick Jesus. They wanted to catch him saying something wrong so that they could have a charge against him."*

Jesus didn't step into their trap. They knew if He let her go, they could accuse Him of not following the law of Moses. But if He said, "Go ahead and stone her," He would be in trouble with the Romans, because, by Roman law, no one except the Roman government could convict a person and carry out capital punishment. Jesus' answer was brilliant. *"Anyone here who has never sinned should throw the first stone at her."* Jesus was the only One present with no sin and therefore, the only One who could have thrown a rock. He chose mercy.

Interestingly, too, is the fact that as the men left the scene, the older men left first. Could it be that the older men knew their own sins, well? In shame, they threw down their rocks and left. When I was young, I was hotheaded with lots of rocks in my hand for others. The longer I live the more rocks I throw down and the more often I walk away in shame, knowing my own sins.

Now, with the book of John, you always have to search for something deeper in Jesus' reply. Jesus didn't care a wit for being politically correct. He didn't allow Himself to be swayed by either the Jewish leaders or public opinion. If it wasn't His time to die, He wasn't going to die. Remember, too, as far as public opinion, He hit rock bottom back in John 6 during the whole sermon about eating His flesh and drinking His blood. In 6:66: *After Jesus said these things, many of his followers left and stopped following him.*

From Luke 19:10 you find: *The Son of Man came to find lost people and save them.*" In that particular scripture in Luke, Jesus had just looked up in a tree at a short man named Zacchaeus and said of him in Luke 19:9-10: *"Today is the day for this family to be saved from sin. Yes, even this tax collector is one of God's chosen people."*

Jesus found a lost man beside Him on the cross and said to him in Luke 23:43, *"I promise you, today you will be with me in paradise."* Luke also tells us a story in chapter 7. A Pharisee invited Jesus to dinner and a sinful woman came and washed Jesus' feet with her tears and dried them with her hair. Jesus told her in verse 48, *"Your sins are forgiven."*

Looking deeper into this particular story of the woman caught in adultery, you find an echo of John 1:16: *...the Word* (Jesus) *was full of grace and truth.*

Grace: *"I don't judge you either..."* This grace means unmerited and undeserved favor. Jesus wasn't a king who granted favors to some poor soul who came groveling into his throne room. He was a king who left His throne room in heaven, came to Earth, and put on flesh *to "find lost people and save them."* Jesus came full of grace.

Truth: *"...but don't sin again."* The sins He forgave the woman of, He no longer wanted her to live in. The word we often hear, repentance, means to turn and no longer go in that direction. The NIV uses this phrase: *"Go now and leave your life of sin."*

What was the lesson to the men who brought the woman to Jesus? Does Jesus mean here that no one should ever point out the sins of another? I believe that Jesus wants us to be a light to the world and to do that, wrong has to be pointed out. He also wants us to judge rightly, with compassion, empathy, and a forgiving spirit. In Matthew 7:1-5 Jesus said:

> *"Don't judge others, and God will not judge you. If you judge others, you will be judged the same way you judge them. God will treat you the same way you treat others.*
>
> *"Why do you notice the small piece of dust that is in your friend's eye, but you don't notice the big piece of wood that is in your own? Why do you say to your friend, 'Let me take that piece of dust out of your eye'? Look at yourself first! You still have that big piece of wood in your own eye. You are a hypocrite! First, take the wood out of your own eye. Then you will see clearly to get the dust out of your friend's eye."*

Justice and Mercy—Another verse comes to mind in dealing with (verse 3), *The teachers of the law and the Pharisees brought a woman they had caught in bed with a man who was not her husband.* I remember both my son, Matt, and my step-son, Paul's life verse, Micah 6:8 (NIV):

> He has shown you, O mortal, what is good.
>   And what does the LORD require of you?
> To act justly and to love mercy
>   and to walk humbly with your God.

Like *grace and truth*, acting justly and loving mercy must proceed from a disciple of the Messiah Jesus in their dealings with others. How does a person do that? I believe the final phrase of Micah 6:8, gives us the answer. We walk in humility before God, applying both justice and mercy and grace and truth to others, knowing we have been offered and given the same by God, through the Messiah Jesus, for our sins. How we treat others is observed by God.

(Second, I Am Statement)

John 8:12-20

"I Am the Light of the World"

12 Later, Jesus talked to the people again. He said, "I am the light of the world. Whoever follows me will never live in darkness. They will have the light that gives life."

13 But the Pharisees said to Jesus, "When you talk about yourself, you are the only one to say that these things are true. So we cannot accept what you say."

14 Jesus answered, "Yes, I am saying these things about myself. But people can believe what I say, because I know where I came from. And I know where I am going. But you don't know where I came from or where I am going. 15 You judge me the way people judge other people. I don't judge anyone. 16 But if I judge, my judging is true, because when I judge I am not alone. The Father who sent me is with me. 17 Your own law says that when two witnesses say the same thing, you must accept what they say. 18 I am one of the witnesses who speaks about myself. And the Father who sent me is my other witness."

19 The people asked, "Where is your father?"

Jesus answered, "You don't know me or my Father. But if you knew me, you would know my Father too." 20 Jesus said these things while he was teaching in the Temple area, near the room where the Temple offerings were kept. But no one arrested him, because the right time for him had not yet come.

Light—With my wife beside me in the passenger seat and our kids in the back seat, we kept waiting for that curve, that last hill. Coming back from Houston, a trip we had made many times, we drove Highway 36 for about seven hours. We were tired, cranky, and hungry, plus everyone had to go to the bathroom. "How much farther is it?" my kids—all kids—inevitably ask.

"Just around the curve and over the hill," I answered, having already seen the 19-mile marker. And there it lay, Abilene, Texas—neither Malibu on the Pacific nor Key West on the Atlantic, but it was home. And those lights that just suddenly spread out as we went over that last hill meant food, rest, and, yes, a bathroom.

The statement in verse 12: *"I am the light of the world,"* is the second in a series of "I am" statements in the book of John. Back in John 1:4-5: *In him there was life, and that life was a light for the people of the world. The light shines in the darkness, and the darkness has not defeated it."*

So, if the life of Jesus is light, what does darkness imply? Since the word light, here, indicates truth, darkness, indicates ignorance. Jesus brings truth to the world about God.

Notice, also, Jesus doesn't say "a" light, but "the" light. The difference between "a" light and "the" light is important in Christian doctrine. **A light** would mean, one of many. **The light** means Jesus is the **One and Only Light,** implying that He is the real and only truth about God. Later, in John 14:6 Jesus will state, *"I am the way, the truth, and the life. The only way to the Father is through me."*

When pressed about who His Father is, Jesus answers in verse 19: "You don't know me or my Father. But if you knew me, you would know my Father too."

Again, when we turn to John 14:8-11, where Jesus' disciples also misunderstand Him, He states something very similar to that above:

> Philip said to him, "Lord, show us the Father. That is all we need."
>
> Jesus answered, "Philip, I have been with you for a long time. So you should know me. Anyone who has seen me has seen the Father too. So why do you say, 'Show us the Father'? Don't you believe that I am in the Father and the Father is in me? The things I have told you don't come from me. The Father lives in me, and he is doing his own work. Believe me when I say that I am in the Father and the Father is in me. Or believe because of the miracles I have done.

The difference in the two responses to Jesus' declaration, though, is dramatic. The disciples were asking for clarification, and the Pharisees were looking for information that would help them prove Him wrong. The disciples believed in Jesus. The leaders did not.

John 8:21-30

[21] Again, Jesus said to the people, "I will leave you. You will look for me, but you will die in your sin. You cannot come where I am going."

[22] So the Jewish leaders asked themselves, "Will he kill himself? Is that why he said, 'You cannot come where I am going'?"

[23] But Jesus said to them, "You people are from here below, but I am from above. You belong to this world, but I don't belong to this

world. ²⁴ I told you that you would die in your sins. Yes, if you don't believe that I AM, you will die in your sins."

²⁵ They asked, "Then who are you?"

Jesus answered, "I am what I have told you from the beginning. ²⁶ I have much more I could say to judge you. But I tell people only what I have heard from the one who sent me, and he speaks the truth."

²⁷ They did not understand who he was talking about. He was telling them about the Father. ²⁸ So he said to them, "You will lift up the Son of Man. Then you will know that I AM. You will know that whatever I do is not by my own authority. You will know that I say only what the Father has taught me. ²⁹ The one who sent me is with me. I always do what pleases him. So he has not left me alone." ³⁰ While he was saying these things, many people believed in him.

Why Can't I Come, Too? —Each of my children said the same thing when it came to being babysat while their mom and I went to dinner, a movie, or just to have some time alone. "Can I come with you?" They didn't so much want to come with us as much as they wanted to be with us.

We would tell them, "No, but we promise we'll be home soon. We won't be gone long." And we weren't. We would always come home, and if they were asleep, we would kiss them while they slept and whisper, "We're close by, and we love you."

That final statement, *"...many people believed in him,"* indicated that it was beginning to dawn on many of the people just what Jesus was talking about. His statements, *"You people are from here below"* (the world)*; "but I am from above"* (heaven). *"Then you will know that I AM."* (the Savior of the world), *"you will die in your sins,"* (die without the salvation I bring).

114

"You will lift up the Son of Man," indicates that He will be crucified on a cross. Many of those present would not only put Him there but would afterward come to realize that He is the Savior of the world. The startling fact is that we have all placed Jesus on the cross for our sins. Read with me Isaiah 53:4-6:

> *The fact is, it was our suffering he took on himself; he bore our pain. But we thought that God was punishing him, that God was beating him for something he did. But he was being punished for what we did. He was crushed because of our guilt. He took the punishment we deserved, and this brought us peace. We were healed because of his pain. We had all wandered away like sheep. We had gone our own way. And yet the LORD put all our guilt on him.*

Finally, Jesus speaks of always pleasing His Father. Verse 29: *"The one who sent me is with me. I always do what pleases him."* Our sins may have put Jesus on the cross, but He also willingly took our place.

Jesus was not only lifted up on the cross at His death, but He was also lifted up from the dead at His resurrection, He was lifted up from the earth to heaven at His ascension, and He was lifted up by the preaching of the gospel by His apostles. How do you lift up Jesus?

John 8:31-32

[31] *So Jesus said to the Jews who believed in him, "If you continue to accept and obey my teaching, you are really my followers. [32] You will know the truth, and the truth will make you free."*

The Truth that Sets You Free—In 1967 I began school at Abilene Christian College. It didn't become a university until the '80s.

Almost all my classes were in the three-story administration building so, I spent a lot of time in that building. I remember, as I would go in the north door there was the inscription In King James language: *"And ye shall know the truth, and the truth shall make you free."* I believe many will see this "Truth that makes you free" as a double meaning. Truth always has a way of shining a light on darkness and ignorance, whether it be social or spiritual. But if you read the inscription on the other door, *"If ye continue in my word, then are ye my disciples indeed; ..."* The three dots after "indeed" makes the meaning clear. Jesus was not speaking of social truths as much as the truth about Himself, who He is, and that His words come from the Father. *"If ye continue in my word, then are ye my disciples indeed; And ye shall know the truth, and the truth shall make you free."*

The final sections of John chapter 8 are six verbal exchanges (debate questions and answers) between Jesus and the people who in John 8:30-31 are said to have believed in Jesus. Not so fast! Jesus challenges these "would-be-disciples" to see if they are really on board with Him.

First Dialog/ "We Have Never Been Slaves"

John 8:33-38

33 They answered, "We are Abraham's descendants. And we have never been slaves. So why do you say that we will be free?"

34 Jesus said, "The truth is, everyone who sins is a slave—a slave to sin. 35 A slave does not stay with a family forever. But a son belongs to the family forever. 36 So if the Son makes you free, you are really free. 37 I know you are Abraham's descendants. But you want to kill me, because you don't want to accept my teaching. 38 I am telling you what my Father has shown me. But you do what your father has told you."

"I Felt Like Two Cents,"—an expression my mom made when she had been caught in a lie. She was not trying to lie. She didn't realize our fat, black dog could jump over the fence.

We were living in a mobile home park at the time, and the park manager had confronted my mom with, "Your dog is jumping over your fence and running around the neighborhood. I had to catch her and put her back inside."

Mom was expressing that she couldn't imagine how that was possible, just as a sonic boom from an air force jet filled the sky. And just at that moment, with my mom and the park manager standing there, our fat, black dog jumped over the fence.

Never Been a Slave? —Verse 33: *"We have never been slaves."* That wasn't exactly true. They had been slaves in Egypt for many years and had been slaves, again, in Babylon for 70 years. And, at the present, while they weren't slaves, they had been conquered and were occupied by Rome. Why would they lie?

Jesus ignores the obvious untruth and speaks of true slavery—the slavery of all humans, including the children of Abraham. That slavery was sin. Then Jesus tells them that He is the true Son and can make them "really" free. Then Jesus casts doubt on who their true father is.

Second Dialog/ "Abraham Is Our Father"

John 8:39-41a

39 They said, "Our father is Abraham."

Jesus said, "If you were really Abraham's descendants, you would do what Abraham did. 40 I am someone who has told you the truth I heard from God. But you are trying to kill me. Abraham did nothing like that. 41 So you are doing what your own father did."

They Didn't Believe Me—Since I was the baby of the family and my sibs were much older than me, I became an uncle at age nine. I remember finding out that my brother Bill and his wife, Eloise had a baby boy, named Mike, and I was, now, his uncle. "Wow! I thought. I can't wait to tell all of my friends."

Now, if you know anything about children, they can be spoilsports when it comes to being happy about your own joy. "You're not an uncle," several of them sneered. "Uncles are much older than you. You're just making it up."

I really was an uncle and these people were literally blood relatives—children—of Abraham. I'm sure most of the people felt insulted. They exclaimed in verse 39: *"Our father is Abraham."*

"No," argues Jesus. "Abraham would not have done that. He isn't your father."

In Matthew 3:7-9, John the Baptist was baptizing and some of these same people came to see what was going on, not because they wanted to change but because they were suspicious of anything out of the norm. Here was John's answer to them:

> *Many Pharisees and Sadducees came to where John was baptizing people. When John saw them, he said, "You are all snakes! Who warned you to run from God's judgment that is coming? Change your hearts! And show by the way you live that you have changed. I know what you are thinking. You want to say, 'but Abraham is our father!' That means nothing. I tell you, God could make children for Abraham from these rocks.*

Claiming that Abraham was their father was not going to cut it with either John the Baptist or Jesus. There was more than blood that makes you a child of Abraham.

Third Dialog/ "God Is Our Father"

John 8:41b-47

But they said, "We are not like children who never knew who their father was. God is our Father. He is the only Father we have."

[42] *Jesus said to them, "If God were really your Father, you would love me. I came from God, and now I am here. I did not come by my own authority. God sent me.* [43] *You don't understand the things I say, because you cannot accept my teaching.* [44] *Your father is the devil. You belong to him. You want to do what he wants. He was a murderer from the beginning. He was always against the truth. There is no truth in him. He is like the lies he tells. Yes, the devil is a liar. He is the father of lies.*

[45] *"I am telling you the truth, and that's why you don't believe me.* [46] *Can any of you prove that I am guilty of sin? If I tell the truth, why don't you believe me?* [47] *Whoever belongs to God accepts what he says. But you don't accept what God says, because you don't belong to God."*

Curly Hair— "You must get your curly hair from me," I teasingly said to my oldest grandson, Fisher.

I first noticed that my hair was somewhat curly when my barber, Georganne, who has cut my hair for twenty years, asked me, "When did your hair turn curly, Darell? It's never been that way before."

It was strange, all right, and she wasn't the only one who noticed. Others in the family asked the same question, and I had to repeat, "I don't know."

One day we were visiting our grandchildren in Ft. Worth. It's Annette's son, Paul, and his wife, Feydra, and their kids. I'm not related. Everyone was commenting on Fisher's cool-looking, black, curly hair. And I joked that it must be the genes he got from me. Everyone laughed but Fisher. He thought about it for a minute, and usually being very literal, seriously replied, "I was wondering whom I got it from." Everyone laughed even harder.

Fisher calls me Papa, not because of any DNA but because ever since he was very young, I have been his Papa. So, it's not always about blood that makes us related to someone in the minds of children. It's whom he has known, loved, and listened to, all these years, and who is married to his Nana.

The people are becoming angry, *"God is our Father."*

"No," Jesus answers, "God isn't your Father, either. Because if He were you would not only listen to Me, you would also love Me. Your real Father is the devil."

Wow! Jesus, did you just say that? You must not be running for public office or trying to win a popularity contest.

But Jesus doesn't stop there. He continues with, "You are his true children. He is a murderer, a liar, and the father of murdering and lying." I love how Jesus described the devil in verse 44, in the NIV. *"When he lies he speaks his <u>native language</u>, for he is a liar and <u>the father of lies</u>."* The first lie recorded in the Bible is in Genesis 3:4, from that ancient serpent, satan himself, when he told Adam and Eve, *"You will not die."*

Fourth Dialog/ Insults

John 8:48-51

48 The Jews there answered, "We say you are a Samaritan. We say a demon is making you crazy! Are we not right when we say this?"

49 Jesus answered, "I have no demon in me. I give honor to my Father, but you give no honor to me. 50 I am not trying to get honor *for myself. There is one who wants this honor for me. He is the judge. ^{51} I promise you, whoever continues to obey my teaching will never die."*

Arguing with Mom—If Mom told me I couldn't go somewhere or do a particular "something" I wanted to do, I could usually wear her down with, "Please, Mom, please, so-and-so is going."

If my dad were listening or had walked up on the discussion, he would look me in the eye and say, "Darell, NO!"

End of discussion!

The people, though, used a tactic that kids use when they have been shut down by other kids and can say no more in their defense. They insult. "Oh yeah, well you are just a half-breed Samaritan. You have a demon. You are crazy."

Jesus is filled, all right, but with the Holy Spirit who came upon Him at His baptism. These people are saying that instead of the Holy Spirit being in Jesus, it is rather, a demon. In Mark 3:28-29, Jesus warns the people who call Him demon possessed: *"I want you to know that people can be forgiven for all the sinful things they do. They can even be forgiven for the bad things they say against God. But anyone who speaks against the Holy Spirit will never be forgiven. They will always be guilty of that sin."*

Fifth Dialog/ "Who Do You Think You Are?"

John 8:52-56

^{52} *The Jews said to Jesus, "Now we know that you have a demon in you! Even Abraham and the prophets died. But you say, 'Whoever obeys my teaching will never die.' ^{53} Do you think you are greater than our father Abraham? He died, and so did the prophets. Who do you think you are?"*

54 Jesus answered, "If I give honor to myself, that honor is worth nothing. The one who gives me honor is my Father. And you say that he is your God. 55 But you don't really know him. I know him. If I said I did not know him, I would be a liar like you. But I do know him, and I obey what he says. 56 Your father Abraham was very happy that he would see the day when I came. He saw that day and was happy."

Outclassed in Debate—When I was in high school, I was part of the debate club. I was teamed up with another guy my age and we were expected to debate this team from another school. Both teams knew the topic ahead of time but what we didn't know is what side of the argument we would present. This was my buddy's and my first debate and the team we were debating with had been debating for a long time. After the other team presented their argument, we both sat there dumbfounded, with our mouths open in disbelief. We just looked at the judge and said, "We don't have anything to say." Everyone laughed, including us, realizing we had been far outclassed. These people had been outclassed by Jesus. They didn't understand what kind of death He was speaking of and so they fall back to, *"Even Abraham and the prophets died."*

Of course, Jesus is speaking of spiritual death. Jesus tries one final time, "I know God, personally. He is my Father and honors Me. You say Abraham is your father. Well, he saw My day coming and was happy about it."

Sixth Dialog/ "I AM!"

John 8:57-59

57 The Jews said to Jesus, "What? How can you say you have seen Abraham? You are not even 50 years old!"

58 Jesus answered, "The fact is, before Abraham was born, I AM." 59 When he said this, they picked up stones to throw at him. But Jesus hid, and then he left the Temple area.

I AM! —The people say their final words, "You aren't old enough to know Abraham." Jesus' final statement, the one that infuriated these would-be believers who had, initially believed Him, *"The fact is, before Abraham was born, I AM."*

My Favorite Movie—Growing up, my favorite movie was The Ten Commandments. Oh, I remember all the adults at church telling us children, "Remember, it is a movie and the movie is making up a dialog that isn't in the Bible." I, of course, knew that because I had listened to my Sunday School teachers throughout the years. But those teachers had never made the Red Sea part like Charlton Heston, playing Moses. But the one part in the whole movie that sent chills down my back and gave me goosebumps, was when Moses saw the burning bush and God spoke to him. I did not know the meaning of *"I AM who I AM"* at the time, but it was done so powerfully and with such a deep, resonating voice, I knew it had to be important. That name had to be holy.

The first question I would ask is, "Why did the people get so mad at the final statement of Jesus that they wanted to stone Him?" Look again at what He said, *"The fact is, before Abraham was born, I AM."* What a strange way of talking, but not if you believe Jesus is God, come to Earth in the form of man; remember the word again, "Incarnation?" Jesus was using the Exodus declaration from the burning bush. *"I Am Who I Am."* The words of Jesus, in John, were not lost on the people. They thought they knew what He was saying earlier, some even believing. Some had claimed discipleship, but like the discourse after the feeding of the 5000, they couldn't handle these words.

When we accept Jesus' gift of salvation, we are in a state where we will not ever die spiritually. But Jesus does have power over both kinds of death. He has, not only, the power to erase sins and spiritual death by His death on the cross, but He has the power over physical death and the grave (Hades, or the place of the dead) by His resurrection. He will raise Lazarus from the dead in chapter 11; the Father Himself after His crucifixion will raise Jesus. And Jesus will raise all of us who are His disciples on the last day. In Revelation 1:17-18, John quotes Jesus: *"Don't be afraid! I am the First and the Last. I am the one who lives. I was dead, but look, I am alive forever and ever! And I hold the keys of death and Hades."*

Astronomy—Science was not always my best subject in school, but I did enjoy astronomy, and I still do. I remember when I was first introduced to the concept that the universe goes on and on it was hard for me to imagine. But then I thought, "If there was an end to space, say a wall, what would be on the other side of the wall?" I had a dilemma. I couldn't understand something that went on and on, but I also couldn't imagine what would be on the other side if there were a stopping point.

When Jesus said, in verse 58: "Before Abraham was, I Am." I found the same dilemma. He was saying, "I have always existed." Jesus had no beginning and no end. Now if He, as God, did have a beginning then what would have been before God? He invaded our world, His creation, and became one of us. "WOW!" "I AM," then sums up the phrase in Revelation 4:8: *"He always was, he is, and he is coming."* No, I don't understand that spiritual truth any more than I understand the physical truth about the universe. But I believe both.

(Sixth Sign)

John 9:1-7

Healing of the Man Born Blind

1 While Jesus was walking, he saw a man who had been blind since the time he was born. 2 Jesus' followers asked him, "Teacher, why was this man born blind? Whose sin made it happen? Was it his own sin or that of his parents?"

3 Jesus answered, "It was not any sin of this man or his parents that caused him to be blind. He was born blind so that he could be used to show what great things God can do. 4 While it is daytime, we must continue doing the work of the one who sent me. The night is coming, and no one can work at night. 5 While I am in the world, I am the light of the world."

6 After Jesus said this, he spit on the dirt, made some mud and put it on the man's eyes. 7 Jesus told him, "Go and wash in Siloam pool." (Siloam means "Sent.") So the man went to the pool, washed and came back. He was now able to see.

"I Was Blind!"— "I couldn't see a thing." Those words, coming from my dad, seemed strange. "I was driving back home when suddenly I couldn't see a thing. Scared, I eased off to the side of the road, hoping I was out of the way of other cars. I didn't know what to do."

"What happened Dad? How did you get home?" were the questions my brothers and I asked our elderly father.

"I just sat there and finally the blackness went away, and I could see again. So, I drove home," he answered, still bewildered.

Becoming suddenly blind, even for a short time caused my dad a lot of anxiety. But just think of the relief and joy he must have felt when his eyesight just as suddenly came back.

Later, we found out that he may have had a minor stroke. Even though he had many other strokes through the final years of his life, he never lost his sight again. We take our eyesight for granted, not thinking about what a blind man or woman must go through.

The thought of Jesus' day, by many, was that if there was something wrong with a person's body or mind someone must have sinned. While some sins do cause calamity—driving drunk can cause an accident, in which someone could be crippled for life, for example—God does not punish people in the womb for sins that they or their parents committed. Sometimes, a child may be affected in the womb by what the mother does while pregnant, such as drinking alcohol or taking illegal drugs. But there is no karma set up by God or the universe that says all bad things will be punished and all good things will be rewarded in this life. The book of Job disputes that belief, in which Job, a good man, had a series of horrible things happen to him. His friends—or not-so-friends—wanted him to repent of some overlooked, grievous iniquity and get back in the good graces of God, so he could, again, be rewarded.

Jesus, repeats what He had said in chapter 8, calling Himself the Light of the World. It probably isn't lost on the disciples that Jesus calls Himself the Light of the World after He heals the man born blind.

What does Jesus mean when He says in verse 4: *The night is coming, and no one can work at night"*?

In the context of the paragraph and especially with verse 5, *"While I am in the world, I am the light of the world."* Jesus is speaking of the days from Friday to early Sunday morning of Passion week when the enemy seems to have won. The disciples are hiding and confused. No one is working because they are afraid. But is there a meaning for us in our own lives? I remember, from my youth, the song, **Work for the Night is Coming?** It was written with the idea that people have only the time they have on earth to do the works of God.

1. Work, for the night is coming,
   Work through the morning hours;
   Work while the dew is sparkling,
   Work 'mid springing flow'rs.
   Work when the day grows brighter,
   Work in the glowing sun;
   Work, for the night is coming,
   When man's work is done.

2. Work, for the night is coming,
   Work through the sunny noon;
   Fill brightest hours with labor,
   Rest comes sure and soon.
   Give every flying minute
   Something to keep in store;
   Work, for the night is coming,
   When man works no more.

3. Work, for the night is coming,
   Under the sunset skies;
   While their bright tints are glowing,
   Work, for daylight flies.
   Work till the last beam fadeth,
   Fadeth to shine no more;
   Work, while the night is dark'ning,
   When man's work is o'er. (Anna Louisa Walker, 1854)

8 His neighbors and some others who had seen him begging said, "Look! Is this the same man who always sits and begs?"

9 Some people said, "Yes! He is the one." But others said, "No, he can't be the same man. He only looks like him."

So the man himself said, "I am that same man."

10 They asked, "What happened? How did you get your sight?"

11 He answered, "The man they call Jesus made some mud and put it on my eyes. Then he told me to go to Siloam and wash. So I went there and washed. And then I could see."

12 They asked him, "Where is this man?"

He answered, "I don't know."

13 Then the people brought the man to the Pharisees. **14** The day Jesus had made mud and healed the man's eyes was a Sabbath day. **15** So the Pharisees asked the man, "How did you get your sight?"

He answered, "He put mud on my eyes. I washed, and now I can see."

16 Some of the Pharisees said, "That man does not obey the law about the Sabbath day. So he is not from God."

Others said, "But someone who is a sinner cannot do these miraculous signs." So they could not agree with each other.

17 They asked the man again, "Since it was your eyes he healed, what do you say about him?"

He answered, "He is a prophet."

18 The Jewish leaders still did not believe that this really happened to the man—that he was blind and was now healed. But later they *sent for his parents. ¹⁹ They asked them, "Is this your son? You say he was born blind. So how can he see?"*

²⁰ His parents answered, "We know that this man is our son. And we know that he was born blind. ²¹ But we don't know why he can see now. We don't know who healed his eyes. Ask him. He is old enough to answer for himself." ²² They said this because they were afraid of the Jewish leaders. The leaders had already decided that they would punish anyone who said Jesus was the Messiah. They would stop them from coming to the synagogue. ²³ That is why his parents said, "He is old enough. Ask him."

Hall Monitors at School—When I was teaching 5ᵗʰ grade at a particular school, my classroom was in a portable building. When my students needed to go to the bathroom, they walked down a particular hall. Now, it was the habit of two teachers who had classrooms along that hall to become self-appointed hall monitors of any child who walked by their classroom. Did the student have the proper documentation—a hall pass—to be there? If not, they would send them scurrying back to me, sometimes in tears. Fortunately, there was another hallway, a little farther away. The teachers in that particular wing were so busy teaching they didn't have time to be bothered with my student's documents or papers permitting them to pass. So, that is where they traveled from then on.

Hall Monitors of the Faith—These, so-called, monitors of the faith in Jesus' day were much like these hall monitors, even deciding that either the miracle hadn't happened, or, if it had, a sinner had performed it.

Nothing can be more devastating than for a family to reject you out of fear. But that seems to be what happened here. Being thrown out of the synagogue meant much more than just not being able to go to church with your friends. It meant that you were ostracized from all that went on in the community. There have been many who became Christians in non-Christian communities, throughout the centuries, who were expelled, not only from their religious societies but from their families, as well.

Is making mud on the Sabbath considered work? Again, Jesus is breaking the 4th Commandment, that is according to these monitors of the faith. Many scholarly "men," over the centuries since the Ten Commandments and the rest of the Law were given by Moses, wrote additions to the Law, especially about Sabbath keeping, to explain what God had considered "work." This was to help the uneducated person of the Jewish faith to keep in line.

One interesting thought! Here they had the Incarnate God (God in human form), right in front of them, showing what the true Law was all about—loving your neighbor as yourself, —and they call Him a sinner.

John 9:24-34

^{24} So the Jewish leaders called the man who had been blind. They told him to come in again. They said, "You should honor God by telling the truth. We know that this man is a sinner."

^{25} The man answered, "I don't know if he is a sinner. But I do know this: I was blind, and now I can see."

^{26} They asked, "What did he do to you? How did he heal your eyes?"

^{27} He answered, "I have already told you that. But you would not listen to me. Why do you want to hear it again? Do you want to be his followers too?"

^{28} At this they shouted insults at him and said, "You are his follower, not us! We are followers of Moses. ^{29} We know that God spoke to Moses. But we don't even know where this man comes from!"

30 The man answered, "This is really strange! You don't know where he comes from, but he healed my eyes. 31 We all know that God does not listen to sinners, but he will listen to anyone who worships and obeys him. 32 This is the first time we have ever heard of anyone healing the eyes of someone born blind. 33 This man must be from God. If he were not from God, he could not do anything like this."

34 The Jewish leaders answered, "You were born full of sin! Are you trying to teach us?" And they told the man to get out of the synagogue and to stay out.

Dublin Dr. Pepper—One day Annette and I were talking about strange events that happen at weddings. Things that, some would think would ruin the celebration. We decided, for our reception, on buying bottles of Dublin Dr. Pepper for everyone, only to forget a bottle opener. She told me that at the wedding of her first husband, Bob, they forgot to sign the marriage certificate until they got back from their honeymoon. They, laughingly, wondered if they had been sinning the whole time they were away. We went to a wedding, not long ago, where the cake was being frosted and decorated during the ceremony. I heard about another where the groom fainted and had to sit in a chair for the rest of the service.

Every wedding seems to have some unforeseen gaffe that may or may not be embarrassing. Sometimes, guests get so caught up in the mistakes that they forget why they are there in the first place— to rejoice with the couple at their wedding. Annette usually tells a bride, embarrassed by some disaster, "At the end of the day you are still married. We came to enjoy your wedding, not nitpick unfortunate mix-ups."

What is sad in this particular miracle, or sign, as John calls them, is that this should be a day of rejoicing and praise. This man could see for the first time. But the parents who raised a blind child could only think of being thrown out of the synagogue. His friends could only argue about if this was the same man who begged. Even his spiritual leaders could only think, "This was not done in the prescribed way." Like there was a prescribed way.

John 9:35-38

[35] When Jesus heard that they had forced the man to leave, he found him and asked him, "Do you believe in the Son of Man?"

[36] The man said, "Tell me who he is, sir, so I can believe in him."

[37] Jesus said to him, "You have already seen him. The Son of Man is the one talking with you now."

[38] The man answered, "Yes, I believe, Lord!" Then he bowed and worshiped Jesus.

The Communion Monitor—When I was growing up in the desert of California, there was a man who came to church who, during the communion service, watched to make sure that everything was done in the prescribed way. You were supposed to have a linen tablecloth over the elements of the communion table because Jesus had a linin cloth placed over his face at his burial. You were supposed to break the bread before serving it because Jesus broke the bread before serving it. You were supposed to always serve the bread first, and then the cup. There were so many rules to pay attention to, I began to wonder if he knew the deeper meaning of this supper of the Lord. While others were worshiping Jesus, he made sure everything was proper. Of course, someone may ask me, "And why were you watching him?" We all seem to nitpick.

John 9:39-41

[39] Jesus said, "I came into this world so that the world could be judged. I came so that people who are blind could see. And I came so that people who think they see would become blind."

⁴⁰ Some of the Pharisees were near Jesus. They heard him say this. They asked, "What? Are you saying that we are blind too?"

⁴¹ Jesus said, "If you were really blind, you would not be guilty of sin. But you say that you see, so you are still guilty."

Blind Preacher, John—We had a blind preacher, John, during part of my teenage years. He had a Braille Bible he would preach out of when he was in the pulpit. There was a funny story my dad told about our preacher. One night my dad and John went up to the church building to retrieve something John needed, and they went into the dark building. John scurried about getting this and that, while my dad was trying to maneuver in the dark. Finally, my dad said to the preacher, "John, will you please turn on some lights? I can't see in the dark like you can!"

Like much of his writing, John is the only gospel writer to include this story. On the surface, the story is about the healing, by Jesus, of a man born blind, which shows glory to God and gives more proof that God sent Him. He heals the man on the Sabbath, which causes a big stir, and ends up with the man being thrown out of the synagogue. Finally, Jesus introduces Himself to the man who in turn worships Him. But as with most of John's writings and Jesus' teachings and signs, there is more than meets the eye (sorry about the pun).

There are several words that Jesus uses over and over: like blindness, darkness, and night; sight, light, and day. Usually, when Jesus uses the former, He is speaking of sin, ignorance, and unbelief, and when He uses the latter, He is speaking of salvation, truth, and faith. Even the mud may represent sin and the washing represent the cleansing of sin.

At the end of the story, we find that Jesus even makes the point that an individual could have two physical eyes and still not be able to see, spiritually. This man had endured blindness from birth. Verse 3: *"He was born blind so that he could be used to show what great things God can do."* Jesus told His disciples in verse 4: *"While it is daytime, we must continue doing the work of the one who sent me."* What is this work of God? Is it to heal the physical person? Is that why Jesus came to this earth? Physical blindness and its healing are incidental to this story. The work of God displayed in this man's life was Jesus' coming as the light of the world, to lead men and women to the Father, to lead them from blindness to sight, from darkness to light, and from night to day.

What about the spitting and the mud? Couldn't Jesus have just touched the blind man's eyes and healed him? Of course, the answer is yes. But remember this miracle, like so many others in the gospel of John was done on the Sabbath. The Pharisees considered making mud, work. And the man going to wash his eyes is also working. Jesus was making a point to these "keepers of details." Is there something more important here than the details of the law? Micah 6:8:

> Human, the LORD has told you what goodness is.
> This is what he wants from you:
> Be fair to other people.
> Love kindness and loyalty,
> and humbly obey your God.

God made the Sabbath a time for humans to rest from their labor. He never meant it to be made into a day that enslaves a person to trivia.

Now about the man himself, surely Jesus didn't heal the man just to prove a point. Like with all of His miracles, Jesus had compassion. He desired to make this man whole, but even with this man, Jesus wanted to give him more. Yes, Jesus was happy to heal the man born blind. But in a sense aren't we all born blind? The end of the story is more important than the beginning. At the end of the story, the man worships Jesus.

This conversation is so much different than the one with the lame man, back in chapter 5. That man, if you remember, gave the impression he didn't want to be healed. And when he was healed, he went and told the authorities about Jesus, because, it too, was done on the Sabbath. The story ended differently, also. Where the man born blind was given the blessing of salvation because of his faith, the lame man was given nothing but a warning. John 5:14: *"See, you are well now. But stop sinning or something worse may happen to you!"*

Two men and two different reactions: One man goes away unthankful and unfilled, his body healed but his heart still bound; the other man goes away worshiping and saved, his eyes and his heart both healed of darkness. What do we desire from Jesus more than anything else—longer life, a whole body? Or do we desire what Jesus came to give, eternal life with Him?

I Was Blind but Now I See—Five thirty comes early any day but especially on a Saturday morning when I could, at least, sleep until seven. But I didn't want to miss it. It was the first day of fall, and I didn't want to miss the sunrise this particular day.

One of my favorite places on earth to spend part of my day is in, believe it or not, Abilene, Texas at Jacob's Dream on the Abilene Christian University campus. This magnificent world-class sculpture was created by Jack Maxwell and dedicated to the university during its centennial in 2006. Part of the sculpture is a metal casting of four, larger-than-life, angels either ascending or descending a ladder into heaven. According to Genesis, Jacob had a dream about this after falling exhausted from his harrowing journey, fleeing the

135

wrath of his older brother, Esau. When Jacob awoke, he called the place Bethel saying, "Surely the LORD is in this place." There are various scriptures on stones, in this small park, that look as if they had been randomly strewn over the area. But each piece of sculpture, every stone, and each scripture is placed in a specific spot. You can walk from one stone to another, reading various Bible passages from both the Old and New Testaments.

Now the reason I came early that Saturday morning was to see the cross. You see if you stand on a particular spot in the park and observe a particular stand of stones, on the west side, you can see the cross within the space between the stones. You cannot see it from any other vantage point other than in that one spot. And on the Autumnal Equinox, or so I had heard, the rising sun can be seen within the space of the cross. I was there to see if—to hope that—it was true.

I went through the McDonald's drive-through, got a cup of coffee, and drove to the spot, hoping no one else was there. Since most people were still in bed, I had the entire park to myself. I sat drinking my coffee and praying for quite a while. As dawn began creeping over the horizon, I sat in anticipation on a stone wall facing east, facing the cross—watching, waiting. But alas, there was no sun peeking through the cross. I stood, thinking that I would have a better vantage point but, to my dismay, saw the sun rising, not to the center, but to one side of the cross. Disappointed, I began thinking it was all a bust—like something you hear as true on the internet, only to find out it was bogus hype.

But then I noticed the words on the ground. I hadn't seen them earlier because of the darkness all around. It was from scripture, quoted from the story of the man born blind in John chapter 9 and from my favorite hymn "Amazing Grace. "I was blind but now I see." How could I have missed it? "I must hurry," I thought. "The sun is rising quickly, now." I quickly moved toward the words and stood on "I see!" And there it was. The sun is positioned in the very center of the cross. In fact, in its brilliance, the risen sun seemed to eclipse the cross itself. And I thought of Easter. The old wooden cross of death, which on Friday had held fast the Savior of the world, now on Sunday stood old and tattered against the risen Son of God. Death had been defeated. Darkness had been replaced with radiant and dazzling light. Christ is risen! He is risen indeed!

John 10:1-6

¹ Jesus said, "It is certainly true that when a man enters the sheep pen, he should use the gate. If he climbs in some other way, he is a robber. He is trying to steal the sheep. ² But the man who takes care of the sheep enters through the gate. He is the shepherd. ³ The man who guards the gate opens the gate for the shepherd. And the sheep listen to the voice of the shepherd. He calls his own sheep, using their names, and he leads them out. ⁴ He brings all of his sheep out. Then he goes ahead of them and leads them. The sheep follow him, because they know his voice. ⁵ But sheep will never follow someone they don't know. They will run away from him, because they don't know his voice."

⁶ Jesus told the people this story, but they did not understand what it meant.

Naming Show Animals —Two of our grandchildren, Ashlyn and Creed Crabtree, are "keepers of show animals" (my terminology) through 4H and FFA. They live with their mom—my daughter, Joanna—and their father, Kyle in the small town of Junction, Texas, at the intersection of US 83 and I-10. Many of the students of the public schools, in Junction, show animals at an annual stock show, and if they win, go on to show in San Antonio, San Angelo, or Kerrville. Some even win prize money for college. Our grandchildren are no exception. Their other grandparents, Marvin and Jo, who live right outside of Junction, usually help them with choosing, sheltering, and transporting their show animals, but it's up to the grandkids to feed, water, and maintain them.

Now, I have heard it said, never name an animal you're going to eat, but since Ashlyn and Creed don't eat the animals—someone else does—I guess that rule doesn't apply. Creed named a pig, "Bacon," once, which reminds me of my usual morning breakfast meat. Ashlyn has also come up with some interesting names for the goats she likes to show; Lily and Crystal are brought to mind.

I remember, once, watching Creed, in a mad dash, chasing his pig round and round the show stage, whacking it with a stick, that's used for directing the pig, not hitting it. And I remember the incident when Ashlyn's goat got tired of being shown and ran off the stage and out the door, with her running wildly after it. But usually, especially since they've gotten older, the grandkids have, not only shown their animals, but have won ribbons, had people with deep pockets buy them, and sometimes even win prize money, put away for college, of course.

The Shepherd King—Throughout the Old and New Testaments there are many stories of shepherds and sheep. King David comes to mind. He was the youngest son of Jesse, when the prophet Samuel was commissioned by God to anoint a new king for Israel. David was tending the sheep, while his brothers and dad were at a feast with the prophet, Samuel, wondering which of the sons would be chosen. It so happened that the new king was not even present, but still tending to the sheep his older brothers had left him in charge of. When David was finally called, he was anointed as the new king. He had, now, become a new sort of shepherd, over a completely different flock of sheep. He was to shepherd his people, Israel, through good and difficult times for 40 years. The animals he shepherded earlier in his life, probably had names, and those sheep knew his voice. They trusted him to care for and protect them. As king, David's new sheep—his people—had names, too, and God knew the names of all of them.

When David was out tending sheep, as a young boy, he likely had a sheep pen to put them in at night, to protect them from robbers and predators, who would try to steal them or do them harm.

Scriptures say, too, in 1 Samuel 17:33-37, that when David saw the giant, Goliath, he told King Saul he would take care of the giant's ranting against God and Israel. The king and young David had this conversation:

> *"You can't go out and fight against this Philistine. You're not even a soldier! Goliath has been fighting in wars since he was a boy."*

> *But David said to Saul, "There were times when I was taking care of my father's sheep that wild animals came to take some sheep from the flock. Once there was a lion and another time, a bear. I chased that wild animal, attacked it, and took the sheep from its mouth. The wild animal jumped on me, but I caught it by the fur under its mouth. And I hit it and killed it. I killed both a lion and a bear like that! And I will kill that foreigner, Goliath, just like them. Goliath will die because he made fun of the army of the living God. The LORD saved me from the lion and the bear. He will also save me from this Philistine."*

As king and shepherd of Israel, David would need to protect his people from the pagan people who were around all of their borders and were waiting for the shepherd king to become distracted with other things. They would then swoop in to steal, kill and destroy his flock.

David wrote many of the Psalms, but his most well-known, even by nonreligious people, is Psalm 23, usually called the Shepherd Psalm. Being a man after God's own heart, David understood that God was the True Shepherd, and also, his Shepherd. Psalm 23:

> The LORD is my shepherd.
>> I will always have everything I need.
> He gives me green pastures to lie in.
>> He leads me by calm pools of water.
> He restores my strength.
>> He leads me on right paths to show that he is good.
> Even if I walk through a valley as dark as the grave,
>> I will not be afraid of any danger, because you are with me.
>> Your rod and staff comfort me.
> You prepared a meal for me in front of my enemies.
>> You welcomed me as an honored guest.
>> My cup is full and spilling over.
> Your goodness and mercy will be with me all my life, and I will live in the LORD's house a long, long time.

(Third I Am Statement)

John 10:7-10

"I Am the Gate for the Sheep"

7 So Jesus said again, "I assure you, I am the gate for the sheep. 8 All those who came before me were thieves and robbers. The sheep did not listen to them. 9 I am the gate. Whoever enters through me will be saved. They will be able to come in and go out. They will find everything they need. ¹⁰ *A thief comes to steal, kill, and destroy. But I came to give life—life that is full and good.*

A Wandering Sheep—I remember reading a newspaper article of "The Strange and the Weird." It told of a place in Australia where there was a sheep station. It seems that one of the sheep escaped his owners and hid in the mountains for several years and then showed up again, out of the blue. It had three years of wool growth on its body and looked more like a giant snowball with a head and feet, than a sheep. When the wool was finally sheared off, the sheep was a third of its size and I'm sure a lot cooler.

I began to wonder, though I don't have facts to back it up, did the escaped sheep wander through the gate or door of the pen where it was kept? Did someone leave the doorway open? Was there no one guarding the door? Was the sheep in the habit of escaping? I guess I will never find out the answers but it does lead to some interesting conclusions about Jesus, the Gate.

Here is the third "I am" statement, from verse 7: "*I am the gate for the sheep.*" It is significate that any shepherd who has put his sheep into a sheep pen or enclosure for the night lays in front of the door to sleep. That individual is both the shepherd and the gate. Jesus, then, makes His point that He is the *"gate."* You can't get into the pen where He keeps His sheep unless you go through Him. He means two things. First, to be one of His sheep, you have to go through Jesus, the Gate. Verse 9: "*Whoever enters through me will be saved.*" But, second, Jesus, the Gate, protects His sheep from thieves, robbers, and wolves. Verse 10: "*A thief comes to steal, kill, and destroy. But I came to give life—life that is full and good.*"

(Fourth I Am Statement)

John 10:11-18

"I Am the Good Shepherd"

11 *"I am the good shepherd, and the good shepherd gives his life for the sheep.* **12** *The worker who is paid to keep the sheep is different from the shepherd. The paid worker does not own the sheep. So when he sees a wolf coming, he runs away and leaves the sheep alone. Then the wolf attacks the sheep and scatters them.* **13** *The man runs away because he is only a paid worker. He does not really care for the sheep."*

14-15 *"I am the shepherd who cares for the sheep. I know my sheep just as the Father knows me. And my sheep know me just as I know the Father. I give my life for these sheep.* **16** *I have other sheep too. They are not in this flock here. I must lead them also. They will listen to my voice. In the future there will be one flock and one shepherd.* **17** *The Father loves me because I give my life. I give my life so that I can get it back again.* **18** *No one takes my life away from me. I give my own life freely. I have the right to give my life, and I have the right to get it back again. This is what the Father told me."*

Close the Gate—I remember seeing a sign on a gate where cattle were being kept in West Texas. "If you open the gate, close the gate." I know it was written by someone who owned the cattle. I, on the other hand, had nothing to lose if I forgot. I was not the rancher and cared nothing for the cattle.

Here, then is the fourth "I am" statement, very closely related to the third. Jesus changes from being the Gate of the sheep pen to become the Good Shepherd. Verse 11: He says, *"I am the good shepherd…"* But He goes on to say in that same verse *"and the good shepherd gives his life for the sheep."* He's not a hired man who runs away from danger. He's not even a shepherd who might fight

142

the enemy but wouldn't die for the sheep. He is the *"good shepherd"* who *"gives his life for the sheep."*

So, we have the enemy described as a wolf, a robber, and a thief. He breaks into the sheep pen: verse 10: *"He comes to steal and kill and destroy;"* he scatters the flock. He is a stranger and the sheep do not recognize his voice. Who is this, then, Jesus is speaking of, who is up to no good when it comes to the sheep?

Jesus is speaking of any person who is pointing to another way to God and away from Him. The enemy is a false messiah, a false prophet, or, in Jesus' time, the teachers of the Law and the Pharisees who were telling the common Jew that Jesus was not the Messiah or the way to God. They thought, falsely, that they knew the way to God. But Jesus said in verse 9: *"Whoever enters through me will be saved. They will be able to come in and go out."*

People have accused Christianity of being narrow as to how a person comes to God. They are correct. In Matthew 7:13-14, Jesus, Himself, states this: *"You can enter true life only through the narrow gate. The gate to hell is very wide, and there is plenty of room on the road that leads there. Many people go that way. But the gate that opens the way to true life is narrow. And the road that leads there is hard to follow. Only a few people find it."*

Verse 10, *"A thief comes to steal and kill and destroy."* Who is the ultimate thief mentioned in this verse? The Apostle Paul says this in Ephesians 6:10-13:

> *To end my letter I tell you, be strong in the Lord and in his great power. Wear the full armor of God. Wear God's armor so that you can fight **against the devil's clever tricks. Our fight is not against people on earth. We are fighting against the rulers and authorities and the powers of this world's***

*darkness. **We are fighting against the spiritual powers of evil in the heavenly places.** That is why you need to get God's full armor. Then on the day of evil, you will be able to stand strong. And when you have finished the whole fight, you will still be standing.*

Watching Sheep from My Fishing Hole—From the time I was old enough to remember, I spent many a summer weekend and a whole lot of short vacations camping with my mom, dad, and two older brothers. We would load up our vehicle and usually drive high into the Sierras of California, just above the small village of Lone Pine, to a stream that ran the entire year, fed from the melting snowpack that lay on the tops of those mountains. The rivulet had an Indian name: Taboose Creek. It was only a couple of yards wide and maybe three or four feet in depth at its deepest, but because of its source and the surrounding steep terrain, the water that coursed its way downward ran cold and hurried. I grew up fishing at a campground along that particular creek. The site was no more than a small area cleared of brush but was large enough for our family to settle in for a weekend excursion. In the 1950s there were few camping spots with the facilities you might expect today.

After wolfing down their breakfasts, Dad, Bill, and Bob would take off, tramping through the underbrush to their various fishing spots, not to be seen again until either hunger or frustration from not getting anything to bite but the mosquitoes, would finally drive them back to camp. They would then quickly devour a sandwich, discuss with each other what kind of luck each was having, and then hike out once again until evening. Stories of an extra-large fish that seemed to have gotten away or a certain hard-fought battle, landing another, became the nightly topic discussed over our evening meal.

Conversely, I fished each day not far away from the watchful eyes of my mom. I had a particular fishing hole close to camp that I had dubbed mine. I was not a very patient child and would constantly reel in my line to either check the bait or to see if a fish had accidentally gotten hooked without my notice. Sometimes I would get my line all tangled up, casting too far and snagging my hook on a tree limb on the opposite bank. Other times I would get that same line so jumbled and knotted that I had to quit fishing until either Dad or one of my brothers would come along to rescue me.

I remember seeing shepherds, each year, leading their sheep to the high country to graze for the summer months. Many times, their flocks would cross the creek not far upstream from where I sat fishing. I would watch the shepherd's dogs running constantly around, corralling the sheep and not letting the little ones stray. The water would be muddied and the fish would scurry to safety as those wooly ovines would wade through a shallow part of the creek. All I could do was wait until the last lamb hopped up on the opposite shore, and then I could begin fishing once again. Other years the sheep would come through our campground, leaving smelly evidence of their presence. We, but mostly Mom, would then have to clean up their mess after their unwelcome visit was over.

Who are the sheep? —The sheep represent anyone who hears and responds to the Good Shepherd's voice. The Good Shepherd's sheep follow the Good Shepherd and ignore the voices of strangers. The sheep are Messiah's true disciples.

Who are the other sheep Jesus has to bring in? They are the Gentile (non-Jewish) nations. The Apostle Peter in Acts chapter 10 is given a command by God to go teach the first Gentile convert of Christianity, Cornelius. He and his whole household received the Holy Spirit and were baptized, beginning the tidal wave of

Gentiles—*"the other sheep"*—that was going to come to Israel's Messiah for salvation. Acts 2:39 states: *"This promise is for you. It is also for your children and for the people who are far away. It is for everyone the Lord our God calls to himself."*

John 10:19-30

[19] *Again the Jews were divided over what Jesus was saying.* [20] *Many of them said, "A demon has come into him and made him crazy. Why listen to him?"*

[21] *But others said, "These aren't the words of someone controlled by a demon. A demon cannot heal the eyes of a blind man."*

[22] *It was winter, and the time came for the Festival of Dedication at Jerusalem.* [23] *Jesus was in the Temple area at Solomon's Porch.* [24] *The Jewish leaders gathered around him. They said, "How long will you make us wonder about you? If you are the Messiah, then tell us clearly."*

[25] *Jesus answered, "I told you already, but you did not believe. I do miracles in my Father's name. These miracles show who I am.* [26] *But you do not believe, because you are not my sheep.* [27] *My sheep listen to my voice. I know them, and they follow me.* [28] *I give my sheep eternal life. They will never die, and no one can take them out of my hand.* [29] *My Father is the one who gave them to me, and he is greater than all. No one can steal my sheep out of his hand.* [30] *The Father and I are one.*

What Would You Do to Save Your Son? —When my oldest son, Jeremy, was about a year old, we took him to a Wednesday evening Bible class at the church we attended. He was in a class for his age group, and I was in the auditorium getting ready to lead the congregation in a song. I looked up to see a hundred eyes looking at the front, not at me, but behind me. I turned around and saw smoke coming from the baptistery area of our building. I knew my son's class was right across the hall from it. I thought about only one thing at that moment: getting my son away from that fire. I ran through the side door and to the entrance of his classroom. The teacher, Leslie Smith, was already passing children out of the window to some ready arms outside. At the door, I saw Jeremy and Kenny Wilkey sitting side by side in their booster chairs. I grabbed Jeremy in one arm and Kenny in the other and headed to an outside door. The first way I tried to get through was blocked with smoke, so I turned and ran in a different direction until we reached safety. I sprinted outside with these two precious bundles just as the fire trucks arrived, sirens blaring. I knew at that moment what it felt like to love another person so much that you would run into a fire to snatch them away. Jesus did just that. His love was so intense for us that He would battle the devil, hell, sin, and the grave to bring us to safety.

Comforting and Disturbing Words—Verse 26: *"But you do not believe, because you are not my sheep."* These are disturbing words to people who thought they had a lock on God—those who looked to their religion as a means to salvation. Jesus, though, tells them differently. "The Father and I are one in thought and action," says Jesus. "When you see one, you see the other."

The words which condemn one group of listeners, though, are a comfort to the others. Verses 28-29: *"I give my sheep eternal life. They will never die, and no one can take them out of my hand"* ...No one can steal my sheep out of his (the Father's) *hand.*

I Am God's Son

John 10:31-42

31 Again the Jews there picked up stones to kill Jesus. 32 But he said to them, "The many wonderful things you have seen me do are from the Father. Which of these good things are you killing me for?"

33 They answered, "We are not killing you for any good thing you did. But you say things that insult God. You are only a man, but you say you are the same as God! That is why we are trying to kill you!"

34 Jesus answered, "It is written in your law that God said, 'I said you are gods.' *35* This Scripture called those people gods—the people who received God's message. And Scripture is always true. *36* So why do you accuse me of insulting God for saying, 'I am God's Son'? I am the one God chose and sent into the world. *37* If I don't do what my Father does, then don't believe what I say. *38* But if I do what my Father does, you should believe in what I do. You might not believe in me, but you should believe in the things I do. Then you will know and understand that the Father is in me and I am in the Father."

39 They tried to get Jesus again, but he escaped from them.

40 Then he went back across the Jordan River to the place where John began his work of baptizing people. Jesus stayed there, *41* and many people came to him. They said, "John never did any miraculous signs, but everything John said about this man is true." *42* And many people there believed in Jesus.

Don't Talk About My Mother—Most people are very protective of the woman in the family who raised them, be it their mother, grandmother, aunt, or older sister. Don't talk about my mother! If you want to insult someone or start a fight, that will do it.

He Has a Demon—Notice, finally, that Jesus is accused of blasphemy (irreverence) because He says in verse 36: *"I am God's Son'? I am the one God chose and sent into the world."* The real blasphemy spoken here was not by Jesus but by the people who say of Jesus in verse 20: *"A demon has come into him and made him crazy."*

There is a great divide between the leaders, who are afraid that their power and way of life will be upset, or completely dismantled, and the people who know that miracles aren't done by demon-possessed people.

Jesus then leaves this place and goes back across the Jordan River. These people hang on to every word of Jesus. The final sentence says it all, verse 42: *"And many people there believed in Jesus."*

Some final questions: In your own life, whose sheep are you? Who is your shepherd? Is it the One who laid down His life for you? Is it the One who can put you in the palm of His hand and say to you: *"I give* (you) *eternal life?* (You) *will never die, and no one can take* (you) *out of my hand.*

(Seventh Sign)

John 11:1-4

Lazarus Raised from the Dead after Four Days

¹ There was a man named Lazarus who was sick. He lived in the town of Bethany, where Mary and her sister Martha lived. ² (Mary is the same woman who put perfume on the Lord and wiped his feet with her hair.) Mary's brother was Lazarus, the man who was now sick. ³ So Mary and Martha sent someone to tell Jesus, "Lord, your dear friend Lazarus is sick."

⁴ When Jesus heard this he said, "The end of this sickness will not be death. No, this sickness is for the glory of God. This has happened to bring glory to the Son of God."

Shooter Kills 21 at Robb Elementary in Uvalde, Texas—My youngest grandson, Owen, a fourth grader, went to an awards assembly on Tuesday at 8:30 AM, just three days before the end of school. Owen and his classmates received several awards from their teacher. I, his Papa, along with his Nana and his mom were there to applaud, take pictures and beam at this end-of-the-school-year event. After the assembly, Mom and Nana went back to work.

Being retired, I went to do Papa things, and Owen and his classmates went back to class to do end-of-the-year stuff, waiting for the final bell. Only two more days and it would be summer vacation.

At that same time, some five hours south of Abilene, nineteen students at Robb Elementary in Uvalde, Texas, also in the fourth grade, had been at an awards assembly. Nanas, papas, moms, and dads applauded, took pictures, and beamed at this end-of-the-school-year event just as we had with Owen. After the assembly, moms, and dads went back to work. Nanas and Papas went to do retired things and nineteen students and two teachers went back to class to do end-of-the-year stuff, waiting for the final bell. Only two more days and it would be summer vacation.

That is where the similarities ceased. Owen would be picked up at 3:15, as usual, safe and sound. He and his sister, Ella, would stay at Dad's in Dallas, swimming at pools and water parks under the hot summer sun, visiting cousins, and going to Nana Camp.

Not so, farther south. In Uvalde, an eighteen-year-old young man, angry about something, changed the summer plans of nineteen children and two teachers at Robb Elementary—no swimming at pools or water parks under the hot summer sun, no visiting cousins or going to Nana camps.

At 11:30 AM, everything changed in this small town. Not long after the assembly, parents, and grandparents would rush to the school, hearing that something terrible had just happened. Police and other first responders would be gathering at the scene, knowing little more than the others who had assembled. Tears would be shed, screams would be heard—screams of relief from some, screams of grief from others. Summer plans would become funerals for the twenty-one and counseling for the living. The

150

atmosphere would change to that of vigils, candles, prayers, embraces, second-guessing, and blaming.

America has been plagued with murder after murder of innocent people. While all murder is horrible, the mass murder of innocent children in public schools is especially horrifying. Many people, including this author, don't seem to have an answer as to why this is happening and what to do about it. We just seem to endure, hoping, maybe, it will not happen again.

Death, the Enemy—Death has been the enemy, the devil's stranglehold over creation since the beginning. Hebrews 2:14-15 says this about Jesus, the devil, and death: *These children are people with physical bodies. So Jesus himself became like them and had the same experiences they have. Jesus did this so that, by dying, he could destroy the one who has the power of death—the devil. Jesus became like these people and died so that he could free them. They were like slaves all their lives because of their fear of death.*

Although the devil has had the *"power of death,"* he didn't cause it. Humans from the beginning of time have been rebellious and their sins led to their death. Romans 6:20-21: *In the past you were slaves to sin, and you did not even think about doing right. You did evil things, and now you are ashamed of what you did. Did those things help you? No, they only brought death.*

Now, we realize innocent children, like the students in Uvalde, who have not sinned also die. Death though is the human condition because of the sinfulness of humankind in general. Romans 5:12: *Sin came into the world because of what one man did. And with sin came death. So this is why all people must die—because all people have sinned.*

But in I Corinthians 15:21-22, we are all made alive again through Christ: *Death comes to people because of what one man did. But now there is resurrection from death because of another man. I mean that in Adam all of us die. And in the same way, in Christ all of us will be made alive again.*

John 11:5-16

⁵ Jesus loved Martha and her sister and Lazarus. ⁶ So when he heard that Lazarus was sick, he stayed where he was two more days ⁷ and then said to his followers, "We should go back to Judea."

⁸ They answered, "But Teacher, those Jews there tried to stone you to death. That was only a short time ago. Now you want to go back there?"

⁹ Jesus answered, "There are twelve hours of light in the day. Whoever walks in the day will not stumble and fall because they can see with the light from the sun. ¹⁰ But whoever walks at night will stumble because there is no light."

¹¹ Then Jesus said, "Our friend Lazarus is now sleeping, but I am going there to wake him."

¹² The followers answered, "But, Lord, if he can sleep, he will get well." ¹³ They thought Jesus meant that Lazarus was literally sleeping, but he really meant that Lazarus was dead.

¹⁴ So then Jesus said plainly, "Lazarus is dead. ¹⁵ And I am glad I was not there. I am happy for you because now you will believe in me. We will go to him now."

¹⁶ Then Thomas, the one called "Twin," said to the other followers, "We will go too. We will die there with Jesus."

First Buffalo, New York, and then Uvalde, Texas—Tuesday turned into Wednesday, then Thursday, and then Friday. I was up early, as usual, reading my Bible and then doing my daily prayer walk around Abilene Christian University. I was so frustrated with the week's events—the senseless act of violence at the grocery store in Buffalo that killed 10, and then this horrible shooting of 19 children and two teachers in Uvalde. I had no more of an idea of what should be done than anyone else. But I knew I was talking, at that moment, with the One who did. I couldn't stop the bloodshed but was there something beyond "my thoughts and prayers" I believed the Lord wanted me to do?

I returned home from my walk, in time to watch the Today Show on Friday morning at 7:00. The news cycle for the school shooting hadn't run its course and more information was forthcoming. I had listened enough. Annette was in the kitchen, half listening to the TV, when I, through tears, told her, matter-of-factly, "I'm going to Uvalde. You can come with me or stay here but I'm going today." Annette, though, a little confused at my outburst, decided that if I was serious, she would go with me.

On the two-and-a-half-hour drive to my daughter's house, in Junction, to spend the night, Annette said, "Help me understand why we are going. What brought this on that you decided that you had to go to this particular school shooting event?"

My response was, "Owen is a fourth grader like many of these children. I taught fourth grade, myself for years, and I would have done anything to protect my students, even standing in front of a gunman. Most of the students I taught were Hispanic, like those in Uvalde. I was friends with their parents. I am a parent but also a grandparent. All of our grandchildren got to go home safely, after their assemblies on Tuesday. These did not. But it is more than that. I felt the Holy Spirit pulling me. I'm not sure what He wants me to do in Uvalde but I guess I will find out when I get there." Verses 14-15: *So then Jesus said plainly, "Lazarus is dead. And I am glad I was*

153

not there. I am happy for you because now you will believe in me. We will go to him now."

Why did Jesus wait two more days? If He had left right away, He would have arrived when Lazarus had been in the tomb for two days, not four. Was it that Jews, like some other races, think that the soul hangs around the body for three days? Maybe He wanted to show that he could raise the dead when there was no question that the person was dead. In verses 38-39, Jesus comes to the tomb where Lazarus' body has been placed and wants the stone removed. Listen to what Lazarus' sister, Martha has to say: *"But, Lord, it has been four days since Lazarus died. There will be a bad smell."* There were many believing and unbelieving people present on this occasion. There was no doubt this man was dead, for his body had begun to decay.

(Fifth I Am Statement)

John 11:17-27

I Am the Resurrection! I Am Life!

[17] Jesus arrived in Bethany and found that Lazarus had already been dead and in the tomb for four days. [18] Bethany was about two miles from Jerusalem. [19] Many Jews had come to see Martha and Mary. They came to comfort them about their brother Lazarus.

[20] When Martha heard that Jesus was coming, she went out to greet him. But Mary stayed home. [21] Martha said to Jesus, "Lord, if you had been here, my brother would not have died. [22] But I know that even now God will give you anything you ask."

[23] Jesus said, "Your brother will rise and be alive again."

[24] Martha answered, "I know that he will rise to live again at the time of the resurrection on the last day."

²⁵ *Jesus said to her, "I am the resurrection. I am life. Everyone who believes in me will have life, even if they die. **²⁶** And everyone who lives and believes in me will never really die. Martha, do you believe this?"*

²⁷ *Martha answered, "Yes, Lord. I believe that you are the Messiah, the Son of God. You are the one who was coming to the world."*

Why Would God Allow This to Happen? —As we entered Uvalde, we had no idea where to begin, so we got GPS directions for Robb Elementary and drove there. The street was blocked off, and a young Sheriff's deputy walked toward our car. I lowered my window and told him we were just trying to find a place where we could pray for all of these people. In an extremely kind voice, he thanked us and directed us to a park in the middle of town, with a fountain in its center. So, that is where we went.

We found a parking place not far from the park. After stopping, I lugged our Ice chest full of iced-down water out of the car and rolled it toward the park. Annette was loaded down with several grocery sacks full of granola, peanuts, and other snacky kinds of food. We also brought five bunches of bananas.

There were several groups of people already there but not a large crowd this early in the morning. A man saw me and walked up to me. With no greeting, he immediately began talking to me. "Why," he asked, "would God allow this to happen?" He was very angry but his anger didn't seem to be directed at me. His words were much like those of Martha in verse 21: *"Lord, if you had been here, my brother would not have died."* I had to admit to myself, I have said those same words to God when unexpected death entered my own life.

He waited for me to reply, and I, trying to formulate a response, asked him, "Do you have family here?"

He replied, waving his hand toward the crosses and the crowd assembled, "We are all family. But why did God, if there is a God, let this happen?"

I had several things run through my head but I knew his question was more rhetorical. Maybe he thought I had some grand response, but all that came out of my mouth was, "I don't know the answer to that." The conversation was over, and the man slowly walked away shaking his head.

"I am the bread that gives life." "I am the light of the world." "I am the gate for the sheep." "I am the good shepherd." "I am the resurrection. I am life." All these descriptions of Jesus, the Son of God. Resurrection and life—what is meant by this fifth "I am" statement of Jesus? The raising of Lazarus would be a preview of the death and resurrection that would take place very shortly.

Jesus would die, and God would resurrect Him. But there is a vast difference between the two risings. Lazarus would one day die once again. The tears shed the first time would be repeated. Lazarus would die again because he was raised back with a physical body as we all have. Jesus, the first fruit of the final resurrection, was raised with a spiritual body, which, unlike our present bodies, was imperishable, glorious, and powerful. In I Corinthians 15:23, the Apostle Paul states this: *But everyone will be raised to life in the right order. Christ was first to be raised. Then, when Christ comes again, those who belong to him will be raised to life.*

And in verses 42-44 of the same chapter, Paul says this:

> *It will be the same when those who have died are raised to life. The body that is "planted" in the grave will ruin and decay, but it will be raised to a life that cannot be destroyed. When the body is "planted," it is without honor. But when it is raised, it will be great*

156

and glorious. When the body is "planted," it is weak. But when it is raised, it will be full of power. The body that is "planted" is a physical body. When it is raised, it will be a spiritual body.

Jesus, who was sinless, takes away the sins of the world. Remember John the Baptist way back in John 1:29-34? Here are his words: *The next day John saw Jesus coming toward him and said, "Look, the Lamb of God. **He takes away the sins of the world**!... I came baptizing people with water so that Israel could know that he is the Messiah... I saw the Spirit come down from heaven like a dove and rest on this man. So this is what I tell people: 'He is the Son of God.'"*

Lazarus would be resurrected at the end of the age. Jesus' resurrection would be the first. He would be the pioneer (**leader**) through death to the other side. Hebrews 12:2: *We must never stop looking to Jesus. He is the **leader** of our faith, and he is the one who makes our faith complete. He suffered death on a cross. But he accepted the shame of the cross as if it were nothing because of the joy he could see waiting for him. And now he is sitting at the right side of God's throne.*

Jesus is the foundation of both the **resurrection**... John 6:37-40:

"The Father gives me my people. Every one of them will come to me. I will always accept them. I came down from heaven to do what God wants, not what I want. I must not lose anyone God has given me. But I must raise them up on the last day. This is what the one who sent me wants me to do. Everyone who sees the Son and believes in him has eternal life. I will

raise them up on the last day. This is what my Father wants."

...and the **Life**, 1 John 5:11-12: *This is what God told us: God has given us **eternal life**, and this **life** is in his Son. Whoever has the Son has **life**, but whoever does not have the Son of God does not have **life.***

John 11:28-35

[28] *After Martha said these things, she went back to her sister Mary. She talked to Mary alone and said, "The Teacher is here. He is asking for you."* [29] *When Mary heard this, she stood up and went quickly to Jesus.* [30] *He had not yet come into the village. He was still at the place where Martha met him.* [31] *The Jews who were in the house comforting Mary saw her get up and leave quickly. They thought she was going to the tomb to cry there. So they followed her.* [32] *Mary went to the place where Jesus was. When she saw him, she bowed at his feet and said, "Lord, if you had been here, my brother would not have died."*

[33] *When Jesus saw Mary crying and the people with her crying too, he was very upset and deeply troubled.* [34] *He asked, "Where did you put him?"*

They said, "Lord, come and see."

[35] *Jesus cried.*

Thinking of My Own Grandchildren—I took out a notebook and made my way around the fountain. There were twenty-one crosses with the names and pictures of each child and teacher who was killed that day. As Annette walked beside me, I wrote, their names in a journal. As I was writing I couldn't help but think of our grandchildren. Their names flashed through my mind—Josiah, Fisher, Ashlyn, London, Ethan, Avyn, Ella, Creed, Kendyl, and Owen.

As I made my way, full circle, having written the names, a young man asked me, in an unpleasant and questioning voice, "What are you writing?"

I answered, "I am writing the names of the students and the teachers."

He said he was from Kerrville, and on Tuesday, after hearing the news about the shooting, he found he was so numb to all of the killings lately that he was beginning to not care. He told Annette and me that that scared him. He wanted to care. He didn't want to become so emotionless that he just went on with his daily routine, chalking this up to another bad day in America. He then grabbed both of us tightly and hugged us for a long time. Annette told me later that she didn't know how he would react but she began praying aloud. We shared tears along with that prayer, as he continued his embrace.

He saw that we brought snacks and water and said he wished he had something to share with the people here. Then he thought about it and said he had just learned to play the guitar. "Maybe I could write a song about today!" He exclaimed.

Why did Jesus cry? He knew He was going to raise His friend: Was it because He had disappointed those whom He loved for not being present earlier? Was the reason because of the tears that were being shed all around Him? The Apostle Paul states this in Romans 12:15: *"When others are happy, you should be happy with them. And when others are sad, you should be sad too."*

I wonder if the tears began much earlier when He first got word, that Lazarus was sick. He knew He was going to wait for a higher purpose; He knew His disciples and His friends would misunderstand; He knew He would watch His friends weep when

159

He could stop the tears. He knew all those things, but He let Lazarus die. Jesus' weeping is God crying because of death!

John 11:36-44

36 And the Jews said, "Look! He loved Lazarus very much!"

37 But some of them said, "Jesus healed the eyes of the blind man. Why didn't he help Lazarus and stop him from dying?"

38 Again feeling very upset, Jesus came to the tomb. It was a cave with a large stone covering the entrance. 39 He said, "Move the stone away."

Martha said, "But, Lord, it has been four days since Lazarus died. There will be a bad smell." Martha was the sister of the dead man.

40 Then Jesus said to her, "Remember what I told you? I said that if you believed, you would see God's divine greatness."

41 So they moved the stone away from the entrance. Then Jesus looked up and said, "Father, I thank you that you heard me. 42 I know that you always hear me. But I said these things because of the people here around me. I want them to believe that you sent me." 43 After Jesus said this he called in a loud voice, "Lazarus, come out!" 44 The dead man came out. His hands and feet were wrapped with pieces of cloth. He had a handkerchief covering his face.

Jesus said to the people, "Take off the cloth and let him go."

Witnessing the Hands, Feet, and Heart of Jesus—As we passed out water and snacks and bananas, we notice many others walking around trying to serve. Most of those we spoke to said they, also, had been led on this day to this place. Annette noticed an old gentleman serving in his own way. He walked around with a box of Kleenex, offering a tissue to all who needed it.

Others wore Chaplin tags helping people with grief. A group brought stuffed animals to give to any child who wanted something soft to hold on tightly to. Another group brought colored chalk, so kids and adults could write scriptures or thoughts or just draw chalk art on all the walkways. There was a church that set up a sign under a canopy that let people know they could come to their table for prayer. There was a church choir that sang and a praise band that played. There was a group of people who brought therapy dogs.

One man, who happened to be a teacher from Abilene, felt the call to just come and sit and watch. He had lived in Uvalde previously. He brought his very large sheep-a-doodle, not really with the intention of it being a therapy dog. Annette told me later, she saw several young boys sobbing, holding on desperately to their parents. One of the boys stopped when he saw the sheep-a-doodle and for twenty minutes or more just ran his hands through the dog's fur, and was comforted.

As the day wore on, there were so many people that we decided it was time to leave. As we left Uvalde, that Saturday afternoon for our trek back home, Annette and I began to process the weekend and especially the hours we spent at the park in Uvalde.

What were our greatest takeaways? As Nana and Papa, we knew that we were fortunate to be able to, this summer, be with all of our grandchildren. We also knew, in the back of our minds we would breathe a sigh of relief as we would hug each a little tighter.

Originally, I thought, though not humbly, that the Holy Spirit was leading just me to Uvalde that Saturday morning. I was pleasantly surprised that God had called an army of people. He had called people to bring the talents He had given them, even handing out tissues for the many who shed tears. I was pleased that within that park, there were no speeches, only prayers; there were no political parties; no brown people, black people, or white people, just one large hurting family. And lastly, the greatest takeaway I witnessed was seeing people being the hands, feet, and heart of Jesus.

Since Adam, men and women have been dying and burying their dead and yes, crying. Sin had caused death, graves, and tears and yet here was God, who came to earth wrapped in flesh, sharing in our humanity and experiencing what sin had caused. He would share in our death, our graves, and our tears, but he also came to put a stop to all of that. Three words would change death to life and tears to joy. Three words would become a preview of what would take place a few days later on an early Sunday morning. Verse 43: *"Jesus...called out in a loud voice,* ***'Lazarus, come out!'"***

 It has been said that Jesus used Lazarus's name; otherwise, there would have been a mass resurrection. This same God of the universe, this Savior of humans, this Messiah Jesus will someday call each of His sheep by name and they, too, will come out of their graves.

John 11:45-57

45 There were many Jews who came to visit Mary. When they saw what Jesus did, many of them believed in him. 46 But some of them went to the Pharisees and told them what Jesus did. 47 Then the leading priests and Pharisees called a meeting of the high council. They said, "What should we do? This man is doing many miraculous signs. 48 If we let him continue doing these things, everyone will believe in him. Then the Romans will come and take away our Temple and our nation."

49 One of the men there was Caiaphas. He was the high priest that year. He said, "You people know nothing! 50 It is better for one man to die for the people than for the whole nation to be destroyed. But you don't realize this."

51 Caiaphas did not think of this himself. As that year's high priest, he was really prophesying that Jesus would die for the Jewish people. 52 Yes, he would die for the Jewish people. But he would also die for God's other children scattered all over the world. He would die to bring them all together and make them one people.

53 That day the Jewish leaders began planning to kill Jesus. 54 So Jesus stopped traveling around openly among the Jews. He went away to a town called Ephraim in an area near the desert. He stayed there with his followers.

55 It was almost time for the Jewish Passover festival. Many people from the country went to Jerusalem before the Passover. They went to do the special things to make themselves pure for the festival. 56 The people looked for Jesus. They stood in the Temple area and asked each other, "Is he coming to the festival? What do you think?" 57 But the leading priests and the Pharisees had given a special order about Jesus. They said that anyone who knew where he was must tell them so that they could arrest him.

Two Completely Different Conclusions—My son, Matt, and I decided we would eat lunch together at my house. "I'll order over the phone and meet you at the house in a few minutes," I said. Matt told me what he wanted and we hung up. "Two hamburgers, an order of fries and two drinks, tea, and a diet coke, under the name Darell," I ordered over the phone.

When I got to the burger stand, I went up to the counter and told the girl behind the counter I had a call-in order under the name of Martin. She began ringing up my order. "Wait a minute," I said, "I didn't order tater tots."

"Yes, you did," she said, "I remember you asking if we had tater tots, and when I said yes, you ordered some."

"Mam," I exclaimed, "I don't even like tater tots. And I noticed you wrote down three hamburgers. I only ordered two."

She seemed exasperated with me and exclaimed. "I just wrote down what you ordered. I wouldn't have written it down otherwise."

"How many drinks do you have written down?" I asked.

"You ordered one tea."

I couldn't figure out how she could have messed up my order so badly. We were both looking at each other with daggers in our eyes, neither of us giving an inch, when one of the other ladies overheard our conversation and came over with another bag and said, "Is this yours, under Darell? That's me I said sheepishly. I guess I forgot what name I put the order under.

Both of us knew what we heard, but we came away with completely different conclusions.

Same Event, Two Different Responses—Two types of people stood at Lazarus' grave that day. Both saw the same event happen, both were astonished, and both knew that a great miracle had taken place, but that is where the similarities ended. Look at the two phrases that describe these two groups. Verses 45-46: *There were many Jews who came to visit Mary. When they saw what Jesus did, many of them believed in him. But some of them went to the Pharisees and told them what Jesus did.*

Even among the Pharisees, there were those honest skeptics who honorably looked at the facts. Others knew the truth but wanted to see what those in positions of authority would do. They feared the Romans more than they feared God. This second group is the people Jesus will speak about later in 12:37: *The people saw all these miraculous signs Jesus did, but they still did not believe in him.*

Each of us has to take in the message and the facts. Do we believe the signs? Do we accept the teachings? Do we believe that Jesus can raise the dead, including me? Or do we fear what others think more than we fear God? God did everything but make us choose. That step is ours to accept or walk away from.

John 12:1-8

¹ Six days before the Passover festival, Jesus went to Bethany. That is where Lazarus lived, the man Jesus raised from death. ² There they had a dinner for Jesus. Martha served the food, and Lazarus was one of the people eating with Jesus. ³ Mary brought in a pint of expensive perfume made of pure nard. She poured the perfume on Jesus' feet. Then she wiped his feet with her hair. And the sweet smell from the perfume filled the whole house.

⁴ Judas Iscariot, one of Jesus' followers, was there—the one who would later hand Jesus over to his enemies. Judas said, ⁵ "That perfume was worth a full year's pay. It should have been sold, and the money should have been given to the poor people." ⁶ But Judas did not really care about the poor. He said this because he was a thief. He was the one who kept the moneybag for the group of followers. And he often stole money from the bag.

⁷ Jesus answered, "Don't stop her. It was right for her to save this perfume for today—the day for me to be prepared for burial. ⁸ You will always have those who are poor with you. But you will not always have me."

Sister Beth—There was one of Jesus' disciples who used to attend Freedom Fellowship where my wife, Annette, and I attend. Her name was Beth. She died several years ago from cancer but is fondly remembered at that small congregation. She had been a drug addict for much of her life but decided to commit herself to the Lord and be baptized.

Beth would dance before the Lord during our song service. When you watched Beth dance you could almost see her partner, Jesus, with a big smile on His face. Since Freedom Fellowship is a satellite church of our larger church, we attend Freedom on Wednesday nights and the big church on Sundays. On a particular Sunday morning, Beth was so caught up in worship she began dancing in the aisle.

While most of us who attended the small church on Wednesday were surprised, we knew Beth, knew her heart, and knew who was dancing with her. Others did not. Many eyes suddenly were riveted in her direction. Some approving, many not. You could almost read minds that day, "We may allow the raising of hands, but dancing…"

Jesus, too, loves our expressions of love whether they are in worship or expressed by what we do for others, even when it sometimes, may seem to others as impractical. Mary must have been some lady. Her brother and sister were doing what most men and women did in that culture. Lazarus sits at the table and eats, and Martha serves the meal. But Mary comes in with expensive perfume and anoints Jesus, not His head, mind you, but His feet.

Luke records another incident with Mary and Martha in Luke 10:38-42:

> While Jesus and his followers were traveling, Jesus went into a town. A woman named Martha let Jesus stay at her house. Martha had a sister named Mary, who was sitting at Jesus' feet and listening to him teach. But Martha was busy with all the work to be done. She went in and said, "Lord, don't you care that my sister has left me alone to do all the work? Tell her to help me."

But the Lord answered her, "Martha, Martha, you are worried and upset about many things. Only one thing is important. Mary has chosen the better thing, and it will never be taken away from her."

Mary wasn't the practical type; I mean she poured a year's wages on feet. She wasn't the type to take a hint; she didn't pay any attention to her sister's dirty looks, coming from the kitchen, about needing Mary's help. But she sure knew what was important. Think of listening at the feet of Jesus, to His words, watching His mannerisms, hearing His voice, seeing the expressions on His face. Mary knew what was best and she didn't listen to her sister, to the badmouthing of Judas, or the raised eyebrows of the people around. And Jesus wasn't embarrassed. He sat there and let Mary express her love and worship.

Here's a question: If you had to describe yourself as a Mary or a Martha, which would you be?

John 12:9-11

[9] *Many of the Jews heard that Jesus was in Bethany, so they went there to see him. They also went there to see Lazarus, the one Jesus raised from death.* [10] *So the leading priests made plans to kill Lazarus too.* [11] *Because of him, many Jews were leaving them and believing in Jesus. That is why they wanted to kill Lazarus too.*

November 22, 1963—I was in a 9th grade English class with a young male teacher all of us thought was cool. Right in the middle of his discussion, our principal came on the intercom and announced that President Kennedy had been shot and killed in Dallas, Texas. He then turned on the radio and let the student body listen to the latest news.

We all sat, unmoving, disbelieving, some even began crying. School was dismissed for the rest of the day. We all went home, unsure of what was going to happen in our safe little world of teenage worries.

I went home, and with my parents, sat glued to the TV set, listening to the nonstop news of the latest events surrounding this tragedy. It was discovered that some guy named Lee Harvey Oswald had been arrested for the crime. On Sunday morning the assassin was shot by another guy named Jack Ruby. At that point, all kinds of conspiracy theories began to surface. "It was the Mafia. It was Castro from Cuba. It was the Russians. It was the CIA. It was Lyndon Johnson, our new president. There were two shooters; one was behind the grassy knoll."

Although, the Warren Commission decided, after reviewing all the evidence, that Oswald was the lone gunman and that there were no others involved, many people were dissatisfied with their conclusion. They were suspicious of our government. They would question, "What was the government trying to cover up?"

The Conspiracy of Getting Rid of Jesus—How do you get rid of Jesus when He keeps doing miracles? Verses 10-11 express a telling tale: *...the leading priests made plans to kill Lazarus too. Because of him, many Jews were leaving them and believing in Jesus. That is why they wanted to kill Lazarus too.*

Talk about a conspiracy; these leaders were not only wanting to kill Jesus for raising a man, who had been dead for four days, but they wanted to kill Lazarus, the formerly dead man also. And all because they were afraid of the Romans more than they feared God.

John 12:12-19

12 The next day the people in Jerusalem heard that Jesus was coming there. These were the crowds of people who had come to the Passover festival. 13 They took branches of palm trees and went out to meet Jesus. They shouted,

"'Praise Him!'

'Welcome! God bless the one who comes in the name of the Lord!'

God bless the King of Israel!"

¹⁴ Jesus found a donkey and rode on it, as the Scriptures say,

¹⁵ "Do not be afraid, people of Zion!
Look! Your king is coming.
He is riding on a young donkey."

¹⁶ The followers of Jesus did not understand at that time what was happening. But after he was raised to glory, they understood that this was written about him. Then they remembered that they had done these things for him.

¹⁷ There were many people with Jesus when he raised Lazarus from death and told him to come out of the tomb. Now they were telling others about what Jesus did. ¹⁸ That's why so many people went out to meet him—because they had heard about this miraculous sign he did. ¹⁹ So the Pharisees said to each other, "Look! Our plan is not working. The people are all following him!"

The Young Man with Downs Syndrome—He was sitting close to where I was that morning for worship. He was singing loudly and very much off-key. He knew most of the words and tried to keep up but was usually a note or two behind the rest of the congregation. And during part of the songs, he seemed to enjoy the most, he would raise his hands as high as he could, and lift his face toward the ceiling. I had tears in my eyes, for I could sense that God's attention was not on me, but was on him. I know the Father was smiling and loving every minute of praise from the lips He had created for this worshipper.

Luke 19:39-40 says this about this entry into Jerusalem on Palm Sunday: *Some of the Pharisees said to Jesus, "Teacher, tell your followers not to say these things."*

But Jesus answered, "I tell you, if my followers didn't say them, these stones would shout them."

A Dancing King—David the king, like the story of Beth above, danced before the Lord and was criticized; Mary poured out her love but was made to feel guilty; children came to sit in Jesus' lap and were told to get away. Here, people waved palm branches and shouted to the Lord, *"Hosanna,"* and were rebuked. None of it was practical or cost-effective, but the Lord loves the praises of His children. In each incident, the Lord accepted the worship and honored the devotion. Psalm 8:2: *From the mouths of children and babies come songs of praise to you. They sing of your power to silence your enemies who were seeking revenge.*

Why a Donkey? Why didn't Jesus ride through town on a white horse? The donkey was a sign of peace. Jesus came to bring peace on earth, not worldly peace, but peace between God and humans, reconciliation between Creator and humanity. His first coming was to deal with sin and bring forgiveness and grace. His second coming brings the white horse and the victorious Christ. Revelation 19: 11-16:

> *Then I saw heaven open. There before me was a white horse. The rider on the horse was called Faithful and True, because he is right in his judging and in making war. His eyes were like burning fire. He had many crowns on his head. A name was written on him, but he was the only one who knew its meaning. He was dressed in a robe dipped in blood, and he was called the Word of God. The*

armies of heaven were following the rider on the white horse. They were also riding white horses. They were dressed in fine linen, white and clean. A sharp sword came out of the rider's mouth, a sword that he would use to defeat the nations. And he will rule the nations with a rod of iron. He will crush the grapes in the winepress of the terrible anger of God All-Powerful. On his robe and on his leg was written this name:

KING OF KINGS AND LORD OF LORDS

John 12:20-22

[20] *There were some Greeks there too. These were some of the people who went to Jerusalem to worship at the Passover festival.* [21] *They went to Philip, who was from Bethsaida in Galilee. They said, "Sir, we want to meet Jesus."* [22] *Philip went and told Andrew. Then Andrew and Philip went and told Jesus.*

Silkworms—As my children were growing up, they would look forward to Dad bringing home that shoebox every spring from his fifth-grade classroom where he taught science. The box would be filled with about thirty or more silkworms, busily eating mulberry leaves. We spent a lot of time in our mulberry tree pulling off leaves for those hungry creatures to eat. And eat, they would. Now a silkworm's job in life is to spin a cocoon made of silk, and the early Chinese would trade that silk with Europe. The cocoon was made so that the silkworm (really a caterpillar) could transform into a beautiful white moth. You could always tell when the silkworm was about to begin spinning its cocoon because it would stop eating and stay very erect, not moving a muscle. (Do silkworms have muscles?) It would stand very still with its head high, and it would stay in that position for about a day, while a change came over it. The silkworm was getting ready to spin a cocoon of silk just like its Creator had created it to do. its whole being was suddenly alert to the task it was about to begin.

Jesus had finished His signs and He would not be distracted from the task He was to begin. His passion, His time, His task was about to begin. Hopefully, these Greek Gentiles would listen alongside all the others as Jesus speaks to all the people present.

Out of Time—One of the things I dreaded the most in school was timed tests. It was like the hands of the clock in the room suddenly began moving double time. My heart raced, my mind went blank and my pencil wouldn't seem to budge. I knew the voice would come—that voice that told me I was out of time.

Philip and Andrew brought some Greeks—probably not Jews, maybe proselytes (new converts to Judaism), or possibly curious Gentiles who accept the Jewish Law, feasts and worship to Jesus. Jesus will announce to all present, in verse 23: *"The time has come for the Son of Man to receive his glory."* The term *"the time"* is important. Jesus spoke of His time or His hour several times in John. In John 2:4: *"It is not yet time."* In John 7:6 and 8: *"The right time."* In John 7:30: *the right time for him had not yet come.* And in John 8:20: *...no one arrested him, because the right time for him had not yet come.* Jesus has come to **"his time."** In John 12:27, Jesus will say: *"Now I am very troubled. What should I say? Should I say, 'Father save me from this time of suffering?"*

The time of His Glory, His Passion had arrived. This was the last week of His life and He was going to prepare Himself and the Twelve, His chosen apostles for His death.

John 12:23-26

23 Jesus said to them, "The time has come for the Son of Man to receive his glory. 24 It is a fact that a grain of wheat must fall to the ground and die before it can grow and produce much more wheat. If it never dies, it will never be more than a single seed. ²⁵ Whoever loves the life they have now will lose it. But whoever is willing to give up their life in this world will keep it. They will have eternal life. ²⁶ Whoever serves me must follow me. My servants must be with me everywhere I am. My Father will give honor to anyone who serves me.

Planting Seeds—I remember teaching in a 5ᵗʰ-grade science class about seeds. We took some pinto bean seeds and put them between two sheets of glass. We laid the seeds on a wet paper towel between the sheets and then stood the whole thing up in a tray of water. The next day the seeds began to sprout.

We watched the seeds through the glass for several weeks as the sprouts became plants and began to grow leaves and roots. Finally, small flowers appeared and from those flowers, small beans began to grow. We looked at the original seeds, and they had fallen off and died leaving a new plant with many seeds. Verse 24: *"It is a fact that a grain of wheat must fall to the ground and die before it can grow and produce much more wheat. If it never dies, it will never be more than a single seed."*

Jesus speaks here of His death but then tells His disciples that they, too, must follow Him. In Luke 9:23-25, Jesus says this: *"Any of you who want to be my follower must stop thinking about yourself and what you want. You must be willing to carry the cross that is given to you every day for following me. Any of you who try to save the life you have will lose it. But you who give up your life for me will save it. It is worth nothing for you to have the whole world if you yourself are destroyed or lost.*

John 12:27-36

27 *"Now I am very troubled. What should I say? Should I say, 'Father save me from this time of suffering'? No, I came to this time so that I could suffer.* 28 *Father, do what will bring you glory!" Then a voice came from heaven, "I have already brought glory to myself. I will do it again."* 29 *The people standing there heard the voice. They said it was thunder.*

But others said, "An angel spoke to him!"

30 *Jesus said, "That voice was for you and not for me.* 31 *Now is the time for the world to be judged. Now the ruler of this world will be thrown out.* 32 *I will be lifted up from the earth. When that happens, I will draw all people to myself."* 33 *Jesus said this to show how he would die.*

34 *The people said, "But our law says that the Messiah will live forever. So why do you say, 'The Son of Man must be lifted up'? Who is this 'Son of Man'?"*

35 *Then Jesus said, "The light will be with you for only a short time more. So walk while you have the light. Then the darkness will not catch you. People who walk in the darkness don't know where they are going.* 36 *So put your trust in the light while you still have it. Then you will be children of light." When Jesus finished saying these things, he went away to a place where the people could not find him.*

Dying on Purpose—I have watched, first, one wife and then a second suffer physically with cancer, through treatments and ultimately death. I have witnessed the mental suffering of children as they lost those same women, their mothers. I have seen others, family, friends, and even strangers go through the suffering of heart, of mind, of body. But I have never known anyone who was born for the purpose of suffering and dying, except Jesus.

174

The writer, John, lets us know that Jesus not only knew His purpose. Verse 27: *"I came to this time so that I could suffer."* He understood from the beginning that it would be on a Roman cross. Verses 32-33: *"I will be lifted up from the earth... Jesus said this to show how he would die."* His suffering was not only known by Jesus, but this suffering would somehow bring glory to God.

The people didn't understand; even His disciples didn't understand this "suffering Messiah." "We thought you were coming to free us from the Romans," they would say. But Jesus came to free them from sin and death. He came so the *"ruler of this world,"* satan and his minions would be judged and overthrown. He came to be *"the Light of the World."* He came to *"draw all people"* to Himself so that they can be *"children of light."*

John 12:37-43

37 The people saw all these miraculous signs Jesus did, but they still did not believe in him. 38 This was to give full meaning to what Isaiah the prophet said:

"Lord, who believed what we told them?
  Who has seen the Lord's power?"

39 This is why the people could not believe. Because Isaiah also said,

40 "God made the people blind.
  He closed their minds.
He did this so that they would not see with their eyes
  and understand with their minds.
He did it so that they would not turn
  and be healed."

41 Isaiah said this because he saw Jesus' divine greatness. So he spoke about him.

42 But many people believed in Jesus. Even many of the Jewish leaders believed in him, but they were afraid of the Pharisees, so they did not say openly that they believed. They were afraid they would be ordered to stay out of the synagogue. 43 They loved praise from people more than praise from God.

Wrong Way—My wife and I pulled out of the convenience store parking lot on our vacation and turned the wrong way. We should have seen the signs we passed but somehow missed them. It wasn't until we were some twenty miles down the road that my wife said, "I remember this place. Those construction workers were redoing that sidewalk by all those stores. Embarrassed, I turned around and drove the way I was going in the first place.

Several groups of people had been listening to Jesus. They had all heard the same message. They had all seen the signs (miracles). But each group came away with a different reaction. The first group was the *"children of light"* mentioned in verse 36. The second group was so rooted in their culture and traditions that they were blind, as the Isaiah passages, above, speak of. God let these blind people stay in their blindness. The third group, I sometimes find myself in. They were the ones who *"loved praise from people more than praise from God."* Verse 43. This group is the saddest to me, to know the truth but to be more fearful of people's reactions than that of God. Which group are you in?

John 12:44-50

44 Then Jesus said loudly, "Everyone who believes in me is really believing in the one who sent me. 45 Everyone who sees me is really seeing the one who sent me. 46 I came into this world as a light. I came so that everyone who believes in me will not stay in darkness.

47 "I did not come into the world to judge people. I came to save the people in the world. So I am not the one who judges those who hear

176

my teaching and do not obey. ⁴⁸ But there is a judge for all those who refuse to believe in me and do not accept what I say. The message I have spoken will judge them on the last day. ⁴⁹ That is because what I taught was not from myself. The Father who sent me told me what to say and what to teach. ⁵⁰ And I know that whatever he says to do will bring eternal life. So the things I say are exactly what the Father told me to say."

So, Am I a Duck? —When I was in the rebellious days of my youth, I acted, talked, and dressed like all of my friends. I remember my Uncle Duane saying, "If it walks like a duck and quacks like a duck, it must be a duck." Not understanding metaphors (symbolic language), and also because of my youth, I passed it off as "old guy's language," but I always remembered what he said. I have also used it several times toward other youths now that I'm an old guy.

7The interesting thought here in both Jesus and my Uncle Duane was that their judgment wasn't what brought people around. It was their words. Words of truth have a way of shining a light in a dark place, even if that dark place is your very own soul. God set the world up to run on earth as it does in heaven but between satan and his people, darkness seems to reign. Jesus' light draws all honest people who love the truth to Jesus Himself and, therefore, to the Father.

John 13:1-3

¹ It was almost time for the Jewish Passover festival. Jesus knew that the time had come for him to leave this world and go back to the Father. Jesus had always loved the people in the world who were his. Now was the time he showed them his love the most.

² Jesus and his followers were at the evening meal. The devil had already persuaded Judas Iscariot to hand Jesus over to his enemies. (Judas was the son of Simon.) ³ The Father had given Jesus power over everything. Jesus knew this. He also knew that he had come from God. And he knew that he was going back to God.

Kids and Potlucks—I remember potluck Sundays when I was growing up. After the amen was said, all of us kids would run ahead pushing and shoving to see who could be first in line at the food table, with never a thought of allowing someone else to go first. We piled our plates high with the fried chicken, mashed potatoes, gravy, and dessert, and then, ran for the nearest table to get a seat. Some of the older people would shake their heads and whisper to each other, "When I was a child…" Of course, our parents would be embarrassed and correct us, but the next time we would forget and rush ahead again.

Here are twelve men, with Jesus, entering a room for the Passover meal, scrambling to their places. Jesus must have noticed the jostling for position. Some of His earlier teachings didn't seem to be sinking in. Mark, in his gospel, wrote of a time when James and John had asked Jesus to allow them to sit at His right and left in the new kingdom. Mark states this in 10:42-44:

Jesus called all the followers together. He said, "The non-Jewish people have men they call rulers. You know that those rulers love to show their power over the people. And their important leaders love to use all their authority over the people. But it should not be that way with you. Whoever wants to be your leader must be your servant. Whoever wants to be first must serve the rest of you like a slave."

John 13:4-5

⁴ So while they were eating, Jesus stood up and took off his robe. He got a towel and wrapped it around his waist. ⁵ Then he poured water into a bowl and began to wash the followers' feet. He dried their feet with the towel that was wrapped around his waist.

The Towel of Service—When I baptized each of my children, I gave them a towel as a gift. It was to remind them that Jesus washed feet. He came to serve not to be served. I wanted each of my children to remember that lesson as they walked the Christian path. As Annette and my grandchildren became old enough to claim the Messiah and be baptized, we made a point to give them that same gift. It became the "towel of service."

There was a towel and a basin of water in the corner at the meal, but none of the disciples washed their feet as they enter the room. The host provided water and a towel. If the host was wealthy, he may even provide a servant to wash his guests' feet. But what happened next was unique in this culture. As the meal was being served, the Host and Creator of the universe stripped down, and with towel and washbasin, proceeded to become the servant and wash His disciples' feet.

He washed the feet of Judas, the traitor, possibly thinking that soon those feet would run to the authorities and turn Him in. He washed the feet of Peter, the one who would deny Him, maybe thinking that soon those feet would stand up in front of thousands as Peter would preach the first gospel sermon. He washed the feet of John, possibly thinking that those feet would someday be old and calloused from spending a lifetime walking roads telling the church to love one another. He washed Thomas, the doubter's feet, and the feet of the other disciples who would, in a few hours, run and hide. And yet all those feet would one day take the gospel to places all over the world. I wonder if Jesus thought of the scripture in Isaiah 52:7 as He washed those feet: *"How beautiful on the mountains are the feet of those who bring good news, who proclaim peace, who bring good tidings, who proclaim salvation, who say to Zion, 'Your God reigns!'"* (NIV) The washing of the disciples' feet that Thursday evening was only the beginning of the love Jesus would show during the next few hours and days.

Jesus Serving in Heaven—There is also a view of the Servant Jesus in heaven, that we are told about in Luke 12:37. Jesus is portrayed as the master who finds His servants watching for Him to come back. Jesus says this: *"I can tell you without a doubt, the master will get himself ready to serve a meal and tell the servants to sit down. Then he will serve them."* The nature of Jesus is to serve, even in heaven. He wants His disciples to have that same nature.

N. T. Wright in his book "John for Everyone" says this: "...for us as for Jesus, we should be looking away from ourselves, and at the world, we are supposed to be serving. Where the world's needs and our vocation meet, is where we ought to be, ready to take on insignificant roles if that's what God wants, or to be publicly visible if that is our calling." (N.T. Wright, 2004)

When Jonathan Storment was pulpit minister at the Highland Church of Christ, he said: "We all try to climb our ladders of successes, seeing if we can be higher in the pecking order than the next guy. But we may find ourselves passing Jesus on our way up as he was climbing down from divinity to servant." (Jonathan Storment, Date Unknown)

John 13:6-17

[6] He came to Simon Peter. But Peter said to him, "Lord, you should not wash my feet."

[7] Jesus answered, "You don't know what I am doing now. But later you will understand."

[8] Peter said, "No! You will never wash my feet."

Jesus answered, "If I don't wash your feet, you are not one of my people."

[9] Simon Peter said, "Lord, after you wash my feet, wash my hands and my head too!"

[10] Jesus said, "After a person has a bath, his whole body is clean. He needs only to wash his feet. And you are clean, but not all of you." [11] Jesus knew who would hand him over to his enemies. That is why he said, "Not all of you are clean."

[12] When Jesus finished washing their feet, he put on his clothes and went back to the table. He asked, "Do you understand what I did for you? [13] You call me 'Teacher.' And you call me 'Lord.' And this is right, because that is what I am. [14] I am your Lord and Teacher. But I washed your feet. So you also should wash each other's feet. [15] I did this as an example for you. So you should serve each other just as I served you. [16] Believe me, servants are not greater than their master. Those who are sent to do something are not greater than the one who sent them. [17] If you know these things, great blessings will be yours if you do them.

My Brother, the Servant—Dad was dying. He was eighty-nine and had congestive heart failure. It could be a week or a month, no one knew for sure, but the doctor said he wouldn't leave the hospital. My two brothers and I and our wives were there, taking turns, as did several of the grandchildren, keeping watch over Dad. Everyone loved this old patriarch, lying peacefully most of the time. I watched my brother, Bill. He was the quiet brother and the eldest, who had learned, as did all of us, about love at our father's feet. I watched him take our dad's false teeth to the bathroom and clean them. Twice a day he would do the same thing so Dad's mouth would feel clean and fresh. He was doing for Dad what Dad had done for us as we were growing up, taking care of our needs. Nothing was too humiliating for Dad in taking care of us, and now the roles were reversed. My brother was quietly doing what the Master had commanded all of us to do. Verse 15: *"I did this as an example for you. So you should serve each other just as I served you."*

There is more than just the washing of the disciples' feet that John has in mind. This is a good introduction to the last nine chapters of the book of John, Jesus' Passion. This, *the time he showed them his love the most,* is the laying down of Himself for all mankind. It is the Master becoming a slave. It is Lord becoming a servant. It is God, come in the flesh—becoming sacrifice—*"Look, the Lamb of God. He takes away the sins of the world!"* John 1:29.

Paul surely was thinking of the servanthood of Jesus in Philippians 2:6-8:

> *He was like God in every way,*
> *but he did not think that his being equal with God*
> *was something to use for his own benefit.*
> *Instead, he gave up everything, even his place with*
> *God.*

He accepted the role of a servant, appearing in
human form.
During his life as a man,
he humbled himself by being fully obedient to God,
even when that caused his death—death on a
cross.

John 13:18-30

18 *"I am not talking about all of you. I know the people I have chosen. But what the Scriptures say must happen: 'The man who shared my food has turned against me.'* **19** *I am telling you this now before it happens. Then when it happens, you will believe that I AM.* **20** *I assure you, whoever accepts the person I send also accepts me. And whoever accepts me also accepts the one who sent me."*

21 *After Jesus said these things, he felt very troubled. He said openly, "Believe me when I say that one of you will hand me over to my enemies."*

22 *His followers all looked at each other. They did not understand whom Jesus was talking about.* **23** *One of the followers was next to Jesus and was leaning close to him. This was the one Jesus loved very much.* **24** *Simon Peter made signs to this follower to ask Jesus who he was talking about.*

25 *That follower leaned closer to Jesus and asked, "Lord, who is it?"*

26 *Jesus answered him, "I will dip this bread into the dish. The man I give it to is the one." So Jesus took a piece of bread, dipped it, and gave it to Judas Iscariot, the son of Simon.* **27** *When Judas took the bread, Satan entered him. Jesus said to Judas, "What you will do— do it quickly!"* **28** *No one at the table understood why Jesus said this to Judas.* **29** *Since Judas was the one in charge of the money, some of them thought that Jesus meant for him to go and buy some* *things they needed for the feast. Or they thought that Jesus wanted him to go give something to the poor.*

30 Judas ate the bread Jesus gave him. Then he immediately went out. It was night.

A Thief! —If anyone had ever asked me if I was a thief, I would have given him or her a disbelieving look and said, "I never stole anything in my life," or so I thought. I enjoyed coin collecting and had several old coins I was proud of. I had a friend, Frank, who shared that hobby with me. He told me about a coin shop close to his house that we could go to and buy some coins. When we arrived at the coin shop the owner had left for a few minutes, leaving her twelve-year-old son in charge. I picked out several coins, as did Frank, and we took them to the front. When the owner's son rang up the price, he charged us only the face value of the coins. Frank started to protest, but I quickly kicked him and motioned for him to let it go. Frank played along, and we walked out with about $50 worth of coins for less than a dollar.

The following day Frank called me, telling me that the owner came back and found out what had taken place and called his mother. We had to take the coins back and face the owner. Greed raised its ugly head when I least expected it, and because of that, I was ripe for satan to tempt me into taking something that wasn't mine.

So Why Did Judas Do It? In verse 2 the devil had already tempted Judas, but in verse 27, after Jesus gives Judas the piece of bread, satan enters into Judas. Judas was ripe for satan. John 12:6 tells us that when Mary put the expensive perfume on Jesus' feet, Judas doesn't like the waste—*But Judas did not really care about the poor. He said this because he was a thief. He was the one who kept the moneybag for the group of followers. And he often stole money* *from the bag.* Satan took the temptation of Judas (greed) and turned it into betraying Christ for thirty pieces of silver.

"That's not me," I protested. "I don't know what came over me but that's not me." Have you ever said those words of objection after being caught doing some outrageous act? Have you heard the world insist that what happened was a mistake and not what is really inside that person? The problem with that statement is that Jesus says differently. In Luke 6:44-45, Jesus makes this statement: *"…evil people bring evil things out of the evil they stored in their hearts. People speak the things that are in their hearts."*

"The man who shared my food has turned against me." Verse 18— The custom of many Middle Eastern people, at that time was to protect all those who come under their roof for a meal, even an enemy. Jesus had invited Judas to His meal, even washing his feet. The master of the banquet, Jesus, not only washed the feet of Judas but He honored Judas by dipping bread in the dish and giving it to him. Judas accepts the gift but quickly leaves to betray his host.

Judas had been with Jesus for three years witnessing the same miracles, hearing the same teachings, and walking the same paths as all the rest, but somehow, he missed what the others received. Somehow his heart was untouched and unchanged. Somehow, he was with the Savior of the world but missed salvation.

Stepping in Dog Poop—During the hotter times of the year, I get up pretty early in the morning several days of the week to water my grass. The temperatures during this particular year have been "well over the century mark," as the weather people like to say. My backyard has two large trees which keep it shady and cooler. The front yard is pretty dead by August.

The problem with walking in my backyard "at night" to change the sprinkler is that our small dog likes to use that same yard for a bathroom. On several occasions, I have come back to the back door with dog poop stuck to the bottom of my shoe. Now, there is nothing worse than having to clean dog poop off of your shoe. It makes you wonder if those shoes will ever be clean again.

Notice, also, in verse 30, *Judas took the bread Jesus gave him and immediately went out.* **It was night.** Let that final sentence burn into your mind. It seems, at first glance, to be insignificant, but John speaks throughout his gospel of darkness and light, night and daylight, and good and evil.

John 13:31-35

31 When Judas was gone, Jesus said, "Now is the time for the Son of Man to receive his glory. And God will receive glory through him. 32 If God receives glory through him, he will give glory to the Son through himself. And that will happen very soon."

33 Jesus said, "My children, I will be with you only a short time more. You will look for me, but I tell you now what I told the Jewish leaders: Where I am going you cannot come.

34 "I give you a new command: Love each other. You must love each other just as I loved you. 35 All people will know that you are my followers if you love each other."

I Love You Grandma—My mom had a stroke several months after she turned 84. She lay dying in the hospital room. The three of us brothers were trying to be with her during those last hours. What was important to say during those final conversations that hadn't been said before? My mom had seen all of her grandchildren claim Jesus as their Savior, being baptized into His name. Jonathan, her youngest grandchild, had received his Lord on his tenth birthday

186

back in March. She had completed her longtime prayer and mission. She could now rest.

My youngest son, Jonathan, his grandma's youngest grandson, wanted to be with her. Would the hospital allow this underage boy into the room? We didn't know but we knew we had to try. As we entered the room the nurse gave us a knowing look and said she could allow a few minutes, no more. Jonathan went to the bed, kissed his grandma, and was on his way out of the room when he turned back to say the most important words a human could speak, "I love you, Grandma." My mom who, for the past day couldn't speak to anyone because of her stroke, was allowed by her Father one last sentence. With all the strength she could muster, and with a loud and clear voice, she responded, "I love you too, Jonathan."

Jesus wanted His disciples to also hear those words and say them over and over to each other. Verses 34-35: *"I give you a new command: Love each other. You must love each other just as I loved you. All people will know that you are my followers if you love each other."*

John 13:36-38

36 Simon Peter asked Jesus, "Lord, where are you going?"

Jesus answered, "Where I am going you cannot follow now. But you will follow later."

37 Peter asked, "Lord, why can't I follow you now? I am ready to die for you!"

38 Jesus answered, "Will you really give your life for me? The truth is, before the rooster crows, you will say three times that you don't know me."

Betraying My Friend—I think her name was Marilyn, but I'm not sure. I do remember that we were friends and played together at recess, both being about eight or nine years old. She had freckles and was a little chunky, but that didn't bother me. It didn't bother me, until that day. You see there were these guys, and I wanted to be part of their group. They made fun of me for being around Marilyn, telling me I had an ugly girlfriend. I wish I could tell you I did the right thing and told them to shove off, but I didn't. I was afraid of what they would think, more afraid of them than I was of hurting my friend. So, I began ignoring her and wouldn't play with her anymore. The last thing I remember about her is one day seeing her run off crying, and I let her go. I had betrayed her; I had betrayed our friendship. Fear makes us do awful things.

Peter didn't want to hear that. He wanted to hear, "Thanks Peter, you are always right there for me, and I know you will fight to the death to protect me." But Jesus had never been one who gave a compliment just to be polite. Luke 22:32 tells us that Jesus said this to Peter: *"I have prayed that you will not lose your faith! Help your brothers be stronger when you come back to me."*

Judas betrays Christ; Peter denies Him. Judas dies full of tears and sorrow but unforgiven. Peter is not only forgiven and reinstated but becomes the leader among the apostles in the early church. Why does Judas get a bad rep? What is the difference between the two?

Judas' sin was premeditated and Peter's was done in a moment of passion. Judas' heart was wrong from the beginning, whereas Peter's was always directed toward the Lord. Judas' sin arose from greed (remember, he was a thief); Peter's arose from fear (he ran away). Judas was devious and underhanded (the kiss of betrayal); Peter was impetuous and upfront (he tried to protect Jesus with a sword).

Repentance is more than saying "I'm sorry." It's more than crying buckets full of tears. Judas and Peter both did that. Repentance is a change of heart. It's accepting the grace of God that only comes through faith in Jesus Christ. Peter had it; Judas did not. 2 Corinthians 7:10 says it this way: *"The kind of sorrow God wants makes people decide to change their lives. This leads them to salvation, and we cannot be sorry for that. But the kind of sorrow the world has will bring death."*

John 14:1-4

[1] Jesus said, "Don't be troubled. Trust in God, and trust in me. [2] There are many rooms in my Father's house. I would not tell you this if it were not true. I am going there to prepare a place for you. [3] After I go and prepare a place for you, I will come back. Then I will take you with me, so that you can be where I am. [4] You know the way to the place where I am going."

I'll Be Home Soon! —Dad spent the first eight years of my life in the Navy, sometimes being aboard ship for as long as six months at a stretch. His vessel would eventually arrive in Long Beach, California, about one hundred eighty miles from our home in the desolate Mojave Desert, and we would make that trip to pick him up. That long-anticipated day was filled with joy and laughter even as we traversed that hot and dry landscape.

As we would arrive at the ship already in the harbor, we would see an assembled throng of Navy families standing on the dock, looking intently for their fathers, husbands, brothers, or sons. There would be noisy shouts and enthusiastic hands frantically waving as a loved one was spotted among the mob of seamen lined up along the ship's rail. The gangplank would be lowered, and the men would begin descending in an orderly fashion until they reached the bottom. The jubilant sailors would then sprint toward welcoming arms.

Dad would come ambling down the gangplank, decked out in his khaki chief petty officer's uniform and wearing a big smile, which spread all over his face. After Mom was held in his arms for a while, he would embrace Bill and Bob. And then he would pick me up and give me a big hug and a peck on the cheek. With my small arms around my daddy's neck, I was happy and contented; and with my head nestled on his large shoulders, I felt safe and secure. Then with expectation, I would whisper in his ear, "What did you bring me?" Since he had been all over the world, he would always have a gift for each of us. On one occasion he brought me a bike from Japan and even took me aboard ship to see it.

Dad would stay home for several months, but when his leave was over, he would once again have to ship out. The journey to take him back to his ship was always sad, and entirely too brief. Seeing tears brimming in our eyes, he would comfort our anguish with these words: "Now don't worry, I'll be home soon, and I'll bring you something when I come back."

I trusted my dad. He did always come back, and he always had a little surprise with him when he saw me. As an adult, years later, after reading Jesus' final words of comfort to His disciples as He was getting ready to leave them, I would smile, thinking of my dad.

Forever! —One of the most wonderful things about life is that it doesn't end. What we fear most is usually death. The only thing we know for sure about death is that when a person dies, he ceases to be with us. We have lots of people who talk about life after death, but no one has ever been on the other side and come back to tell us what it's all about. That is, no one except Jesus. He came from heaven and the Father.

He tells His disciples that He is going away for a while, back to the Father to prepare a place for them. And when it's all ready He will come back and get them. He tells them to trust Him and trust His words, just as they trust God. We don't know a lot about the other side but we do know these comforting words from verses 2-3: *"There are many rooms in my Father's house...I am going there to prepare a place for you...I will come back and take you to be with me so that you may be where I am."*

(Sixth I Am Statement)

John 14:5-14

"I Am the Way, the Truth, and the Life"

⁵ Thomas said, "Lord, we don't know where you are going, so how can we know the way?"

⁶ Jesus answered, "I am the way, the truth, and the life. The only way to the Father is through me. ⁷ If you really knew me, you would know my Father too. But now you know the Father. You have seen him."

⁸ Philip said to him, "Lord, show us the Father. That is all we need."

⁹ Jesus answered, "Philip, I have been with you for a long time. So you should know me. Anyone who has seen me has seen the Father too. So why do you say, 'Show us the Father'? ¹⁰ Don't you believe that I am in the Father and the Father is in me? The things I have told you don't come from me. The Father lives in me, and he is doing his own work. ¹¹ Believe me when I say that I am in the Father and the Father is in me. Or believe because of the miracles I have done.

¹² "I can assure you that whoever believes in me will do the same things I have done. And they will do even greater things than I have done, because I am going to the Father. ¹³ And if you ask for anything in my name, I will do it for you. Then the Father's glory will be shown through the Son. [14] If you ask me for anything in my name, I will do it.

Exclusive—My good friend, Nellie had invited me to dinner with some of her friends. This was no ordinary dinner. It was her religion's equivalent to the Christian Communion service. Nellie belonged to the Baha'i faith. According to Nellie's faith Moses, Jesus, Muhammad, and their spiritual leader, Baha'u'llah were all prophets of One God and each one brought further enlightenment of that One God. Baha'u'llah is just the latest prophet.

As I began to eat the religious meal—more a potluck—with them, several began to ask me questions about my faith. I had decided to try to answer each of their questions, not from my point of view, but from Scripture.

"Is it true," asked one individual, "that Christians believe that theirs is the only religion that is the way to God?"

My reply was, "Jesus said, *'I am the way, the truth, and the life. The only way to the Father is through me.'*"

Although the group was polite and asked me less controversial questions afterward, that one question and answer set the tone for the rest of the evening.

Mom's Inheritance—When my mom passed away in 1999, many people were her friends at the funeral. One lady came whom my mom was especially fond of. And there was that couple whom she and my dad were friends with when he was alive. Many who loved my mom sent beautiful cards or flowers. And the preacher, who had known my parents for years said some touching words that made us all cry. The cars pulled up after the funeral to follow the hearse and the family to the cemetery. I began to notice that just the family rode in the limos. And back at the church, only the family sat in the first few rows of seats. At the cemetery, there were only enough seats for the family. And then there was "the will" some days later that was taken care of. Only the family received her inheritance. Though others knew her, she was very exclusive with what she gave away at her death. We are the family of God through Jesus His Son.

One of the most difficult things to understand for many about the Christian faith is its exclusiveness. Why is Jesus the only way? The words are clear enough. *"I am the way, and the truth, and the life. The only way to the Father is through me."* But, as humans, especially as Americans, we want people to have a choice. We want to come to God on our terms. We want religion to fit our lifestyle and our beliefs. We want God to fit our ideas of what He should be like. We want to decide who gets in and who is left out. And we want it all to be fair.

Look at what Jesus says to Philip in verses 8-10, when Philip says, *"Lord, show us the Father. That is all we need."* Jesus' answer was, *"Philip, I have been with you for a long time. So you should know me. Anyone who has seen me has seen the Father too. So why do you say, 'Show us the Father'? Don't you believe that I am in the Father and the Father is in me?"* In other words, Buddha, Muhammad, Moses, Baha'u'llah, and any other religious leader were just people.

Jesus wasn't just a good man with some nice sayings. He wasn't "a" way to God; He was "the" way. He wasn't one of many voices that have spoken over centuries that lead us a little farther in our search for truth and the meaning of life; He was the Word of God Himself. The Apostle John wrote this "Good News" as a testimony that God the Father and Jesus the Son are one God. Messiah Jesus is God who came to earth with flesh on, to love one is to love the other, to hate one is to hate the other, and to get to one you have to go through the other.

C. S. Lewis says of Jesus, "He is Lord, liar or lunatic. Either he is the greatest liar the world has ever known, he is crazy, or he is who he says he is. And he allows us to make a choice, but he doesn't allow us to ride the fence. We either accept his claim of deity or we reject it." (C.S. Lewis, 1952)

John 14:15-26

[15] *"If you love me, you will do what I command.* [16] *I will ask the Father, and he will give you another Helper to be with you forever.* [17] *The Helper is the Spirit of truth. The people of the world cannot accept him, because they don't see him or know him. But you know him. He lives with you, and he will be in you.*

[18] *"I will not leave you all alone like orphans. I will come back to you.* [19] *In a very short time the people in the world will not see me anymore. But you will see me. You will live because I live.* [20] *On that day you will know that I am in the Father. You will know that you are in me and I am in you.* [21] *Those who really love me are the ones who not only know my commands but also obey them. My Father will love such people, and I will love them. I will make myself known to them."*

[22] *Then Judas (not Judas Iscariot) said, "Lord, how will you make yourself known to us, but not to the world?"*

[23] *Jesus answered, "All who love me will obey my teaching. My Father will love them. My Father and I will come to them and live with them.* [24] *But anyone who does not love me does not obey my teaching. This teaching that you hear is not really mine. It is from my Father who sent me.*

[25] *"I have told you all these things while I am with you.* [26] *But the Helper will teach you everything and cause you to remember all that I told you. This Helper is the Holy Spirit that the Father will send in my name.*

Helper and Truth Speaker—I've been married three times. No, that's not a confession of marriage failures, although I contributed much, to some very big failures within those marriages. Two of my marriages ended in the deaths of my wives, Carolyn, the wife of my youth, and Maryanne, who helped me raise four children, two of mine and two we had together. Currently, I am married to Annette, another "love of my life," and who is Nana to our grandchildren. I have been blessed with three women who loved me and whom I still love deeply.

One of the blessings that all three of these women brought into those marriages, besides love, was that of being a **helper** and a **truth speaker.** They were helpers, in that, each brought styles of marriage expectations, extended family hopes, child-rearing aims, financial goals, and especially godly values. They were truth speakers, in that they "spoke" their minds to me, but more importantly that they "shared" their minds with me. Maturity within marriage comes with time, lots of communication, much prayer, and a "less of self, more of thee," attitude—I don't have to always have it my way.

The Holy Spirit that Jesus had promised His disciples was called the Helper. He would not only assist these inexperienced disciples, but He would also come to dwell, to live right inside them. This Helper has another job. He is the Spirit of truth. These disciples and others would become writers of the New Testament. They would be leaders of the new community of believers, the church, in the not-so-distant future. The Holy Spirit would teach these disciples what to preach about the Messiah. They would be reminded of all the Old Testament Scriptures that prophesied His coming. That is why Jesus promised, in verse 25: *"the Helper will teach you everything and will cause you to remember all that I told you. This Helper is the Holy Spirit whom the Father will send in my name."*

One of Annette's and my morning rituals, when we rise from sleep each morning, is having a daily devotional and prayer time. We also look at each other in the eyes and repeat part of the "Love Chapter" from 1 Corinthians 13: *"Love is patient, love is kind. It does not envy, it does not boast, it is not proud. It is not rude, it is not self-seeking, it is not easily angered, it keeps no record of wrongs. Love does not delight in evil but rejoices with the truth. It always protects, always trusts, always hopes, always perseveres. Love never fails."* NIV

Can You Have Love without Obedience? —I remember at a marriage seminar, I attended many years ago, Paul Faulkner said, "Love is not a noun; it's a verb. Love is not a state of being; it's action. Love is not an idea; it's doing." (Paul Faulkner, Date Unknown)

Jesus equates love with obedience. Verses 23-24: *"All who love me will obey my teaching. My Father will love them. My Father and I will come to them and live with them. But anyone who does not love me does not obey my teaching. This teaching that you hear is not really mine. It is from my Father who sent me."* For three years, Jesus' disciples followed Him, not just hearing Him talk about love, but seeing Him "act" in love. His life, His death, and His resurrection were love in action. So, it's no wonder Jesus tells His disciples that if they love Him, they will keep His commandments. If they love Him, they will follow His teachings. He tells them that His proof of His love for His Father is that He does exactly what His Father commands Him to do. And the proof of their love is obedience to Jesus, which is obedience to the Father.

John 14:27-31

27 "I leave you peace. It is my own peace I give you. I give you peace in a different way than the world does. So don't be troubled. Don't be afraid. 28 You heard me say to you, 'I am leaving, but I will come

back to you.' If you loved me, you would be happy that I am going back to the Father, because the Father is greater than I am. ²⁹ I have told you this now, before it happens. Then when it happens, you will believe.

³⁰ "I will not talk with you much longer. The ruler of this world is coming. He has no power over me. ³¹ But the world must know that I love the Father. So I do exactly what the Father told me to do.

"Come now, let's go."

American Wars—Can you name the wars in which the United States has been involved since its independence? I could list quite a few. Most in the 18th and 19th centuries were to secure lands from the British, the Mexicans, the Spanish, and the French, but mostly, from the Native Americans. And then there was the 20th century when we entered two world wars. We also fought in Korea, Viet Nam and Iraq. Century Twenty-one began with wars in Afghanistan and again in Iraq. We have monument after monument in Washington DC dedicated to the men and women who sacrificed their lives in those wars. Our nation is not alone in its war-making. Most nations on planet Earth have had wars for much of their existence, and people have been killing each other since Cain killed his brother Abel.

Now, just think if there could be one soldier dying, and that sacrifice would bring peace to the whole earth for all eternity. That is what Jesus offers. In verse 27, Jesus says, *"I leave you peace; my peace I give you. I do not give it to you as the world does.* His death will begin the process of peace bringing to the world. You see, the world does not understand peace. The world's definition of peace is the "lack of war." Jesus offers much more. The peace Jesus offers is between God and people and between people and people. His kingdom is based on love, loving God, and loving each other. He even said to those wanting to follow Him, in Matthew 5:9:

"Great blessings belong to those who work to bring peace.
God will call them his sons and daughters."

Jesus realized we have to live in this world, as it is, for the time being. So, He promised His disciples, someone to be with them after His return to the Father, the Holy Spirit.

"Eagerly and patiently," almost seems like a contradiction of terms. We, His disciples, those who have His promised Holy Spirit and a different kind of peace, wait with excitement and with patience— "eagerly and patiently."

The Apostle Paul says this in Romans 8:

> *"The sufferings we have now are nothing compared to the great glory that will be shown to us. Everything God made is waiting with excitement for God to show his children's glory completely...We know that everything God made has been waiting until now in pain, like a woman ready to give birth. Not only the world, but we also have been waiting with pain inside us. <u>We have the Spirit as the first part of God's promise</u>. So we are waiting for God to finish making us his own children, which means our bodies will be made free. We were saved, and we have this hope...and we are waiting for it patiently."*

Jesus tells His disciples that they will receive help in obeying His commands and remembering His teachings after He leaves. The Holy Spirit will be sent to them to remind them of all they are to do and say. That is a good thing for them, but it is also a good thing for us. That means these disciples of Jesus had help from the Holy Spirit when writing their gospel (Good News) accounts—Matthew,

198

Mark, Luke, and John, the history of the first-century church in Acts, the letters of Paul, Peter, John, James, Jude, and others to the churches, and the final Revelation of Messiah Jesus by John. Christians, later put these writings together, in what is now called the New Testament. In 2 Peter 1:21, this author and apostle makes this statement: *"No prophecy ever came from what some person wanted to say. But people were led by the Holy Spirit and spoke words from God."*

I like the way the Apostle Paul tells Timothy, his "son in the faith," in 2 Timothy 3:16-17: *"All scripture is God-breathed and is useful for teaching, rebuking, correcting and training in righteousness, so that the man of God may be thoroughly equipped for every good work."* NIV Although the New Testament had not been written at that writing, and the *"all scripture"* referred to is speaking of the Old Testament, the writings of Paul and others became Scripture or the word of God. The *"Spirit of Truth"* had taught them what to say and write. So, we today, can quote the 2 Timothy passage with confidence and conviction.

That term, *"God breathed,"* reminds us of God breathing into a human the breath of life and that human became a living being, Genesis chapter 2. Later in John 20:22: Jesus *"breathed on them and said, 'Receive the Holy Spirit.'"* There is life in the breath of God, both physical and spiritual. Humans are given the breath of God as they become living beings and are offered the breath of God throughout their lives in the form of God's word and God's Spirit. Without the breath of God, humans die, but God has allowed humans to choose whether or not to accept it. Do you have the spiritual breath of God?

John 15:1-4

¹ Jesus said, "I am the true vine, and my Father is the gardener. ² He cuts off every branch of mine that does not produce fruit. He also trims every branch that produces fruit to prepare it to produce even more. ³ You have already been prepared to produce more fruit by the teaching I have given you. ⁴ Stay joined to me and I will stay joined to you. No branch can produce fruit alone. It must stay connected to the vine. It is the same with you. You cannot produce fruit alone. You must stay joined to me.

Staying Attached to the Vine—My brother, Bob was proud of his watermelon patch even though he only had a few melons growing on the vine. He took us out to see the watermelon he was proud of, though at this point it was only about six inches long. "It will make a nice watermelon for us to eat this summer." My young son, Jeremy, my firstborn, was listening intently to the conversation. As we turned and began walking back to the house, Jeremy ran up to his Uncle Bob with a big smile on his face. He stuck out his hand and gave my brother the watermelon, "Can we eat it now?" You know it's pretty hard to reattach a watermelon.

It's pretty much a rule of nature that if you cut off a branch from a tree, that branch will stop producing fruit. Unless you reattach it or somehow replant it, the branch will wither up and die. It will then be just another stick on the ground to be picked up and burned or a six-inch watermelon that, once detached won't grow any larger. It might as well be thrown away.

In the Old Testament, the nation of Israel was considered a vine that God had planted. Psalm 80:8-11 expresses:

> *When you brought us out of Egypt, we were like*
> *your special vine.*
> *You forced other nations to leave this land, and you*

planted that vine here.
You prepared the ground for it, and it sent its roots
down deep and spread throughout the land.
It covered the mountains, and its leaves shaded
even the giant cedar trees.
Its branches spread to the Mediterranean Sea, its
shoots to the Euphrates River.

Israel failed to live up to the commandments of God in the Law of Moses and had not lived up to the promise of Abraham to be a blessing to the world at large. Israel was supposed to be a *"Light to the Gentiles"* or non-Jewish nations. The problem with humanity is that we don't live up to what we are supposed to do in the world. We tend to be self-centered rather than God-centered. God is pictured in Isaiah chapter 5 as a man who has a vineyard with the hope that good grapes would grow as shown in verses 1-2. But by verse 7 the LORD *All-Powerful* finds only killing and people being treated badly.

Now I will sing a song for my friend, my love song
about his vineyard.

My friend had a vineyard
 on a very fertile hill.
He dug and cleared the field
 and planted the best grapevines there.
He built a tower in the middle
 and cut a winepress into the stone.
He expected good grapes to grow there,
 but there were only rotten ones...

The vineyard that belongs to the LORD All-Powerful
is the house of Israel. The grapevine, the plant he
loves, is the man of Judah.

The Lord hoped for justice but there was only
killing.
He hoped for fairness, but there were only cries
from people being treated badly.

The True Vine—God always had a plan. It wasn't that if plan A didn't work out God would have to resort to plan B. Israel would indeed produce the vine that would produce good grapes, but it would not be the nation itself, but a man, who would represent the nation. Plan A, all along was this mystery, Jesus the Messiah would be *"the true vine"* sent by His Father, who is the gardener. Jesus, alone, does all the Father's will. Only He is the sinless One who can die for the world and become its Savior. That, then, leads us to the 7th and final "I am" statement. Jesus the Messiah is the vine. His disciples, both Jew and Gentile, are His branches.

(Seventh I Am Statement)

John 15:5-8

"I Am the Vine, and You Are the Branches"

5 "I am the vine, and you are the branches. If you stay joined to me, and I to you, you will produce plenty of fruit. But separated from me you won't be able to do anything. 6 If you don't stay joined to me, you will be like a branch that has been thrown out and has dried up. All the dead branches like that are gathered up, thrown into the fire and burned. 7 Stay joined together with me, and follow my teachings. If you do this, you can ask for anything you want, and it will be given to you. 8 Show that you are my followers by producing much fruit. This will bring honor to my Father.

Planting Saturday—Once a year, on the Saturday before Easter Sunday, all of our children and grandchildren get together to plant in Nana and Papa's front or back yards. On one of these Saturday planting days, we planted, or should I say, fathers and daughters—

our granddaughters—planted, rose bushes. Over the years those rose bushes had branches that died. No amount of watering would make a dead branch come back to life. So, Nana or I would cut off those ugly, withered, dead branches and throw them away.

The Seventh "I am" Statement—The main thing Jesus says in this portion of Scripture is what we, His disciples, have to do as branches. We need to stay attached to the vine. Verses 5-6: *"If you stay joined to me, and I to you, you will produce plenty of fruit. But separated from me you won't be able to do anything."* The gardener—the Father—is going to look at us as whether, we, the branches, are producing fruit. If not, he cuts us off. Verse 2: *"He cuts off every branch of mine that does not produce fruit."*

Verse 6 is difficult. *If you don't stay joined to me, you will be like a branch that has been thrown out and has dried up. All the dead branches like that are gathered up, thrown into the fire and burned.* Let's move from a vineyard and a gardener to a farmer planting a field. In Mark chapter 4, Jesus tells a parable of a farmer who scattered seed. As the farmer was scattering the seed, some of it fell on the path. Some seed fell on rocky soil. Some seed fell among thorns. Some seed fell on good soil. In verses 14-20 of Mark 4, Jesus explains the parable:

> *The farmer is like someone who plants God's teaching in people. Sometimes the teaching falls on the path. That is like some people who hear the teaching of God. As soon as they hear it, Satan comes and takes away the teaching that was planted in them.*
>
> *"Other people are like the seed planted on rocky ground. They hear the teaching, and they quickly and gladly accept it. But they don't allow it to go*

deep into their lives. They keep it only a short time. As soon as trouble or persecution comes because of the teaching they accepted, they give up.

"Others are like the seed planted among the thorny weeds. They hear the teaching, but their lives become full of other things: the worries of this life, the love of money, and everything else they want. This keeps the teaching from growing, and it does not produce a crop in their lives.

"And others are like the seed planted on the good ground. They hear the teaching and accept it. Then they grow and produce a good crop—sometimes 30 times more, sometimes 60 times more, and sometimes 100 times more."

The Good Soil—There are a lot of people who seem to be disciples who are not. The word or seed does not become fruitful because of the hardness of their heart, because of giving up the first time there is trouble, or because the world is so attractive to them, they walk away. Notice, though, that good soil is the heart of receptiveness. That soil produces fruit, *"...sometimes 30 times more, sometimes 60 times more, and sometimes 100 times more."* Being joined to Jesus is a matter of faith, not just intellectual belief, but faith that shows itself in the way it obeys Jesus. If someone isn't obeying Jesus, they are not staying joined to Jesus. Branches and soil are two ways Jesus explains fruitfulness. Good branches and good soil produce results.

Sometimes the branches of Ashlyn, Avyn, Ella, and Kendyl's rose bushes are green and healthy but Nana and I realize that to produce lots of roses and to make each bush grow the way we want, we will have to trim and prune, here and there. It might seem, at first like we are trimming so much that we might even kill the plant, but given time, water, and nutrients the roses will come and the bush will thrive and look healthy. If we are fruit-bearing, He prunes us to make us produce even more fruit. Verse 2: *"He also trims every branch that produces fruit to prepare it to produce even more."*

John 15:9-17

9 "I have loved you as the Father has loved me. Now continue in my love. 10 I have obeyed my Father's commands, and he continues to love me. In the same way, if you obey my commands, I will continue to love you. 11 I have told you these things so that you can have the true happiness that I have. I want you to be completely happy. 12 This is what I command you: Love each other as I have loved you. 13 The greatest love people can show is to die for their friends. 14 You are my friends if you do what I tell you to do. 15 I no longer call you servants, because servants don't know what their master is doing. But now I call you friends, because I have told you everything that my Father told me.

16 "You did not choose me. I chose you. And I gave you this work: to go and produce fruit—fruit that will last. Then the Father will give you anything you ask for in my name. 17 This is my command: Love each other.

Sibling Rivalry—Our children, as they were growing up, many times displayed what is called sibling rivalry. They didn't love each other automatically. They had to be nurtured and taught that love, by our example. Mom and Dad want their kids to get along. We want them to love each other as much as we love them. Some get it; others do not. Some brothers and sisters, brothers and brothers, and sisters and sisters never seem to move past damaging childhood memories of hurts, traumas, disloyalties, and distrust.

205

What is the fruit Jesus is speaking of here? Two things are mentioned which seem to be related to the fruit. First are His words, His teachings, or commands, *if you obey my commands, I will continue to love you.* The second is love for each other. *This is what I command you: Love each other as I have loved you.* In Matthew 22:36-39, Jesus was asked this by a man: *"Teacher, which command in the law is the most important?"*

Jesus answered, "'Love the Lord your God with all your heart, all your soul, and all your mind.' This is the first and most important command. And the second command is like the first: 'Love your neighbor the same as you love yourself.'

So, the most important fruit is learning to grow in love, first for God and then for each other. This change, which begins in the believer's life, continues growing throughout their walk on earth. It's much the same as a child beginning to learn in kindergarten, then changing throughout their schooling as they mature, learning more and more until they finally graduate. The child in first grade is not expected to understand algebra. They are learning things that are appropriate to their maturity.

The Christian bearing godly fruit is much the same. The father lovingly teaches his child more and more according to his maturity. What is the main lesson that God the Father wants His children to learn? What is the main fruit that He wants to help us produce in our walk with Him? The answer to both questions is "love." Fruit-bearing does not mean sinlessness. That is why Jesus came to die on the cross. Fruit-bearing means believing, obeying, and allowing God to work in our lives through His Holy Spirit. Judas didn't produce fruit, Peter did. Judas was cut off. Peter was pruned.

Jesus says if we obey His commands, we remain in Him and prove our love for Him. Now this does not mean a legalistic life that obeys commands without any heart in the obedience. Jesus is speaking of lives that are surrendered to Him and want to become more and more like Him every day. *"Love each other as I have loved you."*

The Apostle John writes to the churches about love in one of his letters. I John 4:7-12:

> *Dear friends, we should love each other, because love comes from God. Everyone who loves has become God's child. And so everyone who loves knows God. Anyone who does not love does not know God, because God is love. This is how God showed his love to us: He sent his only Son into the world to give us life through him. True love is God's love for us, not our love for God. He sent his Son as the way to take away our sins.*

> *That is how much God loved us, dear friends! So we also must love each other. No one has ever seen God. But if we love each other, God lives in us. If we love each other, God's love has reached its goal—it is made perfect in us.*

Love is the most important fruit, but are there others? The Apostle Paul, in one of his letters to a new church in the city of Galatia, describes the fruit that the Holy Spirit produces. Galatians 5:22-26:

> *But the fruit that the Spirit produces in a person's life is <u>love, joy, peace, patience, kindness, goodness, faithfulness, gentleness, and self-control</u>. There is no law against these kinds of things. Those who belong to Christ Jesus have crucified their sinful self. They have given up their old selfish feelings and the evil things they wanted to do. We get our new life from the Spirit, so we should follow the Spirit. We must*

not feel proud and boast about ourselves. We must not cause trouble for each other or be jealous of each other.

Pruning—What is this pruning that Jesus is speaking of? There is a funny story about a CEO of a corporation who prayed for patience, so God gave him a secretary who couldn't spell. Pruning is the cutting away of anything in me that God needs to get rid of or clean up to make me more like Him. The branches on a plant that don't produce are called suckers. Suckers use up nutrients but produce no fruit or flowers. The pruning is not always going to feel good or be something I always desire, but it will make me more useful to Him and show Him glory.

When my first wife, Carolyn, was sick with her cancer, we once had a babysitter for my son, Jeremy, then age 4. He was acting up in some way, and the babysitter told him that God wouldn't love him if he kept acting that way. Carolyn heard the rebuke and immediately came to our son's defense, with, "That's not true, Jeremy. God will always love you."

Okay, then, what about Jesus' words above in verse 10, *"If you obey my commands, I will continue to love you"?* Maybe you will remember hearing in the Bible about a story or parable, Jesus told in Luke chapter 15—The Prodigal Son, or The Rebellious Son.

> *Then Jesus said, "There was a man who had two sons. The younger son said to his father, 'Give me now the part of your property that I am supposed to receive someday.' So the father divided his wealth between his two sons.*
>
> *"A few days later the younger son gathered up all that he had and left. He traveled far away to another country, and there he wasted his money living like a*

fool. After he spent everything he had, there was a terrible famine throughout the country. He was hungry and needed money. So he went and got a job with one of the people who lived there. The man sent him into the fields to feed pigs. He was so hungry that he wanted to eat the food the pigs were eating. But no one gave him anything.

"The son realized that he had been very foolish. He thought, 'All my father's hired workers have plenty of food. But here I am, almost dead because I have nothing to eat. I will leave and go to my father. I will say to him: Father, I have sinned against God and have done wrong to you. I am no longer worthy to be called your son. But let me be like one of your hired workers.' So he left and went to his father.

"While the son was still a long way off, his father saw him coming and felt sorry for him. So he ran to him and hugged and kissed him. The son said, 'Father, I have sinned against God and have done wrong to you. I am no longer worthy to be called your son.'

"But the father said to his servants, 'Hurry! Bring the best clothes and put them on him. Also, put a ring on his finger and good sandals on his feet. And bring our best calf and kill it so that we can celebrate with plenty to eat. My son was dead, but now he is alive again! He was lost, but now he is found!' So they began to have a party.

You see, the father in the story never stopped loving his son. The father probably kept the light on and was continually looking down the road. *"While the son was still a long way off, his father saw him* coming and felt sorry for him. So he ran to him and hugged and kissed him." God's love was always there, but the son, in his rebellion, left the father's loving embrace to venture out on his own. If the son had remained in the father's loving hold, he wouldn't have started down the road to rebellion. Besides that, the whole gospel story is about God's love. Remember back in chapter 3 when Jesus was speaking to Nicodemus, we see, probably the most quoted Scripture ever. Verse 16: "...God loved the world so much that he gave his only Son, so that everyone who believes in him would not be lost but have eternal life."

John 15:18-27

[18] "If the world hates you, remember that they hated me first. [19] If you belonged to the world, the world would love you as it loves its own people. But I have chosen you to be different from those in the world. So you don't belong to the world, and that is why the world hates you.

[20] "Remember the lesson I told you: Servants are not greater than their master. If people treated me badly, they will treat you badly too. And if they obeyed my teaching, they will obey yours too. [21] They will do to you whatever they did to me, because you belong to me. They don't know the one who sent me. [22] If I had not come and spoken to the people of the world, they would not be guilty of sin. But now I have spoken to them. So they have no excuse for their sin.

[23] "Whoever hates me also hates my Father. [24] I did things among the people of the world that no one else has ever done. If I had not done those things, they would not be guilty of sin. But they have seen what I did, and still they hate me and my Father. [25] But this happened to make clear the full meaning of what is written in their law: 'They hated me for no reason.'

26 *"I will send you the Helper from the Father. The Helper is the Spirit of truth who comes from the Father. When he comes, he will tell about me. 27 And you will tell people about me too, because you have been with me from the beginning.*

The Missionary—Before I remarried, my second wife, Maryanne was an apprentice missionary in the Philippines. Maryanne had the opportunity to help a Filipina (a female in the Philippines) and her baby who was very dehydrated and about to die if he didn't receive medical help. The family could not afford a hospital stay or a doctor, so, Maryanne used some of her own money to put the baby under a doctor's care. The mother stayed night and day with the baby, as did Maryanne, trying to be Jesus to them. The baby lived and Maryanne was invited by the woman to her house to meet her husband.

Now came the rub. The husband was a Moslem who hated Americans. When Maryanne came in and introduced herself, the Moslem began to rant and rave about President Reagan (he was president at that time) and his policies. He saw all Americans as servants to what he thought was an evil President. It didn't make sense to him that this American woman would help him and his family since he saw her as an enemy, but he did say he was grateful.

That Is Why the World Hates You—Much of this last part of the chapter is speaking mostly to the disciples themselves. Jesus is warning them that being sent out by Him is not going to be easy. They will be hated even more than Jesus was. But Jesus will not leave them by themselves. He will provide the Holy Spirit to guide them in telling the world about Him. *"He will tell about me."* Jesus uses the words *"Advocate"* and *"testify,"* in verses 26-27: *"When the Advocate comes, whom I will send to you from the Father—the Spirit of truth who goes out from the Father—he will testify about*

211

me. And you also must testify, for you have been with me from the beginning. NIV

Advocate and Testify—Those two words make me think of lawyers and court and of telling the truth under oath. The Advocate—a lawyer from God, the Holy Spirit—will testify— *"tell"* the truth— about Jesus to the disciples who will, in turn, testify—tell the truth—about Jesus to the world. They are under oath, to tell the truth about what they have heard and seen from the beginning of Jesus' ministry, through His death, burial, and resurrection. They will have the Spirit's help in remembering what they witnessed and heard.

Remember back in chapter 14? *"But the Helper will teach you everything and cause you to remember all that I told you. This Helper is the Holy Spirit that the Father will send in my name."* The disciples, who witnessed the resurrected Messiah, would, later, write letters to the new churches telling them how to live. These letters would form what we, today, call the New Testament.

John 16:1-4

¹ "I have told you all this so that you won't lose your faith when you face troubles. ² People will tell you to leave their synagogues and never come back. In fact, the time will come when they will think that killing you would be doing service for God. ³ They will do this because they have not known the Father, and they have not known me. ⁴ I have told you all this now to prepare you. So when the time comes for these things to happen, you will remember that I warned you.

The Snake—"Darell, don't pick up that snake. It'll bite you," my mom warned. My dad, mom, and I had just passed this beautiful bullsnake along the side of the road, and I loved snakes. No matter the pleadings of my mom, "Doyle, don't stop the car or Darell will get out and try to pick up that snake," he did, and I did.

The males in our family, there were four, (three brothers and a dad), outnumbered my mom and she was talking into the wind. My dad stopped the car, and I got out, with promises to my mom that I would be careful. Now I knew better, but the only place I could get hold of the snake was by the tail, so that's what I went for. I lifted the snake, so my smiling dad and my mom, just shaking her head, could get a better look. "Ow! It bit me," I yelled as I dropped the snake as quickly as I had picked it up.

"See what I told you. No one listens to me," my mom kept saying as both she and my dad took me to the doctor. The doctor showed me lots of pictures of snakes, but I already knew the one that bit me wasn't venomous.

After the doctor was satisfied, he gave me a tetanus shot, but also directed a frown at my sheepishly looking dad, saying, "I should give this shot to you for stopping." My mom just smiled.

I don't want to compare Mom and Dad to "Good Advice" and "Bad Advice," but I guess, "if the shoe fits…" My dad, being a dad and wanting his son to experience life, stopped the car and trusted me to do the right thing. My mom, on the other hand, being a mom, trusted me to a point but sure didn't trust the snake. Snakes are, by nature, going to bite if provoked.

Jesus continues to warn His disciples about those who will persecute them, believing they are doing God's will as they do it. If you read the book of Acts there is incident after incident that describes the persecution that the early Christians went through, from the martyrdoms of Stephen and the Apostle James to the incarcerations of many of the early Christian leaders in Roman and Jewish prisons: Paul and Silas, and Peter and John come to mind.

Why did Jesus tell them of these coming events? Verse 4: *"I have told you all this now to prepare you. So when the time comes for these things to happen, you will remember that I warned you."* Jesus has always warned His followers of persecution so they wouldn't give up. My mom warned both me and my dad. But we didn't listen. But Jesus' warning is not just for the disciples He taught while He was on earth, but for all of us, His disciples who have lived the 2000 years since that warning.

In Matthew 5:10-12 Jesus tells his disciples:

> *"Great blessings belong to those who suffer persecution for doing what is right.*
>
> *God's kingdom belongs to them.*
>
> *"People will insult you and hurt you. They will lie and say all kinds of evil things about you because you follow me. But when they do that, know that great blessings belong to you. Be happy about it. Be very glad because you have a great reward waiting for you in heaven. People did these same bad things to the prophets who lived before you."*

In Luke 10:18-20, Jesus gave this promise to His disciples:

> *Jesus said to them, "I saw Satan falling like lightning from the sky. He is the enemy, but know that I have given you more power than he has. I have given you power to crush his snakes and scorpions under your feet. Nothing will hurt you. Yes, even the spirits obey you. And you can be happy, not because you have this power, but because your names are written in heaven."*

The apostle Paul says it this way in 2 Corinthians 4:7-9;16-18:

214

"We have this treasure from God, but we are only like clay jars that hold the treasure. This is to show that the amazing power we have is from God, not from us. We have troubles all around us, but we are not defeated. We often don't know what to do, but we don't give up. We are persecuted, but God does not leave us. We are hurt sometimes, but we are not destroyed...That is why we never give up. Our physical body is becoming older and weaker, but our spirit inside us is made new every day. We have small troubles for a while now, but these troubles are helping us gain an eternal glory. That eternal glory is much greater than our troubles. So we think about what we cannot see, not what we see. What we see lasts only a short time, and what we cannot see will last forever."

John 16:5-15

[5] Now I am going back to the one who sent me. And none of you asks me, 'Where are you going?' [6] But you are filled with sadness because I have told you all this. [7] Let me assure you, it is better for you that I go away. I say this because when I go away I will send the Helper to you. But if I did not go, the Helper would not come.

[8] "When the Helper comes, he will show the people of the world how wrong they are about sin, about being right with God, and about judgment. [9] He will prove that they are guilty of sin, because they don't believe in me. [10] He will show them how wrong they are about how to be right with God. The Helper will do this, because I am going to the Father. You will not see me then. [11] And he will show them how wrong their judgment is, because their leader has already been condemned.

12 "I have so much more to tell you, but it is too much for you to accept now. 13 But when the Spirit of truth comes, he will lead you into all truth. He will not speak his own words. He will speak only what he hears and will tell you what will happen in the future. 14 The Spirit of truth will bring glory to me by telling you what he receives from me. 15 All that the Father has is mine. That is why I said that the Spirit will tell you what he receives from me.

Newbie on the College Scene—When I came to Abilene Christian College in the fall of 1967, I was a newbie. I knew absolutely nothing about the college scene except what I learned from my cousin Barbara, who was a year older than I. The first couple of days at college, we Freshmen had to take all kinds of tests, which I hated. But we had fun too. There was a tug-a-war with a mud pit in the middle, there were parties put on by the college. We also met a lot of upperclassmen.

These upperclassmen were our helpers for the next few days. They were part of our orientation, to our college life. We found out about the cafeteria, dubbed "The Bean." They took us to the post office where we would get our mail. We got to go to the dorms to see where we would be living. Some of the older student helpers would even tell us the names of the hard teachers, whom to avoid, if possible, and the names of the ones everyone wanted as their professors. These helpers were very important to us Freshmen so we wouldn't flounder during our first semester.

Jesus is promising His disciples that they will receive the Holy Spirit. It is a promise of His love for them, and it is a promise of things to come.

Luke tells us, after the resurrection, Jesus spent forty days on earth and then ascended to heaven. Just before Jesus ascended, He told his disciples in Acts 1:3-5:

...The apostles saw Jesus many times during the 40 days after he was raised from death. He spoke to them about God's kingdom. One time when Jesus was eating with them, he told them not to leave Jerusalem. He said, "Wait here until you receive what the Father promised to send. Remember, I told you about it before. John baptized people with water, but in a few days you will be baptized with the Holy Spirit."

In Acts chapter 2 the apostles were baptized or overwhelmed with the Holy Spirit. Peter promised the same Holy Spirit to all who would become Jesus' disciples. Peter tells his listeners in wrapping up his first gospel sermon in verses 38-39: *"Change your hearts and lives and be baptized, each one of you, in the name of Jesus Christ. Then God will forgive your sins, and you will receive the gift of the Holy Spirit. This promise is for you. It is also for your children and for the people who are far away. It is for everyone the Lord our God calls to himself."*

Early disciples went everywhere preaching the gospel of Jesus, and God was with them. We have within the New Testament the words that the Holy Spirit guided the writers to write, and Christians believe that these are the very words of God. Verses 13-14, above: *"But when the Spirit of truth comes, he will lead you into all truth. He will not speak his own words. He will speak only what he hears and will tell you what will happen in the future. The Spirit of truth will bring glory to me by telling you what he receives from me.*

In verse 8, Jesus said of the Spirit: *"When the Helper comes, he will show the people of the world how wrong they are about **sin**, about **being right with God**, and about **judgment**."*

The NIV uses the word "convict"—to find guilty or to condemn—so the Spirit will find guilty or condemn the world in three areas: sin, righteousness, and judgment.

Jesus went on to explain the three areas: The Holy Spirit will convince the world about the sin of people because they don't believe in Jesus. John 1:29 says, He *"takes away the sins of the world!"*

The Holy Spirit will reveal to people their lack of righteousness (being right with God). Romans 3:22-24: *"God makes people right through their faith in Jesus Christ. He does this for all who believe in Christ. Everyone is the same. All have sinned and are not good enough to share God's divine greatness. They are made right with God by his grace. This is a free gift. They are made right with God by being made free from sin through Jesus Christ."*

The world is found guilty and condemned as far as judgment is concerned; verse 11: *"because their leader,"* satan, *"has already been condemned."* The one who first deceived the world to sin now stands condemned because of Jesus' death on the cross. The world he deceived also stands condemned without Jesus Christ. Matthew 25:41: *"Then the king will say to the evil people on his left, 'Get away from me. God has already decided that you will be punished. Go into the fire that burns forever—the fire that was prepared for the devil and his angels."*

John 16:16-24

16 "After a short time you won't see me. Then after another short time you will see me again."

17 Some of the followers said to each other, "What does he mean when he says, 'After a short time you won't see me. Then after another short time you will see me again'? And what does he mean when he says, 'Because I am going to the Father'?" 18 They also asked, "What does he mean by 'a short time'? We don't understand what he is saying."

¹⁹ Jesus saw that the followers wanted to ask him about this. So he said to them, "Are you asking each other what I meant when I said, 'After a short time you won't see me. Then after another short time you will see me again'? ²⁰ The truth is, you will cry and be sad, but the world will be happy. You will be sad, but then your sadness will change to happiness.

²¹ "When a woman gives birth to a baby, she has pain, because her time has come. But when her baby is born, she forgets the pain. She forgets because she is so happy that a child has been born into the world. ²² It is the same with you. Now you are sad, but I will see you again, and you will be happy. You will have a joy that no one can take away. ²³ In that day you will not have to ask me about anything. And I assure you, my Father will give you anything you ask him for in my name. ²⁴ You have never asked for anything in this way before. But ask in my name, and you will receive. And you will have the fullest joy possible.

Moving Houses and Losing Our Dog—After the death of my wife, Maryanne, I decided that my 16-year-old son, Jonathan, and I needed to move from the house we had shared. There were too many memories. Good memories, yes, but the last several years had brought heartaches along with those good memories, and, at the moment, they were too overwhelming.

Jonathan and I moved to a very small house. We had only a carport, so after bringing the furniture and appliances into our house we filled the carport with things we needed to take our time with. We had two dogs. Frisky, the larger of the two, was an outside dog, and since we had a fenced-in yard, she immediately had a place to go.

219

Dipper Doodle, Jonathan's and his mother's dog, was kept in the house.

During one of our loads of furniture, it began pouring down rain. At the same time, Dipper Doodle somehow got out of the door of our new house and decided to go explore the neighborhood. I ran after her but she was too fast for me. I finally came home wet, deciding the best option was for me to go look for her in the car. Jonathan and I were both very distraught, knowing this was a new place and she could become lost. She was his dog but more than that, she was his mom's dog. She was his tie to his mom.

We worried, too, because she didn't know the neighborhood. How would she find her way home? Worse she might get run over. A very busy street was not far from where we lived. I got in the car with Jonathan and we searched everywhere we could think. My heart ached for Jonathan, and I didn't know what to do. Finally, with the rain still pouring down and the sun quickly setting, we decided to go back home and search again the next day. With heavy hearts we drove back to our new house, and "lo and behold" there sat Dipper Doodle, scared, wet, and shaking because she was cold. Our grief had turned into joy.

Jesus had been telling His disciples about His death, all along, but somehow, they didn't understand His cryptic (mystifying, perplexing, confusing) message. There was still the thought that Messiah wouldn't die. Again, here in these verses, Jesus uses language the disciples don't understand. He says this in verses 19 and 20: *"Are you asking each other what I meant when I said, 'After a short time you won't see me. Then after another short time you will see me again'? The truth is, you will cry and be sad, but the world will be happy. You will be sad, but then your sadness will change to happiness."*

Jesus, of course, is telling His disciples that He will be killed, and they won't see Him. But in a short time, He will be raised from the dead and they will see Him again. Their grief will turn into joy, a reminder of Psalm 30:11-12:

> You have changed my sorrow into dancing.
> *You have taken away my sackcloth*
> *and clothed me with joy.*
> *You wanted me to praise you and not be silent.*
> *LORD my God, I will praise you forever!*

Jesus makes another promise here, "I will give you everything you need to be successful in the mission I send you on." This is an allusion to the Holy Spirit that He promised would be with them. "All of this is only possible if I go to the Father," Jesus tells them. He then comforts them with this in verse 24: "...*you will have the fullest joy possible.*"

John 16:25-30

25 "I have told you these things, using words that hide the meaning. But the time will come when I will not use words like that to tell you things. I will speak to you in plain words about the Father. 26 Then you will be able to ask the Father for things in my name. I'm not saying that I will have to ask the Father for you. 27 The Father himself loves you because you have loved me. And he loves you because you have believed that I came from God. 28 I came from the Father into the world. Now I am leaving the world and going back to the Father."

29 Then his followers said, "You are already speaking plainly to us. You are not using words that hide the meaning. 30 We can see now that you know all things. You answer our questions even before we ask them. This makes us believe that you came from God."

A Child's Game—I recall, as a child, playing a game where a parent would write messages and hide them in various places in the house or yard. The other children would have to follow the trail as the first message would indicate where the next message was located. One message might sound like this: "Go to the plant that has thorns and red flowers. Dig in the dirt next to the plant to find the next message." Each message would be a little cryptic but not too difficult and finally, there would be a prize at the end.

Why did Jesus use cryptic messages when speaking to the people, especially His disciples? A couple of ideas come to mind. Many of the people who listened to Jesus had their agendas (plans) of the way things ought to be, and Jesus wasn't following their agendas. Back in 12:37-40, Jesus confronted some of these individuals who wouldn't believe:

> *The people saw all these miraculous signs Jesus did,*
> *but they still did not believe in him. This was to give*
> *full meaning to what Isaiah the prophet said:*
>
> *"Lord, who believed what we told them?*
> *Who has seen the Lord's power?"*
>
> *This is why the people could not believe. Because*
> *Isaiah also said,*
>
> *"God made the people blind.*
> *He closed their minds.*
> *He did this so that they would not see with their*
> *eyes*
> *and understand with their minds.*
> *He did it so that they would not turn*
> *and be healed."*

But why did Jesus speak to His disciples in this cryptic way, also? Throughout the book of John, Jesus' disciples slowly, over time, discovered who He was. They realized why He came and where He was going. Kind of like a person working for a secretive government organization, these disciples were, at this point on their journey, on a "need-to-know" basis. I am reminded of Moses' final speech to Israel before he died. He is telling Israel of its future. But there are some things, at this point, they aren't to know. In Deuteronomy 29:29, Moses says this: *"There are some things that the LORD our God has kept secret. Only he knows these things. But he told us about some things. And these teachings are for us and our descendants forever. And we must obey all the commands in that law.*

Not a Puzzle, but a Purpose—I read this recently in a Bible Study Fellowship lesson on the book of Revelation: "In the Bible, a mystery is not a puzzle to be solved but a purpose of God that was once hidden but now is revealed." (BSF lesson, 2015)

We have to realize, though, sometimes Jesus isn't speaking cryptically. We just don't get it. We don't get it because of prejudices, culture, sins, pride, or maybe, as Jesus once asked His disciples in Matthew 15:16: *"Do you still have trouble understanding?"* The NIV uses the phrase, *"Are you still so dull?"*

John 16:31-33

31 Jesus said, "So now you believe? 32 Listen to me. A time is coming when you will be scattered, each to his own home. In fact, that time is already here. You will leave me, and I will be alone. But I am never really alone, because the Father is with me.

33 "I have told you these things so that you can have peace in me. In this world you will have troubles. But be brave! I have defeated the world!"

Terry and His PSA Numbers—I eat breakfast with my good friend, Terry St. Pierre, and three others on Tuesday at a local taco establishment. We talk about the weather, football, and the price of gas but mainly we are accountability partners in our walk with God. Sometimes the conversation is lighthearted, and we laugh a lot. Other times challenging things come up that we know we need to stop and pray about.

Terry had been concerned for a while about his PSA numbers and had been in touch with his doctor about his concerns. The doctor, after doing all kinds of doctor-type tests came up with a diagnosis—prostate cancer. After he broke the news, we stopped and prayed.

Terry began a regiment of radiation therapy. He had 44 radiation treatments during a short period of time. The treatment took its toll on Terry and took away energy from this once energetic man. Then came the final treatment. It was finally over, and as other cancer patients have done after treatment was over, Terry got to ring the bell while all who were present applauded.

I Have Defeated the World—Back in chapter 13, Jesus had predicted that His disciples would run away when Jesus was arrested. Here in chapter 16, Jesus tells them again: *"A time is coming when you will be scattered, each to his own home... You will leave me, and I will be alone."* Jesus always tells the truth. He doesn't mince words. But along with the gentle rebuke comes words of comfort. True peace is only found in Him. It is interesting in Verse 33, that Jesus, knowing their upcoming cowardly behavior, strengthens them with: *"Be Brave!"* He follows that exclamation with words that have comforted the disciples of Jesus for 2000 years. *"I have defeated the world!"*

That "defeat of the world," Jesus is speaking of, begins with crucifixion. How could killing the Messiah be seen as defeating the world's rule? As commentator Paul Harvey used to say: "And now for the rest of the story." The disciples were still in hiding, all through Saturday. But then on Sunday morning, Jesus was raised from the dead. In Philippians 2:8-11, the apostle Paul quotes an early Christian hymn showing how the Messiah defeated the world:

> *He humbled himself by being fully obedient to God,*
> *even when that caused his death—death on a cross.*
> *So God raised him up to the most important place*
> *and gave him the name that is greater than any other name.*
> *God did this so that every person will bow down to honor the name of Jesus.*
> *Everyone in heaven, on earth, and under the earth will bow.*
> *They will all confess, "Jesus Christ is Lord,"*
> *and this will bring glory to God the Father.*

John 17:1-5

¹ After Jesus said these things, he looked toward heaven and prayed, "Father, the time has come. Give glory to your Son so that the Son can give glory to you. ² You gave the Son power over all people so that he could give eternal life to all those you have given to him. ³ And this is eternal life: that people can know you, the only true God, and that they can know Jesus Christ, the one you sent. ⁴ I finished the work you gave me to do. I brought you glory on earth. ⁵ And now, Father, give me glory with you. Give me the glory I had with you before the world was made.

Sending Me to College—My dad never went to college, but he wanted me to go. He sent me from California to Abilene, Texas to attend Abilene Christian College. It was a long way to travel, and I was excited, mainly because I was traveling by train, and I was going to be on my own for the first time. Now I went to college to get an education, so I could teach school someday. But I also went because my dad wanted me to go. He was proud, and I was proud that he was proud. I'll never forget the smiles on their faces as my name was announced, and I walked across the stage, four years later, to receive my diploma. I know they felt it was as much for them as it was for me.

Thirty years later I got to watch my daughter, Joanna, walk across that same stage. I watched as my wife stood behind her and draped a white hood around her neck. Flashbulbs lit up the auditorium. Cheers from those around us echoed, as each graduate, in turn, heard their name called from the front. This graduation was as much for her mom and me as it was for her. The pride in her accomplishment was also the pride in our accomplishment. Her glory became our glory.

Jesus began a long prayer to His Father, first for Himself. Jesus spoke in the prayer of the glory He had with the Father before He came to earth. He spoke of the glory He brought with Him to the earth because He finished the work the Father gave Him to do. Even though He hadn't yet died, He spoke as if it was a certainty. Because of the glory He gave the Father by His obedience even unto death, the Father gave the Son the authority to give eternal life. What is eternal life? It is knowing and living with the Father and His Son, Jesus the Messiah, forever!

John 17:6-19

6 "You gave me some people from the world. I have shown them what you are like. They belonged to you, and you gave them to me. They have obeyed your teaching. 7 Now they know that everything I have came from you. 8 I told them the words you gave me, and they accepted them. They realized the fact that I came from you and believed that you sent me. *9* I pray for them now. I am not praying for the people in the world. But I am praying for these people you gave me, because they are yours. *10* All I have is yours, and all you have is mine. And my glory is seen in them.

11 "Now I am coming to you. I will not stay in the world, but these followers of mine are still in the world. Holy Father, keep them safe by the power of your name—the name you gave me. Then they will be one, just as you and I are one. *12* While I was with them, I kept them safe by the power of your name—the name you gave me. I protected them. And only one of them was lost—the one who was sure to be lost. This was to show the truth of what the Scriptures said would happen.

13 "I am coming to you now. But I pray these things while I am still in the world. I say all this so that these followers can have the true happiness that I have. I want them to be completely happy. *14* I have given them your teaching. And the world has hated them, because they don't belong to the world, just as I don't belong to the world.

15 "I am not asking you to take them out of the world. But I am asking that you keep them safe from the Evil One. *16* They don't belong to the world, just as I don't belong to the world. *17* Make them ready for your service through your truth. Your teaching is truth. *18* I have sent them into the world, just as you sent me into the world. *19* I am making myself completely ready to serve you. I do this for them, so that they also might be fully qualified for your service.

Being a Hippie—When I went to college, I wish I could tell you I always made my dad happy, but being eighteen and away from home for the first time does something to a young man's mind. When I arrived at school in 1967, being a hippie was a big deal, so I began dressing like one, talking like one, and even listening to the kind of music a hippie would listen to. And most of the people I hung around with looked a lot like me. My dad would always tell me that the world was a difficult place to live in but if I would remember I was "set apart," I would most likely honor God and in turn honor him. He would always quote me the same scripture. Romans 12:2 *"Be not conformed to this world but be ye transformed."* KJV Another way of saying it I found out later was "Don't let the world fit you into its mold."

Not of this World—The Twelve, minus Judas, were going to be left to fend for themselves after Jesus left. Well, not exactly. Jesus prayed that His disciples who were going to take His message to the world would be strong. Jesus did not ask God to remove them from the world but to strengthen them. They had accepted Him as Messiah and were going to be a target for everything satan could throw at them. Jesus' disciples were not "of this world," meaning that they didn't fit into the devious ways of the world—the politics, the culture, and the immorality.

Jesus asks the Father to *"set them apart"* for the special purpose Jesus has for them. These men had been set apart by the Father just as the Father had set apart Jesus, His Son. How did He do this? In verse 17 Jesus asked the Father to *"make them ready for your service through your truth. Your teaching is truth."* Knowing and teaching the truth about God sending His Son, Jesus the Messiah, to die for the world, sets these disciples apart from the world because the world does not know nor believe this truth. These disciples, beginning in Acts 1, will take the good news of the gospel of Jesus to the world so that all who believe its truth will, also, be set apart from the world and toward God.

John 17:20-23

[20] *"I pray not only for these followers but also for those who will believe in me because of their teaching.* [21] *Father, I pray that all who*

228

believe in me can be one. You are in me and I am in you. I pray that they can also be one in us. Then the world will believe that you sent me. **22** *I have given them the glory that you gave me. I gave them this glory so that they can be one, just as you and I are one.* **23** *I will be in them, and you will be in me. So they will be completely one. Then the world will know that you sent me and that you loved them just as you loved me.*

The Legacy—One year, just before Easter, I had our children and their children place some stepping stones on a pathway. On each stepping stone were two footprints, one a mother's and one a father's. The stones began with great-grandparents, then grandparents, followed by parents, and finally our grandchildren.

There is a song "Find Us Faithful" by Steve Green, which I have included below, that I copied onto each of the stepping stones, a few lines on each one. The stones were to remind, not only the grandchildren but each of us family members that we must leave a legacy (heritage) to the following generation of our faithfulness to Jesus and His gospel.

> "We're pilgrims on the journey of the narrow road
>
> And those who've gone before us line the way
>
> Cheering on the faithful, encouraging the weary
>
> Their lives a stirring testament to God's sustaining grace
>
> Surrounded by so great a cloud of witnesses.
>
> Let us run the race not only for the prize
>
> But as those who've gone before us
>
> Let us leave to those behind us

The heritage of faithfulness passed on through godly lives.

Oh, may all who come behind us find us faithful,

May the fire of our devotion light their way.

May the footprints that we leave, lead them to believe

And the life we live inspire them to obey.

Oh, may all who come behind us find us faithful.

After all our hopes and dreams have come and gone and our children sift through all we've left behind

May the clues that they discover and the memories they uncover

Become the light that leads them to the road we each must find.

Oh, may all who come behind us find us faithful

Oh, may all who come behind us find us faithful."
(Steve Green, 1988)

The Legacy Jesus Left—Jesus taught His disciples for three years. During those three years, Jesus sent them out to practice what they heard. They taught about the kingdom and repentance, and they healed and performed miracles. Then Jesus went back to the Father and left them to preach to the world about sin and forgiveness, grace and truth, baptism and the promised Holy Spirit, heaven and hell, the Kingdom of God, and the New Jerusalem. These disciples went out and taught their fellow Jews and the unbelieving Gentiles. And they taught the next generation the same message of salvation, who then taught the next until the world was full of the message of the Father's love for His creation and His Son's sacrifice for our redemption.

Jesus' prayer now turns to all believers who will come to know the truth through the message that His disciples will preach. Jesus' prayer is for unity. Now this is not just wishful thinking on His part or some dream that someday... No, this is a reality. We are family because of Jesus. We don't choose our physical family, and we can't pick our spiritual family either. The Father makes us one. What Jesus is praying for is that in our God family, we need to act as one. Just as a father of a family might tell his kids who are fighting with each other, "Listen up, we are family; we are one; start acting like it!" Why? Because the world is watching and we want the world to believe that the family of God loves each other. This love is the same love the Father has for the Son and the Son for the Father. His prayer here, and earlier in 15:12 is this: *"Love each other as I have loved you."*

John 17:24-26

[24] "Father, I want these people you have given me to be with me in every place I am. I want them to see my glory—the glory you gave me because you loved me before the world was made. [25] Father, you are the one who always does what is right. The world does not know you, but I know you, and these followers of mine know that you sent me. [26] I showed them what you are like, and I will show them again. Then they will have the same love that you have for me, and I will live in them."

Mine and My Dad's Hands—I was looking at my hands one day and couldn't believe how much they look like my dad's hands as he got older. I have certain mannerisms of my dad and find myself saying some of his same words and phrases as much as I didn't want to when I was a young man. Some of the things we do and say, both good and bad, remind us of whom we came from and the lessons we learned.

Mannerisms of Jesus—Jesus promises that *"I will live in them."* He lives in us by His Holy Spirit, which He promised to all believers. Now this is not having mannerisms, ways of speaking, or how our hands might remind us of our dad's hands. This is Jesus coming to live right inside us as our Helper and Guide as we teach His gospel of salvation and as we live a holy life before God. His Holy Spirit will teach us, by His word and through His leading, how to love each other, how to love the lost world, and how to love even our enemies. Jesus didn't want His followers to try to weather the world's storms or satan's fury alone. He wanted us to be one body, one church, one faith, and be filled with the same Holy Spirit.

John 18:1-3

¹ When Jesus finished praying, he left with his followers and went across the Kidron Valley. He went into a garden there, his followers still with him.

² Judas, the one responsible for handing Jesus over, knew where this place was. He knew because Jesus often met there with his followers. ³ So Judas led a group of soldiers to the garden, along with some guards from the leading priests and the Pharisees. They were carrying torches, lanterns, and weapons.

Daily Routine—I am a person who enjoys a routine. I get up at a certain time and go to bed at a predetermined hour. When I get up in the morning our dog, Daisy, knows she has about ten minutes before she will come into the kitchen to find me. After getting out of bed, I leave the bedroom door cracked just enough for her to get out. The first thing I do is start the coffee, I drink a glass of Metamucil mixed with water, eat a banana, get out the frying pan and go to the fridge and get bacon to cook for Annette and me.

When I open the drawer that has both bacon and cheese, Daisy is at my feet, begging for the piece of cheese she always gets every morning. After eating the cheese, she looks at me once again for the second treat, a dog bone. She then turns and goes to the back door. I let her out so she can do her business. When she returns, she goes back to the bedroom and again, climbs in bed with Annette.

At 2:40 in the afternoon, I go pick up my grandson, Owen, a 5th grader at an elementary school, not far from my house. I park my car in a line, behind other cars, waiting until we can move forward to pick up our student. When Owen gets into the car, I have an old cell phone all charged up in the back seat so he can play games on it. We usually stop, at his request, to buy something to eat or drink. Usually, it's something Moms wouldn't buy but Papas do. We drive home and he eats his snack, plays on the phone, and waits for Mom to get off work to come and get him. Karyn, Owen's mom, always looks at me with a smile when she sees the evidence of the snack she wouldn't buy. I, with a sheepish look on my face, always tell her something along the lines of "Papas have a hard time saying no to grandchildren." She, knowingly, nods her head.

Jesus' Routine:

Luke 22:39-40: *Jesus left the city and went to the Mount of Olives. His followers went with him. (He went there often.) He said to his followers, "Pray for strength against temptation."*

Mark 1:35: *The next morning Jesus woke up very early. He left the house while it was still dark and went to a place where he could be alone and pray.*

Luke 6:12: *A few days later, Jesus went out to a mountain to pray. He stayed there all night praying to God.*

Luke 4:16: *Jesus traveled to Nazareth, the town where he grew up. On the Sabbath day he went to the synagogue as he always did. He stood up to read.*

Matthew 26:55: *Then Jesus said to the crowd, "Why do you come to get me with swords and clubs as if I were a criminal? Every day I sat in the Temple area teaching. You did not arrest me there.*

Luke 19:47: *Jesus taught the people in the Temple area every day.*

John 18:2: *Judas, the one responsible for handing Jesus over, knew where this place was. He knew because Jesus often met there with his followers.*

John 18:4-6

⁴ Jesus already knew everything that would happen to him. So he went out and asked them, "Who are you looking for?"

⁵ They answered, "Jesus from Nazareth."

He said, "I am Jesus." (Judas, the one responsible for handing Jesus over, was standing there with them.) ⁶ When Jesus said, "I am Jesus," the men moved back and fell to the ground.

Running From a Pack of Dogs—When I was about ten years old a friend of mine and I were walking across a field. There was hay stacked up in rectangular bales that we had just passed on our way from his house. About halfway through the field a pack of dogs—there must have been five or six, but it seemed like twenty at the moment—began chasing the two of us. My friend ran toward his

234

house, and I ran in the other direction toward those bales of hay. Wouldn't you know it, every one of those dogs went after me? I was running as hard as I could with those dogs nipping at my heels. I saw the hay bales stacked so that there was no way for me to climb to the top without a lot of effort, and they still were far enough away that the dogs were bound to catch up with me. But fear is a great motivator making a person do fantastic feats. I don't know how, but I found myself at the top of that stack of hay bales where the dogs could not come. I don't know about you, but if the Lord Jesus said in my presence, *"I am Jesus,"* I would have fallen to the ground out of utter fear.

The Men Fell to the Ground—John doesn't tell us of the prayer in the garden when Jesus asks that the cup of suffering pass from Him, as the other gospel writers do. John also doesn't go into much detail about Judas betraying Him. You may remember hearing about the kiss of greeting that Judas gives his master. But, again, that story is told by Matthew, Mark, and Luke but left out of John. The gospel of John, as usual, has other details left out of the other three. The strangest detail to me is when Jesus told the detachment of soldiers that He was the one they were looking for. Verse 5 ends the sentence with: *the men moved back and fell to the ground.*

That would have been a sight to see. I have often wondered why they fell back. Could the reason have been that Jesus' presence was so intimidating and powerful that they couldn't bear to stand in front of Him? Or was it something the Father did in honor of His Son's sacrifice?

Another thought is the phrase, *"I am Jesus."* Could they have thought that He was using the phrase, *I am,"* as it has already been used by the author, John, in other passages in his book meaning God—the Great I Am? Fear does a lot of things to the body. The

Easy-To-Read footnotes from Bible Gateway say this about John 18:5:

> *"I am Jesus"* Literally, "I am," which could have the same meaning here that it has in 8:24, 28, 58; 13:19. Also in verse 8. (Easy-to-Read Footnotes, 2004)

John 18:7-11

⁷ He asked them again, "Who are you looking for?"

They said, "Jesus from Nazareth."

⁸ Jesus said, "I told you that I am Jesus. So if you are looking for me, let these other men go free." ⁹ This was to show the truth of what Jesus said earlier: "I have not lost anyone you gave me."

¹⁰ Simon Peter had a sword, which he pulled out. He struck the servant of the high priest and cut off his right ear. (The servant's name was Malchus.) ¹¹ Jesus said to Peter, "Put your sword back in its place! I must drink from the cup the Father has given me."

Sword Fighting with Cactus—Growing up in the Mojave Desert you would probably guess that we had cactuses. There was one particular type that was rather plentiful. Each plant had short spines everywhere. If you ever brushed up next to it, the spiny section would seem to jump at you, and once it had you there was no getting away.

My cousin Barbara and I were always together during our teenage years. I had just gotten a new fishing knife, and to show off to her I began sword fighting with one of those cactuses. I was winning, slicing off parts of the cactus this way and that when I suddenly stopped. The cactus seemed to explode. Cactus parts and sticky spines were everywhere, most of them landing on me. I had cactus on my hand, cactus on my feet, and cactus on my pants. I tried to grab the part that landed on my hand and both hands became stuck

236

together. I tried to walk and my feet stuck together. I must have looked like Brer Rabbit fighting the tar baby, and I was hurting all over.

Of course, Barbara was standing there laughing about the way I looked, which I thought was pretty rude since I was in so much pain. All I could do was yell, "Go get my mom!" I could hear her laughing all the way to the house. A few minutes later my mom came running toward me with a large butcher knife and began trying to hack the prickly things away from my skin. We pulled thorns out of my skin for quite a while, and I guess I looked, I know I felt, pretty silly for several days as I healed from my wounds. I suppose if I had been there the night Jesus was betrayed if I hadn't already run away, I would have rushed headlong into the fracas, like I did when I fought the cactus, having Jesus have to clean up after me. Come to think of it, I guess my Lord has done that quite a lot for me over the years.

More Powerful than a Jedi Knight—I always wonder why the disciples, especially Peter, weren't arrested that night. I mean Peter had just committed attempted murder. At Jesus' word, the guards just let them go. I remember seeing Star Wars, as a younger man, and there were these hero-type people called Jedi Knights who had been trained to get into a weak person's brain. They would make suggestions, "These aren't the men you are looking for. Let them go." Now there is here someone more powerful than a Jedi Knight. It makes me wonder if the I Am part of Jesus—the Deity—controlled what these men did, or in this case, did not do. He told this small army in verse 8: *"Let these other men go free."* And that is what those soldiers did.

Parallel Plots

John 18:12-27

Jesus

¹² Then the soldiers with their commander and the Jewish guards arrested Jesus. They tied him ¹³ and brought him to Annas, the father-in-law of Caiaphas. Caiaphas was the high priest that year. ¹⁴ He was also the one who had told the other Jewish leaders that it would be better if one man died for all the people.

Peter

¹⁵ Simon Peter and another one of Jesus' followers went with Jesus. This follower knew the high priest. So he went with Jesus into the yard of the high priest's house. ¹⁶ But Peter waited outside near the door. The follower who knew the high priest came back outside and spoke to the gatekeeper. Then he brought Peter inside. ¹⁷ The girl at the gate said to Peter, "Are you also one of the followers of that man?"

Peter answered, "No, I am not!"

¹⁸ It was cold, so the servants and guards had built a fire. They were standing around it, warming themselves, and Peter was standing with them.

Jesus

¹⁹ The high priest asked Jesus questions about his followers and what he taught them. ²⁰ Jesus answered, "I have always spoken openly to all people. I always taught in the synagogues and in the Temple area. All the Jews come together there. I never said anything in secret. ²¹ So why do you question me? Ask the people who heard my teaching. They know what I said."

22 When Jesus said this, one of the guards standing there hit him. The guard said, "You should not talk to the high priest like that!"

23 Jesus answered, "If I said something wrong, tell everyone here what was wrong. But if what I said is right, then why do you hit me?"

24 So Annas sent Jesus to Caiaphas the high priest. He was still tied.

Peter

25 Simon Peter was standing at the fire, keeping himself warm. The other people said to Peter, "Aren't you one of the followers of that man?"

Peter denied it. He said, "No, I am not."

26 One of the servants of the high priest was there. He was a relative of the man whose ear Peter had cut off. The servant said, "I think I saw you with him in the garden!"

27 But again Peter said, "No, I was not with him!" As soon as he said this, a rooster crowed.

Finding Nemo—Do you remember seeing the computer-generated animation "Finding Nemo"? It was an animated fish story about Nemo, a clownfish, and his family and friends. Back in 2003, the movie grossed $871 million, worldwide. Our kids were too old for the movie, and their kids hadn't yet been born. But our grandchildren did enjoy seeing the film years later since it stayed a hit for a long time.

One of the characteristics of the film is that it has, what is called, a parallel plot (two stories going on at the same time). There is the story of Marlin, Nemo's father, trying to find his son after Nemo was captured in a net. And there is Nemo's story of trying to escape the dentist's fish aquarium. The parallel plot runs until near the end when father and son are, happily, reunited.

John's Parallel Plot—John has a parallel plot in verses 12-27, Jesus' trial, and Peter's denial. You can witness, in your mind's eye, first one story and then the other, playing out at the same time. In Luke's gospel, chapter 15, verses 61-62 we can see the parallel stories come together in dramatic fashion: *"Then the Lord turned and looked into Peter's eyes. And Peter remembered what the Lord had said, "Before the rooster crows in the morning, you will say three times that you don't know me." Then Peter went outside and cried bitterly."*

An interesting point in the story is the relationship between Annas and Caiaphas. Caiaphas was married to Annas' daughter. Rome had removed Annas as high priest in 15 AD and the job was given to Caiaphas. Many in Jerusalem still regarded Annas as the high priest.

Now look at the paradoxes (contradictory stories) that are in these parallel plots. Jesus is before Annas, being questioned about His teachings, answering honestly, while Peter is hiding in a corner trying not to be noticed. Jesus was not afraid to teach openly in the temple and synagogues, even saying in verse 20: *"I have spoken openly to the world."* The Jewish leaders, on the other hand, arrested Him at night, behind everyone's back, for fear of the people.

It is interesting, too, that Peter denies Jesus three times, and yet, rather than hiding at home, he continues to follow his master's movements throughout the night.

My Crowing Rooster—I had all kinds of pets when I was growing up. I had dogs, snakes, lizards, horned toads, water turtles, desert tortoises, fish, a bird, and a horse (never cats). My parents were not cat people. We did have some chickens. We raised about twenty, one time, that we, eventually, ended up eating. But there were two other chickens, Bandies, that were pets.

A Bandy is smaller than most chickens and lays very small eggs. I had a hen and a rooster. The hen was pretty and brown and had the sweetest disposition. The rooster was completely different, very colorful, proud, arrogant, and just plain ornery. He loved to peck me any time he got a chance. Whenever I had to go into the chicken hut to feed and water or check for eggs, I had to watch my backside. But there was one thing this rooster could do better than any other; he could crow. He would come out every morning just at sunrise and crow his old head off. You never had to worry about sleeping late with that rooster.

Peter and the Crowing Rooster—Was it always a reminder to Peter, when he heard a rooster crow? Did it remind him of that night? Did he think of his denial of the Messiah in some of his later years, or did it, instead, remind him of the love his Savior showed him, by not only dying for his sins but also giving him another chance? The tears Peter shed that night must have been more than any other time in his life. The grief must have been overwhelming. To betray your best friend and teacher must have made him feel that he could never be forgiven.

All four gospel accounts include Peter's denial. John leaves it rather abruptly but seems to allude to it later after Jesus is resurrected when Jesus asks Peter three times in 21:15, 16, and 17: ***"Simon, son of John, do you love me?"*** Matthew, Mark, and Luke conclude this portion with Peter going away crying. Matthew and Luke use the word *"bitterly"* which suggests that he felt guilt and grief deep within his very soul.

I love what Mark's gospel says after Jesus' resurrection. The women who come to the tomb early that Sunday morning are greeted by an angel who tells them that Jesus has been raised from the dead. And then the angel says, in Mark 16:7: *"Now go and tell his followers. And be sure to tell Peter..."* I'm glad Mark included that part about telling Peter. Can you imagine what Peter must have been thinking all along? "He'll forgive the others, but how could He forgive me?" The disciples were gathered as the women brought the news. Peter must have looked up and said, "He actually said, *'Tell Peter?'"* I'm sure Jesus knew what Peter must have felt like. He also knows what we feel like when we commit that sin we think we could never be forgiven of.

John 18:28-40

28 Then the guards took Jesus from Caiaphas' house to the Roman governor's palace. It was early in the morning. The Jews there would not go inside the palace. They did not want to make themselves unclean, because they wanted to eat the Passover meal. 29 So Pilate went outside to them and asked, "What do you say this man has done wrong?"

30 They answered, "He is a bad man. That is why we brought him to you."

31 Pilate said to them, "You take him yourselves and judge him by your own law."

The Jewish leaders answered, "But your law does not allow us to punish anyone by killing them." 32 (This was to show the truth of what Jesus said about how he would die.)

33 Then Pilate went back inside the palace. He called for Jesus and asked him, "Are you the king of the Jews?"

34 Jesus said, "Is that your own question, or did other people tell you about me?"

³⁵ Pilate said, "I'm not a Jew! It was your own people and their leading priests who brought you before me. What have you done wrong?"

³⁶ Jesus said, "My kingdom does not belong to this world. If it did, my servants would fight so that I would not be handed over to the Jewish leaders. No, my kingdom is not an earthly one."

³⁷ Pilate said, "So you are a king."

Jesus answered, "You are right to say that I am a king. I was born for this: to tell people about the truth. That is why I came into the world. And everyone who belongs to the truth listens to me."

³⁸ Pilate said, "What is truth?" Then he went out to the Jewish leaders again and said to them, "I can find nothing against this man. ³⁹ But it is one of your customs for me to free one prisoner to you at the time of the Passover. Do you want me to free this 'king of the Jews'?"

⁴⁰ They shouted back, "No, not him! Let Barabbas go free!" (Barabbas was a rebel.)

Accused but Innocent—What six-year-old boy wants to sit in a beauty shop waiting for his mom to finish getting her hair fixed? Certainly not me, but that is exactly what happened once a week if my older brothers were not home to babysit me.

I hated this part of the week worse than a shot at the doctor's office. But there was one thing that made it bearable. There was a small 5 and 10 (that's what my generation called a dollar store), just down the street from the beauty shop, and Mom would give me some money so I could go buy some candy. I thought it was a pretty good trade-off, so I always looked forward to that part of the hour or two. I even got to know the lady at the counter that checked me out. She would always talk kindly to me, and I thought we had become fast friends.

One day I visited the little store as I usually did and went back to Mom at the beauty shop. A few minutes later the lady that was my friend from the store, came to my mom and told her that I had stolen some candy and taken it outside to pass out to some friends. Now, I don't know who she saw stealing the candy, but I do know it wasn't me. I told my mom that the lady was mistaken and that she must have mixed me up with someone else. My mom didn't know what to believe. She wanted to believe me, but there stood an adult accusing me. My mom did the wise thing. She didn't accuse me, but she also told me never to go back to that store.

I was devastated. I knew I didn't steal the candy, but I also knew adults are believed before kids. I remember carrying that incident with me down through the years until one day, as an adult myself, I asked my mom if she remembered the situation. She did. I told her, "Mom, I didn't steal the candy."

She said, "I believe you." And I was satisfied. The main person, all these years ago, I didn't want to disappoint was my mom. If she believed me, no one else's opinion mattered.

Not Believing Jesus—Many on this day didn't believe Jesus was the Son of God and therefore their Savior. There were others, even His friends and family, who didn't understand. No one else's opinion mattered except for His Father's who had sent Him.

The Jews were not against stoning a person. If they wanted to, even though legally they were not allowed to, they would do it. Later in the book of Acts, the Jews stoned Stephen for preaching about Jesus. But it had been prophesied that Jesus would die by being crucified. Zechariah 12:10: *"They will look on me, the one they have* pierced, and they will mourn for him as one mourns for an only child." Isaiah 53:5 *"But he was pierced for our transgressions..."* Psalm 22:16 *"...a band of evil men has encircled me, they have pierced my hands and my feet."* Jesus also predicted the kind of death He would die. John 3:14: *"It is the same with the Son of Man. He must be lifted up too."* John 8:28 *"You will lift up the Son of Man. Then you will know that I AM."* John 12:32-33: *"I will be lifted up from the earth. When that happens, I will draw all people to myself." Jesus said this to show how he would die.*

The Nervous Governor—Pilate seemed to get a little nervous here, not only by being put on a spot by the Jewish leaders but because there was something different about this man, Jesus. Did he feel what many others felt when they were around Him? John 7:46: *"We have never heard anyone say such amazing things!"* Or was it because of his wife? In Matthew 27:19, we find: *While Pilate was sitting there in the place for judging, his wife sent a message to him. It said, "Don't do anything with that man. He is not guilty. Last night I had a dream about him, and it troubled me very much."*

Pilate then asks Him in verse 33: *"Are you the king of the Jews?"* This is followed by Jesus stating in verse 36: *"My kingdom does not belong to this world. If it did, my servants would fight so that I would not be handed over to the Jewish leaders. No, my kingdom is not an earthly one."*

The Kingdom of God or the rule of God, is of heaven, not of this world. It is a spiritual kingdom but physical people belong to it. In this world, the kingdom is the church, the believers or disciples of Jesus the Messiah. Yet this spiritual kingdom will ultimately replace, not only Rome but also, every other kingdom, especially the kingdom of darkness.

In Daniel 2:31-35:

"King, in your dream you saw a large statue in front of you that was very large and shiny. It was very impressive. The head of the statue was made from pure gold. Its chest and the arms were made from silver. The belly and upper part of the legs were made from bronze. The lower part of the legs was made from iron. Its feet were made partly of iron and partly of clay. While you were looking at the statue, you saw a rock that was cut loose, but not by human hands. Then the rock hit the statue on its feet of iron and clay and smashed them. Then the iron, the clay, the bronze, the silver, and the gold broke to pieces all at the same time. And all the pieces became like chaff on a threshing floor in the summertime. The wind blew them away, and there was nothing left. No one could tell that a statue had ever been there. Then the rock that hit the statue became a very large mountain and filled up the whole earth."

The gold head was the Babylonian empire and was located in modern-day Iraq. The silver arms and chest represent the Medes and Persians who defeated the Babylonians and were located in modern-day Iran. The bronze thighs represent Greece, which defeated the Medo-Persian Empire. The iron legs and the feet made of iron and clay represent the Roman Empire and the rest of the kingdoms of men, which are broken to pieces by the rock, the Kingdom of God. The Kingdom of God then becomes so big it fills the whole earth and the kingdoms of men are all like chaff, blown away by the wind.

So here stands Pilate, who represented all the power of Rome and of the kingdoms of men, and Jesus the Messiah, who is the King of the Kingdom of God. One looks like he has the power but doesn't. The other, who looks defeated, really has the power. The Apostle John writes in another book, visions from a glorified Jesus many years in the future, speaking of the powerful Roman Empire. Rome in the following passage is renamed Babylon in prophetic language. Revelation 18:1-2:

> *Then I saw another angel coming down from heaven. This angel had great power. The angel's glory made the earth bright. The angel shouted with a powerful voice,*
>
> *"She is destroyed!*
>
> *The great city of Babylon is destroyed!*

Jesus will make one final exchange with Pilate, in chapter 19, which will let him know where the real power lies:

> *Pilate said, "You refuse to speak to me? Remember, I have the power to make you free or to kill you on a cross."*
>
> *Jesus answered, "The only power you have over me is the power given to you by God. So the one who handed me over to you is guilty of a greater sin."*

Finally, there is Barabbas, a criminal, who should have been crucified that day with the two thieves. Instead, the crowd asks that he be released and Jesus be crucified. We are Barabbas. We deserve death. Jesus not only took Barabbas' place that day but He took ours. Isaiah 53:5: *But he was being punished for what we did. He was crushed because of our guilt. He took the punishment we deserved, and this brought us peace. We were healed because of his pain.*

John 19:1-5

¹ Then Pilate ordered that Jesus be taken away and whipped. ² The soldiers made a crown from thorny branches and put it on his head. Then they put a purple robe around him. ³ They kept coming up to him and saying, "Hail to the king of the Jews!" And they hit him in the face.

⁴ Again Pilate came out and said to the Jewish leaders, "Look! I am bringing Jesus out to you. I want you to know that I find nothing I can charge him with." ⁵ Then Jesus came out wearing the crown of thorns and the purple robe. Pilate said to the Jews, "Here is the man!"

A Different Kind of Crown—Kids can find the strangest things to entertain themselves. I remember weaving long runners of St. Augustine grass together into a crown and wearing it on my head. One time, after hearing the story of Messiah's crucifixion, I found a thorny vine. I tried to weave it together into a crown, puncturing my fingers and hand in the process. After a long torturous time, I finally succeeded in forming the thorny vine into some semblance of a crown. I looked at it, wondering, in a childlike way, how much it would hurt to have someone push it down on my head. Years later, I have thought many times of the crown I wove and realized, not only the pain, but the ridicule Jesus went through because of my sins. *"He was pierced for our transgressions."* He gave up the crown of heaven to wear a crown of thorns.

Pilate tries one last time to release Jesus. Prisoners who were crucified were not usually flogged, but in Jesus' case, Pilate thought that just a flogging might appease the crowds. Now when the Jews flogged a man, they gave him thirty-nine lashes. By their law, they were allowed forty, but they were such sticklers that the law be kept and were afraid that the person counting lashes might miscount. Because of that, they would only allow thirty-nine. The Romans had no such law. A man could be beaten to death or just short of death. Jesus was beaten, brutally. I can't help but think that each time the whip went across his back it was for one of my sins, *"...by his wounds we are healed."*

John 19:6-16

⁶ When the leading priests and the Jewish guards saw Jesus they shouted, "Kill him on a cross! Kill him on a cross!"

But Pilate answered, "You take him and nail him to a cross yourselves. I find nothing I can charge him with."

⁷ The Jewish leaders answered, "We have a law that says he must die, because he said he is the Son of God."

⁸ When Pilate heard this, he was more afraid. ⁹ So he went back inside the palace and asked Jesus, "Where are you from?" But Jesus did not answer him. ¹⁰ Pilate said, "You refuse to speak to me? Remember, I have the power to make you free or to kill you on a cross."

¹¹ Jesus answered, "The only power you have over me is the power given to you by God. So the one who handed me over to you is guilty of a greater sin."

¹² After this, Pilate tried to let Jesus go free. But the Jewish leaders shouted, "Anyone who makes himself a king is against Caesar. So if you let this man go free, that means you are not Caesar's friend."

¹³ When Pilate heard this, he brought Jesus out to the place called "The Stone Pavement." (In Aramaic the name is Gabbatha.) Pilate sat down on the judge's seat there. ¹⁴ It was now almost noon on Preparation day of Passover week. Pilate said to the Jews, "Here is your king!"

15 They shouted, "Take him away! Take him away! Kill him on a cross!"

Pilate asked them, "Do you want me to kill your king on a cross?"

The leading priests answered, "The only king we have is Caesar!"

16 So Pilate handed Jesus over to them to be killed on a cross.

The soldiers took Jesus.

Angry Bumblebees—When my first granddaughter, Ashlyn, was a little over a year old, her mother, Nana, and I—her Papa—went to Tennessee to visit my youngest son, Jonathan at a young men's Christian Camp called Narrowgate. The four of us had traveled from Texas to the site and were staying in what was called the big house, where we ate and slept.

A day or two into our visit I was outside on the porch with many of the young men, including my son, while Nana, Ashlyn, and Joanna—Ashlyn's mother—were taking a walk not far away, near some trees. In one of those trees hung a gourd, made into a birdhouse. Nana, wondering if the home was made of plastic or was a real gourd, innocently tapped the side of it. Unexpectedly, a nest of bumblebees that had taken up residence in the gourd, swarmed out and began to swarm around Ashlyn, who had recently learned to walk. Joanna and Nana immediately reached for Ashlyn, and Joanna who is a little closer swooped her up and began running away from the hive. Nana swatted bees with both hands trying to help Joanna and Ashlyn and at the same time keep them away from herself.

Quickly, the angry bees began stinging Nana and Joanna, but both of Joanna's hands were wrapped tightly as she cradled her baby daughter. I heard the screaming and ran toward the sound, watching Nana and Joanna being attacked, viciously, by the stinging insects. I ran to Joanna, as she was fleeing the melee, and was able to take Ashlyn and run to the house. Finally, with both of her hands now free, Joanna was able to fight back as we all ran toward the safety of the house. Nana was close behind.

Joanna had taken the brunt of the attack by keeping her hands, arms, and body cradled around her daughter. She had been stung ten times, Ashlyn only once. That evening, Joanna vomited throughout the night, finally getting rid of most of the toxins. Jesus did the same for each of us as He took the brunt of the stinging arrows meant for us.

Angry Men—When you look at the life of Jesus, we get our information almost entirely from the four gospels. From Matthew and Luke, we learn information about His birth. Matthew chapter 2 tells us that there was another king, Herod the Great, who first heard about the birth of Jesus from the wise men. There was no room for two kings in Herod's domain, and we learn that the king tried to murder the boy, Jesus, by sending soldiers to kill every boy under the age of two in Bethlehem. Jesus' family escaped but many children were slain because of another king's jealousy.

Now we have Pilate, who represents another king, the Roman emperor, Tiberius. Pilate knows that to claim to be a king is treasonous but he also realizes that the Jewish leaders are jealous of the man, Jesus. He walks a tightrope trying to appease the leaders of Jerusalem and not give in to their petty demands.

Jesus is brought out to the crowd, Pilate thinking, "Maybe this will be enough for them." But it isn't. When the crowd sees Jesus dressed as a king, they know that Pilate is mocking them, and they cry louder than ever, *"Kill him on a cross! Kill him on a cross!"*

By then, Pilate could see that he was losing the crowd and wouldn't be able to save Jesus, so he taunted them one last time, *"Do you* want me to kill your king on a cross?" And the Jewish priests answer, *"The only king we have is Caesar!"*

So, where Herod failed, Caesar succeeds, for the time being anyway. The main power any king has over a would-be usurper (one who takes illegal power by force) is death. For a Roman citizen, the treasonous act would be punished by death by being beheaded. For a non-Roman, the penalty was the tortuous death of crucifixion.

Rome, Caesar, Pilate, and the Jewish leaders have no power over Jesus except what God allows. What will be found in just a few short days is that even death and the grave are defeated, showing they have no lasting power either. Therefore, Jesus will bring into effect the new way through death to a new and everlasting life. Paul says of this death in 1 Corinthians 15:54-55:

> *Death is swallowed in victory."*
>
> *"O death, where is your victory?*
> *Where is your power to hurt?"*

John 19:17-24

17 He carried his own cross to a place called "The Place of the Skull." (In Aramaic the name of this place is "Golgotha.") 18 There they nailed Jesus to the cross. They also nailed two other men to crosses. They put them on each side of Jesus with him in the middle.

19 Pilate told them to write a sign and put it on the cross. The sign said, "JESUS OF NAZARETH, THE KING OF THE JEWS." 20 The sign was written in Aramaic, in Latin, and in Greek. Many of the Jews read this sign, because the place where Jesus was nailed to the cross was near the city.

21 The leading Jewish priests said to Pilate, "Don't write, 'The King of the Jews.' But write, 'This man said, I am the King of the Jews.'"

²² Pilate answered, "I will not change what I have written."

²³ After the soldiers nailed Jesus to the cross, they took his clothes and divided them into four parts. Each soldier got one part. They also took his tunic. It was all one piece of cloth woven from top to bottom. ²⁴ So the soldiers said to each other, "We should not tear this into parts. Let's throw lots to see who will get it." This happened to make clear the full meaning of what the Scriptures say:

"They divided my clothes among them,
    and they threw lots for what I was wearing."

So the soldiers did this.

Naked—I have an unnamed family member who permitted me to tell a humiliating story about him. He was living in California as a young married husband. Because of the California heat, he usually slept naked. His wife had already gone to work, and he was suddenly awakened by two puppies that needed to instantly, go outside and do their business. He rushed them to his backyard, only to have the backdoor slam behind him. He found a small covering and sneakily walked to the neighboring fence. Fortunately, his neighbor was in the backyard, and our friend asked him if he could borrow some clothes and use his cell phone. Everything worked out, but the embarrassment and family laughter still follow him to this day.

Naked on the Cross—When we look at the paintings of Jesus on the cross, the artists, almost always, place a small white covering over His private parts. Ever since God first made clothes for Adam and Eve, after they had sinned in the garden, humans in most cultures have worn some type of clothing. Much of the time it was for warmth, but it was also for modesty. Being exposed, especially

Jesus was naked on the cross. He was naked in front of His mother, the other women, and John. He was naked in front of all who came by to ridicule and mock Him. He was naked before His God. Where Adam and Eve were clothed by God, Jesus was allowed to have His clothes removed. Where Adam and Eve's sin had revealed their nakedness, Jesus, who never sinned, hung naked because of our sin.

Psalm 22 is what is called a Messianic Psalm (Jesus Psalm). This Messianic Psalm foretells the Messiah's death on the cross 1000 years before Jesus was born, lived, and died on this earth. Yet it depicts the humiliation and alienation Jesus must have felt as He was dying. Look at verses 3-8 and 16-20, and picture with me the crucifixion scene:

> "God, you are the Holy One.
>   You sit as King upon the praises of Israel.
> Our ancestors trusted you.
>   Yes, they trusted you, and you saved them.
> They called to you for help and escaped their enemies.
>   They trusted you and were not disappointed!
> But I feel like a worm, less than human!
>   People insult me and look down on me.
> Everyone who sees me makes fun of me.
>   They shake their heads and stick out their tongues at me.
> They say, "Call to the LORD for help.
>   Maybe he will save you...
>   If he likes you so much, surely he will rescue you!"
>
> The "dogs" are all around me—
>   a pack of evil people has trapped me.
>   They have pierced my hands and feet.

I can see each one of my bones.
   My enemies are looking at me;
   they just keep staring.
   They divide my clothes among themselves,
      and they throw lots for what I am wearing."

25 *Jesus' mother stood near his cross. Her sister was also standing there with Mary the wife of Clopas, and Mary Magdalene.* **26** *Jesus saw his mother. He also saw the follower he loved very much standing there. He said to his mother, "Dear woman, here is your son."* **27** *Then he said to the follower, "Here is your mother." So after that, this follower took Jesus' mother to live in his home.*

28 *Later, Jesus knew that everything had been done. To make the Scriptures come true he said, "I am thirsty."* **29** *There was a jar full of sour wine there, so the soldiers soaked a sponge in it. They put the sponge on a branch of a hyssop plant and lifted it to Jesus' mouth.* **30** *When he tasted the wine, he said, "It is finished." Then he bowed his head and died.*

Watch Out for Mama—That last year, my dad knew he was dying. He had suffered two strokes, a broken hip, and now had congestive heart failure. He told each of us boys, but especially my oldest brother, Bill, "Watch out for Mama." He didn't have to remind us, but I know it made him feel better to say it.

John tells of the words Jesus in verses 26-27, directed to him and Mary, Jesus' mother: *Jesus saw his mother. He also saw the follower he loved very much standing there. He said to his mother, "Dear woman, here is your son." Then he said to the follower, "Here is your mother." So after that, this follower took Jesus' mother to live in his home.*

We're not told why Jesus asked John to take care of Mary since Jesus had brothers, but there must have been a close relationship, not only between Jesus and John but also Mary and John. It must have been painful for Mary to watch her first-born son dying in front of her and not being able to do anything except to be there. And where would his mother be other than close by? I have to wonder if Mary had thought of another time when a man had predicted to her that she would go through this. Luke 2:34-35: *Then Simeon blessed them and said to Mary, "Many Jews will fall and many will rise because of this boy. He will be a sign from God that some will not accept. So the secret thoughts of many will be made known. And the things that happen will be painful for you—like a sword cutting through your heart."*

Again, let's read more from Psalm 22. Look at verses 9-10, as Jesus makes this request of John for His mother:

> *"God, the truth is, you are the one who brought me into this world.*
> *You made me feel safe while I was still at my mother's breasts.*
> *You have been my God since the day I was born.*
>
> *I was thrown into your arms as I came from my mother's womb."*

Seasick—It was Christmas break. I, along with my high school senior son, Jonathan, his older brother, Jeremy, and my older brother, Bill, decided to go fishing in south Texas, out in the Gulf of Mexico. We paid our fee which included fishing equipment, a boat with an operator and guide, and a six-hour trip. Two hours were spent going to the fishing spot, two hours fishing, and two more on the return trip. I forgot to start the Dramamine the night before and spent five of those six hours, either throwing up over the side of the boat or lying prone on a bench seat. I suffered from a terrible headache and stomachache, wishing the trip would hurry and be over.

Annette and I married in September after that Christmas break. During the following Christmas break, Annette and I decided to celebrate a late honeymoon on a cruise of the Caribbean. This time I was ready. I asked my family doctor for a motion sickness patch that I could wear for the whole voyage, and it worked as far as sea sickness. I felt great in the stomach and head department. But the tradeoff was, I was sleepy the first few days, and I had the driest mouth I had ever experienced. For the whole excursion, I was constantly drinking water to keep my tongue from sticking to the roof of my mouth and to lubricate my parched lips.

"I am thirsty." John includes these words of Jesus to show that the Son of Man was human through and through. God? Yes! But on the cross, Jesus felt the pain of the nails, the heat of the sun, the panic of not being able to get a breath, loneliness, embarrassment, sorrow, hunger, and yes, thirst. In verses 14-15 of Psalm 22, we read of the Messiah's thirst:

> *"My strength is gone,*
> * like water poured out on the ground.*
> *My bones have separated.*
> *My courage is gone.*
> *My mouth is as dry as a piece of baked pottery.*
> *My tongue is sticking to the roof of my mouth.*
> *You have left me dying in the dust."*

The Debt Has been Paid—I have made many mistakes in my life that ended up costing a lot of money. I remember telling our children, as they were growing up, that education is expensive, but if you learn from your mistake, the money was worth it. Not long after I married Maryanne, I made a very expensive mistake when our new blended family left Texas and moved to California. I took my twelve years of teacher retirement funds out of the Teacher Retirement System of Texas (TRS), to the dismay of my brother, Bob, who had warned me not to do it. My thought, at the time, was that we would never move back to Texas and we could use the money.

Three years later, we moved back to Texas, and I had to begin all over with adding to my retirement. I had always planned to replace that money later on but just never had the resources to do it. Sometime after my dad passed away in 1997, I asked my mom if I could borrow the money to repay TRS. We worked out an agreement where I would pay her so much a month, taken directly out of my bank account. My oldest brother, Bill, worked out all the arrangements so Mom would not be hurt for money while I was paying her back.

I began making the payment on time and regularly when Mom had a stroke and passed away. I had hardly made a dent in the money I owed her. Bill was the executor of her will. When it came time to divvy up the inheritance, I expected to pay the estate back the money I still owed Mom. When I told Bill my intention, he told me that Mom and he had discussed the loan before she died and she had said, "If I die before Darell pays the loan back, he is to be forgiven the entire debt.

I said, "Bill, that is not fair to you and Bob. Let me put the money from my part of the inheritance back into the estate."

He said, "Darell, I am just the executor. I will do what Mom has told me to do. **The debt is paid!** And the inheritance will be divided up equally, in three ways, as Mom has directed. So, stop arguing."

Over, Done, Paid in Full— *"It is finished."* John includes these three wonderful words, not just because Jesus can now let go, not having

258

to endure anymore, but because the work that God had planned before the creation of the world is finally finished (through, over, ended, done, completed). Another phrase that fits the definition of **"It is finished"** is "paid in full."

> "He paid a debt he did not owe;
>
> I owed a debt I could not pay;
>
> I needed someone to wash my sins away.
>
> And now I sing a brand-new song, Amazing Grace.
>
> Christ Jesus paid the debt that I could never pay." (Anonymous, Date Unknown)

This is the first verse of a contemporary song by an anonymous writer. Humans have always tried to work themselves to God, whatever they perceived God to be. But God's plan for all humanity has always been that the work was God's; the response is ours. Ephesians 2:8-10:

> *I mean that you have been saved by grace because you believed. You did not save yourselves; it was a gift from God. You are not saved by the things you have done, so there is nothing to boast about. God has made us what we are. In Christ Jesus, God made us new people so that we would spend our lives doing the good things he had already planned for us to do.*

And Romans 6:23: *When people sin, they earn what sin pays— death. But God gives his people a free gift—eternal life in Christ Jesus our Lord.*

"It is finished." Implies another marvel. Jesus was in complete control over His crucifixion and death. Look, again, at John 10:17-

18: *"The Father loves me because I give my life. I give my life so that I can get it back again. No one takes my life away from me. I give my own life freely. I have the right to give my life, and I have the right to get it back again. This is what the Father told me."*

Finished and Completed—There are three times in Scripture that the finished work of God reveals something brand new, creation, the crucifixion, and the new heaven and the new earth.

Genesis 2:1-3: *So the earth, the sky, and everything in them were finished. **<u>God finished the work he was doing</u>**, so on the seventh day he rested from his work. God blessed the seventh day and made it a holy day. He made it special because on that day he rested from all the work he did while creating the world.*

John 19:28-30: *Later, Jesus knew that everything had been done. To make the Scriptures come true he said, "I am thirsty." There was a jar full of sour wine there, so the soldiers soaked a sponge in it. They put the sponge on a branch of a hyssop plant and lifted it to Jesus' mouth. When he tasted the wine, he said, **"It is finished."** Then he bowed his head and died.*

Revelation 21:1-7:

> *Then I saw a new heaven and a new earth. The first heaven and the first earth had disappeared. Now there was no sea. And I saw the holy city, the new Jerusalem, coming down out of heaven from God. It was prepared like a bride dressed for her husband.*
>
> *I heard a loud voice from the throne. It said, "Now God's home is with people. He will live with them. They will be his people. God himself will be with them and will be their God. He will wipe away every tear from their eyes. There will be no more death, sadness, crying, or pain. All the old ways are gone."*

The one who was sitting on the throne said, "Look, I am making everything new!" Then he said, "Write this, because these words are true and can be trusted."

*The one on the throne said to me, **"It is finished! I am the Alpha and the Omega, the Beginning and the End. I will give free water from the spring of the water of life to anyone who is thirsty. All those who win the victory will receive all this. And I will be their God, and they will be my children.***

Another completion comes with God finishing His work with each one of His children. Look with me at this marvelous verse, Philippians 1:6: *I am sure that the good work God began in you will continue until he completes it on the day when Jesus Christ comes again.*

John 19:31-37

31 This day was Preparation day. The next day was a special Sabbath day. The Jewish leaders did not want the bodies to stay on the cross on the Sabbath day. So they asked Pilate to order that the legs of the men be broken. And they asked that the bodies be taken down from the crosses. 32 So the soldiers came and broke the legs of the two men on the crosses beside Jesus. 33 But when the soldiers came close to Jesus, they saw that he was already dead. So they did not break his legs.

34 But one of the soldiers stuck his spear into Jesus' side. Immediately blood and water came out. 35 (The one who saw this happen has told about it. He told about it so that you also can believe. The things he says are true. He knows that he tells the truth.) 36 These things happened to give full meaning to the

Scriptures that said, "None of his bones will be broken" [37] and "People will look at the one they stabbed."

What Is Your Favorite Season? —I have been asked on several occasions, "What is your favorite season of the year?" My answer is usually, "Spring, after a cold winter, and fall, after a hot summer." In the autumn, pecans begin to fall from our two trees in the backyard, and I remember paying my young grandchildren a penny a pecan to pick them up. Sometimes, I would take them to a place that buys pecans to sell them so the grandkids could make some extra money. I remember on several occasions I would sit and crack some for my granddaughter, Ella, who loved to sit beside me and eat them as I handed the nut to her.

I also pay several of my grandkids to rake my backyard leaves into large piles. Two of the grandkids, Owen and Ella, who live in Abilene, would come over in the late afternoon and spend an hour jumping in those leaves. Teenage, Ella, still enjoys that tradition.

I have planted several kinds of plants in my backyard over the years, which would begin to flower in the early fall. Some, like a large patch of Greg's Mist Flower, attract monarch butterflies. Others are just pretty. Ruellia is one of those pretty plants I transplanted, about ten years ago, from FaithWorks, where I used to teach. I planted them in a section of the yard next to the neighbor's fence. They are so fruitful that they not only filled in the section I had set up for them but, my sweet neighbor, laughingly, revealed to me that they are taking over his side of the yard also.

Granddaughter Ella especially likes to water the Ruellia with me because I have dubbed them Ella's plant since the name of the plant sounds a lot like her own name. Ruellia grows on a two-to-three-foot thin stock over the spring and summer to produce pretty purple flowers in early fall that later produce seeds. These plants have an interesting way of scattering their seeds. When the seed pods get wet, like, for instance, watering them, they will shoot their seeds everywhere, sometimes hitting you in the face.

Pecans, leaves, butterflies, and seeds are beautiful reminders of the fall. But autumn is also a reminder of death and renewal. The squirrel, hiding nuts for later, plants new trees. The fall leaves decay, becoming mulch for new plants and grass. The butterfly lays her eggs to repeat their life cycle. And the seed that falls to the earth becomes buried to produce new flowers. The death of the pecan, the leaf, the butterfly, and the seed all will bring brand new life. Jesus made a statement back in John 12:23-24, that speaks of His death in much the same way. Only in death will there be glory: *Jesus said to them, "The time has come for the Son of Man to receive his glory. It is a fact that a grain of wheat must fall to the ground and die before it can grow and produce much more wheat. If it never dies, it will never be more than a single seed.*

John 19:38-42

38 Later, a man named Joseph from Arimathea asked Pilate for the body of Jesus. (Joseph was a follower of Jesus, but he did not tell anyone, because he was afraid of the Jewish leaders.) Pilate said Joseph could take Jesus' body, so he came and took it away.

39 Nicodemus went with Joseph. He was the man who had come to Jesus before and talked to him at night. He brought about 100 pounds^e *of spices—a mixture of myrrh and aloes. 40 These two men took Jesus' body and wrapped it in pieces of linen cloth with the spices. (This is how the Jews bury people.) 41 In the place where Jesus was killed on the cross, there was a garden. In the garden there was a new tomb. No one had ever been buried there before. 42 The men put Jesus in that tomb because it was near, and the Jews were preparing to start their Sabbath day.*

Cemeteries—Annette and I have been married to other spouses who died way too young. Those precious people are buried in the same cemetery. Each Easter, we and other family members, go to that cemetery to read about resurrection. Annette's daughter, Andrea, blows the kudu horn that Annette bought me several years back for these occasions. The sound of the horn is a reminder to death that it doesn't get the final word. All present then yell, "Christ Is Risen! He Is Risen Indeed!"

I have thought, several times, as I visit that cemetery, how many tears have been shed to water that ground. Christians believe that this Man, who was buried on Friday conquered death and the grave, not only for Himself but also for all who believe. There will be a day when cemeteries will no longer be needed, and tears will cease to flow.

Joseph of Arimathea—We don't know a lot about Joseph of Arimathea. We do know from the gospel of Matthew that he was rich and that Joseph placed the body of Jesus in his own tomb. Mark's gospel tells us in 15:43: *...he was brave enough to go to Pilate and ask for Jesus' body. Joseph was an important member of the high council. He was one of the people who wanted God's kingdom to come.*

And from the gospel of Luke, 23:51, this is also said of Joseph: *But he did not agree when the other Jewish leaders decided to kill Jesus.*

John adds this in verse 39 above. *Nicodemus went with Joseph.* Remember him coming by night to talk to Jesus in the third chapter of John?

These men had been secret disciples until now. They had been afraid of their fellow council members until now. But now they made the decision to take the body of Jesus, wrap it with linen and spices according to tradition, and bury Him in a new tomb. They also showed their love by touching the body before the special Sabbath, for now, they were ceremonially unclean, according to their law, and could not partake of the Passover with their family.

Matthew's gospel adds one important detail. The Jewish leaders asked Pilate for a guard at the tomb because they feared Jesus' disciples would steal the body and claim He had been resurrected. A guard was posted and the tomb was sealed. **And then came SUNDAY!**

John 20:1-9

1 Early on Sunday morning, while it was still dark, Mary Magdalene went to the tomb. She saw that the large stone was moved away from the entrance. 2 So she ran to Simon Peter and the other follower (the one Jesus loved very much). She said, "They have taken the Lord out of the tomb, and we don't know where they put him."

3 So Peter and the other follower started going to the tomb. 4 They were both running, but the other follower ran faster than Peter and reached the tomb first. 5 He bent down and looked in. He saw the pieces of linen cloth lying there, but he did not go in.

6 Then Simon Peter finally reached the tomb and went in. He saw the pieces of linen lying there. 7 He also saw the cloth that had been around Jesus' head. It was folded up and laid in a different place from the pieces of linen. 8 Then the other follower went in—the one who had reached the tomb first. He saw what had happened and believed. 9 (These followers did not yet understand from the Scriptures that Jesus must rise from death.)

Grandkids Go to a Play—"The Thorn," a play about the life of the Messiah, was planned to be performed at The Hills Church of Christ in Ft. Worth, close to Easter, five years in a row. What makes this play unique is that there is a mixture of professional and nonprofessional actors who play the parts. Church members get to play the non-speaking parts but get to dress in the costumes of the time period along with the regular actors. One year my stepson, Paul, got to play a Roman soldier. His wife, Feydra, played one of the many town's people. Grandson Fisher played the twelve-year-old Jesus, his younger brother London played one of the many children, and granddaughter Avyn played a little girl in a dancing circle around Jesus who was welcomed by Jesus.

In the final year that the play was performed, that family of five, watched from the audience along with all their aunts, uncles, cousins, and grandparents. Avyn was so excited for her six cousins to finally get to see the play that she sat explaining every move the actors were making. She talked about the parts her family had played and even sang some of the songs along with the cast. Avyn so excited her cousins that they sat enthralled through the long production.

Avyn would have been good at playing Mary Magdalene had she been a little older. Better yet, I can see Mary with Avyn's charismatic and spontaneous personality, taking charge and going to tell Peter and the other men who still were in hiding, "Peter, John, go find out what has happened to the body of the Lord."

There are several Marys in the New Testament. Of course, Mary the mother of Jesus is one. But several others show up from time to time: Mary, the mother of James and Joseph; Mary, the sister of Martha and Lazarus; Mary, the wife of Cleopas; Mary, the mother of John Mark; and Mary Magdalene.

Who is Mary Magdalene? —There have been several fables told about this Mary. One of the main stories is that Mary Magdalene was a prostitute but there is no indication of that in scripture. Let's see what the New Testament says that we know is true. First,

Magdalene is not Mary's last name. She was probably from the town of Magdala on the coast of the Sea of Galilee. According to Luke 16:1-3, Mary Magdalene had seven demons cast out by Jesus. In the same verses, we find that she, along with some other women, helped support Jesus and His disciples during their missionary journeys. According to John 19:25, Mary was at the cross when Jesus died and saw the tomb where His body was laid. John 20:1-2 tells us that she was the first to the tomb after the resurrection, notices there is no body, and goes to tell Peter. Finally, and most importantly, John tells us in 20:11-18, that Mary Magdalene is the very first person to witness the resurrected Messiah and the first to announce she has seen the resurrected Lord.

John 20:10-18

10 Then the followers went back home. 11 But Mary stood outside the tomb, crying. While she was crying, she bent down and looked inside the tomb. 12 She saw two angels dressed in white sitting where Jesus' body had been. One was sitting where the head had been; the other was sitting where the feet had been.

13 The angels asked Mary, "Woman, why are you crying?"

Mary answered, "They took away the body of my Lord, and I don't know where they put him." 14 When Mary said this, she turned around and saw Jesus standing there. But she did not know that it was Jesus.

15 He asked her, "Woman, why are you crying? Who are you looking for?"

She thought he was the man in charge of the garden. So she said to him, "Did you take him away, sir? Tell me where you put him. I will go and get him."

[16] *Jesus said to her, "Mary."*

She turned toward him and said in Aramaic, "Rabboni," which means "Teacher."

[17] *Jesus said to her, "You don't need to hold on to me! I have not yet gone back up to the Father. But go to my followers and tell them this: 'I am going back to my Father and your Father. I am going back to my God and your God.'"*

[18] *Mary Magdalene went to the followers and told them, "I saw the Lord!" And she told them what he had said to her.*

Another Strong Female in Our Family—"I want to be baptized," nine-year-old Kendyl shared with her mom and dad. They decided to talk to her about what baptism meant, and what she felt about Jesus being her Lord and Savior. Together, they decided to wait for the Saturday before Easter, while they and their cousins were visiting Papa and Nana for their special Planting Saturday. On that day Kendyl, her brother, and cousins would help plant Papa's garden, as they did during that time every year. They would then go to a small pool of water on the campus of Abilene Christian University and I, her Papa, would get to baptize her.

Ethan, her twelve-year-old brother said, "Hey, I think I want to be baptized too."

"Let's discuss that with your Papa," answered Jeremy, his father.

"I don't see a problem with it," I said. "There were 3000 baptized on Pentecost. I'm sure some were being baptized because friends and family were. Cornelius' whole household was baptized at the same time. I don't think every family member of Cornelius' household had the same maturity of understanding." And so, Kendyl and Ethan were baptized on that day before Easter Sunday, Ethan by his mother, Holly, and Kendyl by me. Their cousin Ella decided afterward to follow suit and she was baptized by her mom, Karyn.

Several years earlier, the same type of situation came up with another set of grandchildren. Avyn, the youngest of three children and the only girl decided she wanted to be baptized. Mother's Day was coming up and she thought the day would be extra special if she also received her Lord and was baptized. Her brothers, Fisher and London, chose to follow their baby sister and receive Jesus, also, on that special day.

Women, and especially young girls, most of the time are not given the credit they deserve. In many countries in the world, females are thought of as second-class people. Even in our nation, women's right to vote came slightly over a hundred years ago. But here are two girls, my granddaughters, each the youngest in their family, who led their older brothers to acknowledge Jesus as Lord and Savior. Praise God for women!

Mary Is First to Witness the Resurrection—Jesus' first appearance was not to one of His apostles, as you might expect, or even to a man. His first appearance is to a woman. Mary had been a faithful disciple for a long time and when she mistook Him for someone else, He spoke her name. *"Mary."*

There is something about saying someone's name when you have been away that makes the person feel good all over. Don't all of us want to hear our names as we enter heaven?

Have you ever gone from deep grief to overwhelming joy in an instant? Someone you thought wouldn't be at a particular event, is suddenly there. That is what happened to Mary. Jesus said her name, and suddenly, everything in her world was right.

Jesus says to her in verse 17: *"You don't need to hold on to me!"* Or as one version states *"Quit clinging to me!"* Isn't that a strange thing to say? And yet it makes me think that Jesus was telling her, "Mary, don't just keep me for yourself. You have great news to tell. Go tell all my friends. Go tell my other disciples. Go tell the world. **I HAVE RISEN!"**

John 20:19-23

19 The day was Sunday, and that same evening the followers were together. They had the doors locked because they were afraid of the Jewish leaders. Suddenly, Jesus was standing there among them. He said, "Peace be with you!" 20 As soon as he said this, he showed them his hands and his side. When the followers saw the Lord, they were very happy.

21 Then Jesus said again, "Peace be with you. It was the Father who sent me, and I am now sending you in the same way." 22 Then he breathed on them and said, "Receive the Holy Spirit. 23 If you forgive the sins of anyone, their sins are forgiven. If there is anyone whose sins you don't forgive, their sins are not forgiven."

Blessing Our Unborn Children—Each of my four children is unique in many ways, but there is one thing they have in common. When each child was still in their mother's womb, I would put my hand on my wife's belly and pray, giving each a blessing from me. My wife and I would then try to pick out a name for each child that would be a blessing to that child. One example is that of my daughter. Because we almost lost her, she was named Joanna, meaning "God's precious gift" or "God's gracious gift." After each child was born, my wife and I would give them the name we had chosen, and a promise. We would place our hands on them and pray a blessing, dedicating each one to the Lord. They didn't receive their promised name on paper, making it official, until they were born, but they each received the promised name in their mother's womb.

Receive the Holy Spirit—Jesus had promised the apostles that they would receive the Holy Spirit. Later, in the book of Acts Jesus tells His disciples to stay in Jerusalem until the Holy Spirit comes. Those last statements of Jesus are challenging to understand. Since the baptism of the Holy Spirit on the church did not happen until Pentecost, what did Jesus mean here in verse 22, when He said, *"Receive the Holy Spirit"?* Remember, also, Jesus had told the disciples earlier in John 16:7: *"Let me assure you, it is better for you that I go away. I say this because when I go away I will send the Helper* (The Holy Spirit) *to you. But if I did not go, the Helper would not come."*

Another statement that may be difficult also in verse 22 is: *"If you forgive the sins of anyone, their sins are forgiven. If there is anyone whose sins you don't forgive, their sins are not forgiven."* What did Jesus mean? Maybe Jesus is giving these apostles an understanding of people's hearts as they preach the gospel. In Acts, chapter 5, two believers named Ananias and Sapphira lied to Peter about a gift they had brought to God. Peter told them they had actually lied to the Holy Spirit, and each of them died on the spot.

In Acts chapter 8, Peter is asked by Simon the Sorcerer if he can buy the ability to give the Holy Spirit to others by laying on of his hands. Peter tells him, *"You and your money should both be destroyed because you thought you could buy God's gift with money."*

In Acts chapter 9, Paul is accosted by a Jewish sorcerer named Elymas as he is trying to convert a proconsul name, Sergius Paulus. Paul, filled with the Holy Spirit called him a *"child of the devil"* and struck him blind.

In Matthew, there are two instances when Jesus tells the twelve (Matthew 16:19 and 18:18): *"I will give you the keys to God's* kingdom. When you speak judgment here on earth, that judgment will be God's judgment. When you promise forgiveness here on earth, that forgiveness will be God's forgiveness."

Could this be the same thing Jesus is saying in John when Jesus breathes on His apostles? He is commissioning them in a new area of responsibility.

Let me give you one final scripture. In Matthew 19: 28 Jesus says: *"When the time of the new world comes, the Son of Man will sit on his great and glorious throne. And I can promise that you who followed me will sit on twelve thrones, and you will judge the twelve tribes of Israel."*

John 20:24-29

[24] *Thomas (called Didymus) was one of the twelve, but he was not with the other followers when Jesus came.* [25] *They told him, "We saw the Lord." Thomas said, "That's hard to believe. I will have to see the nail holes in his hands, put my finger where the nails were, and put my hand into his side. Only then will I believe it."*

[26] *A week later the followers were in the house again, and Thomas was with them. The doors were locked, but Jesus came and stood among them. He said, "Peace be with you!"* [27] *Then he said to Thomas, "Put your finger here. Look at my hands. Put your hand here in my side. Stop doubting and believe."*

[28] *Thomas said to Jesus, "My Lord and my God!"*

[29] *Jesus said to him, "You believe because you see me. Great blessings belong to the people who believe without seeing me!"*

Doubting Dipper Doodle—When my two youngest boys were growing up, we owned a little dog, a poodle, named by my youngest son, Jonathan. Her name was Dipper Doodle, to the irritation of his older brother, Matt. For the first four years of her life, she had a ritual every morning. I would open the door to her kennel, which was by our bed, where she slept. She would run to our back door, which I would open for her, and she would go outside to poop and pee. I would leave her out just long enough to take a quick shower. I would then, open the door, and she would run into the house, scamper to the bedroom, jump up on the bed and plop herself amongst the covers beside my wife, who would reach over, still half asleep, and rub Dipper Doodle's head.

Once, I discovered a hole in our wooden fence just big enough for a small poodle, and I thought, "I need to fix that fence before Dipper gets out." But being a man, I put the job off until I forgot all about it.

One morning, the dog and I went through the first part of our ritual as usual with one exception. She found the hole in the fence and squeezed through. She also found that she couldn't squeeze back through to come back into the yard. I called and called her, to no avail. Then I remembered my neglected patchwork and ran to open the back gate. There sat Dipper Doodle, hunched up, tail between her legs, quivering from the cold temperatures and fright. The dogs, from all over the neighborhood, were barking at her, and she knew it was at her, which was scaring her to death. She was used to having a six-foot fence between her and the scary world while she chased away garbage trucks, stray dogs, or an occasional person who happened to be going down the alley.

Dipper Doodle scooted inside the house as fast as she could to reclaim her throne in the covers of our bed. All was well again in her world. Now, I guess you would call my dog Doubting Dipper Doodle because she had to see for herself what was outside the fence and probably thought that I had forgotten all about her. But when I, her master, opened the gate and she saw my face, she ran to me, knowing she was safe.

Doubting Thomas—Forever, because of this incident, Thomas gets the nickname "Doubting Thomas." And yet there is a part of me that also likes proof of those things I have never witnessed. I, too, wonder at times if I can really trust the Master to be there for me, especially when He isn't answering me.

In verse 29, Jesus does tell those who haven't seen and yet have believed that they have *"Great blessings."* I also wonder if Jesus will have the marks of crucifixion that He showed to Thomas, throughout eternity, for us to see the evidence of His everlasting love?"

To give Thomas credit for something, he did make one of the most telling remarks about the divinity of Jesus Christ. ***"Thomas said to Jesus, 'My Lord and my God!"*** I speculate he said it with awe but also a sigh of relief. He was glad he had been wrong. He was secure again, seeing his Master's face and knowing all is really right in his world.

John 20:30-31

The Purpose of the Gospel of John

30 Jesus did many other miraculous signs that his followers saw, which are not written in this book. 31 But these are written so that you can believe that Jesus is the Messiah, the Son of God. Then, by believing, you can have life through his name.

Shake the Trees—When my middle son, Matt, was still at home, he had an experience during a Wednesday night Bible class that none of us will forget. He got into our car, with an excited look on his face. He explained that his eighth-grade Bible class had taken a field trip to a park just outside of town. He wanted us to go back out there now with him, "to see," he said, "a beautiful sight."

His older sister, Joanna, and younger brother, Jonathan, had just gotten in the car. Matt's mom, always wanting to encourage anything spiritual in our children, looked at me and said, "Let's go see what this is all about."

We drove outside of town to the small park, stopped the car, and the four of us followed Matt as he walked ahead excitedly yelling back, "Hurry, before it gets dark." And we hurried.

He took us to a bunch of trees and said, "What do you see?"

I answered, "A whole bunch of trees."

He laughed and yelled, "Watch this!" He proceeded to shake the trees, and thousands upon thousands of Monarch Butterflies flew off the trees flying this way and that. It was one of the most beautiful sights I had ever seen. All of us began shaking trees with, "Ohs and ahs," until darkness forced us back to our car.

Now, some twenty-five years later, I plant Greg's Mist Flower, a delicate purple flower that spreads and will fill any area you plant it. The Monarchs are attracted to this flower and every year around mid-September, the butterflies come and find their nectar. This year has been a particularly warm fall, and here in mid-November we still haven't had a freeze, allowing the Monarchs to stay for a longer period. There are probably fifty or more of these orange and black insects in the two areas of our yard where the flowers grow.

We found out that Monarchs actually migrate down several corridors to a certain spot in central Mexico, and the central part of Texas, where we live, is one of those corridors.

They begin as an egg, laid by a female Monarch, on the stem of a milkweed plant. (We planted some of those too.) They hatch to become a pretty multicolored caterpillar that spends its time around the milkweed eating to its heart's content.

Then a change takes place. The caterpillar climbs to a spot and attaches itself with a little silk, which it spins. A shell forms around the caterpillar and soon becomes hard. Within that transparent chrysalis, a metamorphosis is taking place, changing this earth-bound worm into a beautiful butterfly that will travel thousands of miles from its home.

Now think of the tomb of Jesus. It is only a cocoon or chrysalis in which His earthbound body that felt hunger, thirst, pain, tiredness, loneliness, and sadness lay. A metamorphosis has taken place and now an incorruptible body that is no longer earthbound but free of Earth's gravity and the world's fallen nature is free. Jesus has just been resurrected, never to die again. One day, He, the pioneer, will come back and shake the trees for the rest of us to fly away with Him to the home He has prepared.

Others have been brought back from the dead. Jesus raised several including Lazarus. Even in the Old Testament, there were several cases where people were brought back from the dead. But all of those cases were simply resuscitations. All of those people would eventually die again. But this is resurrection. Jesus conquered death forever. The Apostle Paul said this in 1 Corinthians 15:20: *But Christ really has been raised from death—the first one of all those who will be raised.* Because Jesus was raised, you and I can now be raised. Death no longer has the final say! Death has now been reversed!

Epilogue/ John 21:1-25

The Reinstatement of Simon Peter

The final chapter of John seems like an addendum (P.S., postscript, addition). According to our Preacher Shane, "The gospel of John could have ended very comfortably with: *Jesus did many other miraculous signs that his followers saw, which are not written in this book. But these are written so that you can believe that Jesus is the Messiah, the Son of God. Then, by believing, you can have life through his name.* But the Apostle John doesn't do that. He has to take care of one last thing, something very important—the reinstatement of Simon Peter." (Shane Hughes, 2023)

Peter had denied his Lord three times. Remember the three conversations?

Girl at the Gate — *"Are you also one of the followers of that man?"*

Peter— *"No, I am not!"*

Some People — *"Aren't you one of the followers of that man?"*

Peter— *"No, I am not."*

Bystanders— *"I think I saw you with him in the garden!"*

Peter— *"No, I was not with him!"*

So, let's take a look at this incredible event as this final story unfolds. Maybe you are a believer already in the Messiah Jesus and you have denied your Lord in some grievous way. Perhaps the interactions above could be yours at various points in your life. Possibly you have allowed other things to get in the way of your relationship with the Son of God. If that is true, this final story is for you. Jesus, the Good Shepherd, wants to search for all His lost sheep who seem to be wandering. Listen for His voice. You've heard it before; you recognize it. Listen! Listen! He is calling you back as He did His precious disciple Simon Peter.

John 21:1-3

¹ Later, Jesus appeared again to his followers by Lake Galilee. This is how it happened: ² Some of the followers were together—Simon Peter, Thomas (called Didymus), Nathanael from Cana in Galilee, the two sons of Zebedee, and two other followers. ³ Simon Peter said, "I am going out to fish."

The other followers said, "We will go with you." So all of them went out and got into the boat.

They fished that night but caught nothing.

Fishermen Grandsons—I have always been a so-so fisherman. I enjoy the sport when I'm fishing but I've never been really good at it. Now, having said that I have enjoyed, especially fishing with several of my grandsons. London likes to fish, off by himself. He's not a talker, he's a watcher. He observes how other fishermen are working on their skills and tries to imitate them if they are successful. He leaves his line in the water and waits patiently. He came to fish.

When I take Owen fishing, he's a talker. He is the friendly type who wants to know how many fish you've caught and where you caught them. He likes to pull in his line every five minutes or so, just to see if it's still baited or if there is an accidental fish attached to his hook. When he sees someone pull in a fish from a particular spot, he is ready to cast his hook in that same spot. He loves the action of casting but is not a patient fisherman. He came to talk and to cast his line.

Ethan likes the comradery (being with people) when he fishes. His whole point in going fishing is to have a good time and maybe catch a fish in the meantime. He likes it when there is a whole lot of family doing the same thing. He enjoys the conversation but not necessarily about fishing. He came to be with people. But like the other two, I've mentioned, he is very happy if, at the end of the day, he's caught a fish or two.

Several disciples are together after the resurrection. Peter, always the leader, announces that he is going fishing. The others respond that they will accompany him. This was not a sport like with my grandsons and me, but a job, a way of making a living. I've never sold a fish I've caught, but for these fishermen, I doubt they have ever not fished for food or money. They would have been appalled at "catch and release." They used a large net and worked together, where I and my grandsons use a pole, reel, line, hook, and bait. They fish all night and many times catch nothing. I give up after not getting a bite for an hour or two and go back to the house.

These fishermen are doing what they do best, catching fish. But remember, Jesus had told them three years before they would be doing a different sort of fishing. Matthew 4:19 says this about His earlier encounter with some of these same fishermen: *Jesus said to them, "Come, follow me, and I will make you a different kind of fishermen. You will bring in people, not fish."* He's about to show up again and talk with them over breakfast.

John 21:4-7

⁴ Early the next morning Jesus stood on the shore. But the followers did not know it was Jesus. ⁵ Then he said to them, "Friends, have you caught any fish?"

They answered, "No."

⁶ He said, "Throw your net into the water on the right side of your boat. You will find some fish there." So they did this. They caught so many fish that they could not pull the net back into the boat.

⁷ The follower Jesus loved very much said to Peter, "That man is the Lord!" When Peter heard him say it was the Lord, he wrapped his coat around himself. (He had taken his clothes off to work.) Then he jumped into the water.

My Daily Walk—I walk two miles a day around Abilene Christian University, along a cement track made especially for that purpose. It's usually dark when I walk and even though the university has placed lights along the path, you can't always make out who may be walking the other way, toward you. But you get to know many of the people you meet, not always by name, but by the way they walk or the dog they have leashed beside them. One man has a dog that kind of jumps or hops as it walks beside its master as if it has a limp. Most people have a certain gait in their walk that makes you able to identify them way before you can see their faces. My wife, one morning, accused me of walking like an old man. I retorted, "I am an old man!"

The Apostle John, the writer of this gospel, never mentions his own name, not even once. Here he uses the identifier in verse 7: *The follower Jesus loved very much...* How does John recognize Jesus? Something very similar happened much earlier when some of these disciples met Jesus. In Luke 5:1-7 the story goes:

> As Jesus stood beside Lake Galilee, a crowd of people pushed to get closer to him and to hear the teachings of God. Jesus saw two boats at the shore of the lake. The fishermen were washing their nets. Jesus got into the boat that belonged to Simon. He asked Simon to

push off a little from the shore. Then he sat down in the boat and taught the people on the shore.

When Jesus finished speaking, he said to Simon, "Take the boat into the deep water. If all of you will put your nets into the water, you will catch some fish."

Simon answered, "Master, we worked hard all night trying to catch fish and caught nothing. But you say I should put the nets into the water, so I will." The fishermen put their nets into the water. Their nets were filled with so many fish that they began to break. They called to their friends in the other boat to come and help them. The friends came, and both boats were filled so full of fish that they were almost sinking.

John remembered the incident and sudden recognition dawns on him and he yells to all present, *"That man is the Lord!"*

Have you ever done an unkind or downright stupid something to someone you loved and weren't quite sure how to broach the subject and get back in their good graces? I have been that person, several times, especially with my wife. I tend to intentionally go be around her without saying anything, at first. I want to kind of test the waters, so to speak, to look at her face, to get a sense if she is in a forgiving mood. I want to say, "Sorry," but I'm not sure where the conversation will go. Now, please don't get me wrong. I'm not saying that's the best way to ask forgiveness but sometimes it's my way.

Notice Simon Peter. He's not being lazy, jumping in the water and leaving his friend to row ashore with all those fish. He's excited. It's

Jesus on the shore. He wants to go and be close by. Maybe he can finally tell Jesus how sorry he is.

John 21:8-10

8 The other followers went to shore in the boat. They pulled the net full of fish. They were not very far from shore, only about 100 yards. 9 When they stepped out of the boat and onto the shore, they saw a fire of hot coals. There were fish on the fire and some bread there too. 10 Then Jesus said, "Bring some of the fish that you caught."

Frying Bacon and Brewing Coffee—Two things I love to smell in the morning, bacon frying and coffee brewing. They bring back lots of memories of my childhood, raising my own children, drinking coffee with my grown daughter, Joanna, and more recently, times with grandkids. Annette and I love our morning coffee. Early on, our grandchildren, also, learned to drink coffee because of our early morning routine. Nana even bought each grandchild, with their help, a cup that would be only theirs. Their coffee was more milk and sugar than coffee, but they were satisfied. We began putting green food coloring in their coffee, at some point, calling it alligator milk. We later had to use other colors, as well, and came up with flamingo milk (pink), whale milk (blue), and bumblebee milk (yellow).

I have, for most of my adult life, been an early riser. My oldest grandson, Fisher, also loves to get up early and he has always been a talker. So, when he came visiting, we would be up an hour before anyone else, eating bacon, drinking coffee, and talking. I mostly listened and he mostly talked so it made for a good arrangement. Our conversations were of a wide variety, mostly about school friends, sometimes about the Bible. I loved the way he explained things and how he would exaggerate his exploits. He would make me laugh out loud much of the time. He had, and still has, one of those personalities that makes you laugh even when he's not trying to be funny. He is very literal and you, much of the time, have to explain a joke or sarcasm. He is like me, in that he wakes up happy and raring to go. I always look forward to my mornings with Fisher.

Annette, on the other hand, remembers her coffee times with our second grandson, Fisher's younger brother, London. He and Annette, London's Nana, are late sleepers. They get up gradually, not talking, first thing until they have had time to get the fog of sleep out of their brains.

We have a treehouse right outside of our backyard French windows that has a bottom story for the granddaughters and a top story, with an open top, for the grandsons. London would drag the kids' table and chairs to the top floor. He and his Nana would then climb the ladder—a funny sight—to that open-aired cafe, coffee in hand, carefully, so as not to spill any, and sit in those tiny kid chairs—a funnier sight. There they would drink their coffee and talk about Nana and grandson stuff.

Breakfast with Friends—I know the disciples and Jesus didn't eat bacon for breakfast and I doubt they drank coffee, but I bet that fish smelled good cooking over that open fire. Jesus, though, didn't provide everything—I'm sure He could have—but asked the men to bring their contribution to the breakfast in verse 10 with: *"Bring some of the fish that you caught."*

I can't help but wonder what interaction Jesus and Peter had when Peter steps onto shore and runs to the fire. I'll bet it was awkward on Peter's part. Peter had seen Jesus two times before this story, according to the timeline of the other gospel accounts and verse 14, below. But had they gotten to be alone? Had Peter wanted to raise the subject before but couldn't because the others were around? Had he wanted to tell his Lord how sorry he was but it was never the right moment? All of this is supposition on my part, but I have lived long enough to know human nature—my nature.

John 21:11-14

11 Simon Peter got into the boat and pulled the net to the shore. It was full of big fish—153 of them! But even with that many fish, the net did not tear. 12 Jesus said to them, "Come and eat." None of the followers would ask him, "Who are you?" They knew he was the Lord. 13 Jesus walked over to get the bread and gave it to them. He also gave them the fish.

14 This was now the third time Jesus appeared to his followers after he was raised from death.

Trying to Begin Making Amends—Sometimes, if I've said that unkind word to my wife and she goes to the store before we makeup, I am listening for the car to drive up. In a form of penance, I have run outside offering to carry in all the groceries—my way of beginning the "I'm sorry," conversation. Peter runs back to the boat, and all by himself drags the net full of fish on shore. In fact, he counts them—153. At least, someone did. What was that about?

Bread and Fish—Where have we seen that menu before? Remember John 6, the feeding of the 5000? Jesus fed a whole lot of people. Here, again with the contribution of His disciples, He feeds them breakfast.

The Unforgettable Meal—Thinking about fish, I remember when I was about sixteen my two older brothers and I hiked in some of the Sierra Nevada Mountain Range of California to a small, beautiful lake. We caught some native golden trout (how did they get there) and cooked them almost immediately. I still remember the taste of those fish fried over a campfire, so hot you could barely pinch off a piece and pop it in your mouth. I still remember the aroma of those fish frying in that grease and covered in cornmeal. And I can remember that it was undoubtedly the best meal I've ever had. But more than the meal, I remember the conversation, the kidding, and the laughter between my brothers and me. I can't remember the words so much but I remember the sound of their voices and the love we felt for each other. I remember us sitting on the ground getting the back of our jeans dirty and wiping our greasy hands on our pant legs. I remember the warmth of the sleeping bag and watching the embers of the fire until I fell asleep.

I'm glad John put this incident in his gospel. Here is the humanity of the Messiah; Jesus was eating breakfast with His friends. I'll bet over the years they never forgot that morning. Just think of having God fix your breakfast and then sitting down and eating it with you. I can't wait for heaven! And I hope God allows bacon and coffee.

John 21:15-17

15 When they finished eating, Jesus said to Simon Peter, "Simon, son of John, do you love me more than these other men love me?"

Peter answered, "Yes, Lord, you know that I love you."

Then Jesus said to him, "Take care of my lambs."

16 Again Jesus said to him, "Simon, son of John, do you love me?"

Peter answered, "Yes, Lord, you know that I love you."

Then Jesus said, "Take care of my sheep."

17 A third time Jesus said, "Simon, son of John, do you love me?"

Peter was sad because Jesus asked him three times, "Do you love me?" He said, "Lord, you know everything. You know that I love you!"

Jesus said to him, "Take care of my sheep.

The Conversation—Jesus now pulls Peter aside for "the conversation." It's time for that difficult process of amends making, but not to get back into the love of his Lord. Jesus had just gone through death and resurrection to prove that. And it wasn't for Jesus' sake. He already knew Peter's heart. Jesus did it for Peter's sake because humans need that time to make things right, to <u>feel</u> loved again. It is the conversation Peter both wanted and dreaded.

Do You Love Her More than Me? —My brother Bill had just gotten married. I was thirteen years younger than him and he could see that I was troubled. Bill asked, "Darell, what's wrong?"

"Do you love Eloise more than you do me?" I asked him.

Always wise in his answers, my oldest brother hugged me and replied, "I love her in a different way than I love you. I love you like a brother; I love her like a wife." I was satisfied, but over the years I have always remembered the tender way he dealt with me.

Many people have asked over the years, "Why did Jesus ask Peter three times, 'Do you love me?'" Some think that the reason Jesus asked three times is that Peter denied his Lord three times. That sounds reasonable.

Jesus also told Peter to feed His sheep. Was that because Peter was considered the chief of the apostles and he would take care of the rest after Jesus was gone? Maybe! Was it because he was given the keys to the kingdom of heaven and would open the doors to three groups of sheep—Jews in Acts 2, Samaritans (half-Jews) in Acts 8, and Gentiles in Acts 10? Could be! Whatever the reason, Jesus saw within Peter a man who was a leader, a man who was not afraid to get dirty, and a man who loved his Lord. And Jesus seemed to add to Simon Peter's resumé of fishing for people; he was now a shepherd, also. Whatever Jesus meant, Peter must have understood for in 1 Peter 5:1-4, Peter wrote these words:

286

Now I have something to say to the elders in your group. I am also an elder. I myself have seen Christ's sufferings. And I will share in the glory that will be shown to us. I beg you to take care of the group of people you are responsible for. They are God's flock. Watch over that flock because you want to, not because you are forced to do it. That is how God wants it. Do it because you are happy to serve, not because you want money. Don't be like a ruler over those you are responsible for. But be good examples to them. Then when Christ the Ruling Shepherd comes, you will get a crown—one that will be glorious and never lose its beauty.

John 21:18-24

18 *The truth is, when you were young, you tied your own belt and went where you wanted. But when you are old, you will put out your hands, and someone else will tie your belt. They will lead you where you don't want to go." **19** (Jesus said this to show how Peter would die to give glory to God.) Then he said to Peter, "Follow me!"*

20 *Peter turned and saw the follower Jesus loved very much walking behind them. (This was the follower who had leaned against Jesus at the supper and said, "Lord, who is it that will hand you over?") **21** When Peter saw him behind them, he asked Jesus, "Lord, what about him?"*

22 *Jesus answered, "Maybe I want him to live until I come. That should not matter to you. You follow me!"*

23 *So a story spread among the followers of Jesus. They were saying that this follower would not die. But Jesus did not say he would not die. He only said, "Maybe I want him to live until I come. That should not matter to you."*

24 That follower is the one who is telling these things. He is the one who has now written them all down. We know that what he says is true.

This Is How You Are Going to Die—If you could know how and when you were going to die, would you want to know? I guess you could do a lot of planning and making amends. I guess I wouldn't mind, so much, if like some of the patriarchs in the Old Testament, I would be told I would die as a very old man, with my children and grandchildren around my bed, singing, as I comfortably slip into the next world. Jesus is telling Peter, here in verses 18-19, that he will die for him, and in a way, Peter wouldn't choose nor want. History tells us that Peter was crucified under Emperor Nero, "upside down," because he didn't feel worthy to die like his Lord.

Mind Your Own Business—Sometimes it's hard for me to mind my own business. Is it because I'm just curious or do I sometimes want to know some juicy gossip? Maybe I want to know what someone else is getting to do that I'm not. Then there are other times I feel it should be my business.

My first wife, Carolyn died of adrenal cancer when she was twenty-eight. I was left to raise a son and an infant daughter. Maryanne and I married three and a half years later, and she helped me raise our two oldest along with two of our own. We discovered in 1999 that Maryanne had ovarian cancer. She was given two years to live. She prayed for eight more so she could raise our youngest two boys. She was given five and a half. We lost the battle on March 12, 2005. Maryanne, surrounded by her four children and me, went to meet her Lord. Don't get me wrong, I'm grateful for the extra three years I had with my wife. But there are times I can't help asking the Lord, "Why?"

Peter turns around and gets into John's business by saying in verses 21-22: *"Lord, what about him?"* And Jesus has to rebuke him again, *"Maybe I want him to live until I come. That should not matter to you. You follow me!"*

I then realize Jesus didn't let my children or me in on the tomorrows of Carolyn, Maryanne, or even of my present wife, Annette. He gives me only this day. But He does promise what He says in Matthew 28:20: *"You can be sure that I will be with you always. I will continue with you until the end of time."* And so, I try very hard to mind my own business.

John 21:25

Enough Said!

[25] *There are many other things that Jesus did. If every one of them were written down, I think the whole world would not be big enough for all the books that would be written.*

Some Final Words from the Author

My Older Brother, Bob—My middle brother, Bob, has always been my rescuer and the one I wanted to emulate and follow. When I was just a toddler, learning to walk, we went fishing as a family. Bob was already at the lake casting in a line when he heard small feet running in his direction. I was running, but not to him; I was running past him toward the water. And I didn't stop at the shore but proceeded to run into the lake. Bob, quickly dropped his pole and ran into that very cold Sierra Nevada Mountain lake water, to rescue me.

Being ten years older than me, I expected a lot out of my older brother. On fishing trips, when I was five and he was fifteen, he seemed to know how to unravel my fishing line when it was tangled in a bush or tree. He also had the wisdom to know when the line had gotten so tangled that the best thing I could do was to "cut bait" and begin again. I think that the last fishing example became a metaphor for how I needed to handle some of life's other challenges.

He taught me simple things like how to change the oil and filters, sparkplugs, and belts in my car. And he helped me navigate becoming independent from my parents without destroying my relationship with them. Once when we were mowing lawns together as a summer job he even gave me advice as I was running past him followed by a swarm of bumblebees. I had disturbed their hive and they were bent on chasing and stinging me, as I was yelling to my brother, "HELP, Help, help," as I ran past. "Get in the car and roll up the windows!" he advised. I did and it worked.

I went to Abilene Christian College because he had ten years earlier. I also followed him in the teaching profession after seeing how much joy teaching brought him. I experienced that same joy in my teaching experience.

Bob baptized me when I was nine, listening to my confession of faith that Jesus was my Lord and Savior. He listened to me, more recently as a much older man, as I confessed a grievous sin that had haunted me much of my life, reminding me of God's amazing grace. He sat with me at the church and cemetery, as I buried my first wife, Carolyn, and was in the room, standing next to me as my second wife, Maryanne slipped into the next world. He cried with me both times.

As many times as Bob had rescued me, his younger brother, and as much as I tried to emulate him, there were many things he could never do or be. He couldn't be the bread that gives me life or the light that shines in the darkness; he couldn't be the gate I needed to go through for safety or the good shepherd that guided my way;

he wouldn't be the one who would raise me from the dead or give me eternal life; he couldn't be the Way, the Truth and the Life that led me to the Father, nor could he be the vine to which my branch was attached.

Oh, Bob was a great brother and a good example for me to follow on my path of life on Earth. But as John the Baptist confessed of himself, only Jesus is the Lamb of God. Only Jesus takes away sins, not only my sins but the sins of the world.

What the apostle John wrote about are accounts of how real people in his gospel reacted to meeting this Messiah Jesus. What I wrote in between John's accounts are stories of how real people 2000 years later also reacted to John's message, his gospel of Jesus the Lamb of God. My prayer for you who have read John's gospel and my narrative is "That You Can Believe," and that John's story of Jesus will impact your life as it has mine.

Acknowledgments

Thanks be, first to God, my Abba, who first breathed into me the breath of life and then His own Spirit; to Jesus, my elder brother, full of grace and truth, who is the Word become flesh and the Lamb of God who takes away the sins of the world; and to the Spirit who has led me all of my life, convicts the world of sin, who inspired John to write this Gospel, and who indwells the children of God.

Thanks to my favorite apostle, John, who wrote my favorite book— the Good News of Messiah Jesus.

Thanks to Dad who taught me a love of Scripture and Mom who taught me to pray.

Thanks to Annette, my wife, confidant, and partner in this world. I love you. Thank you for your constant encouragement and for always thinking out of the box.

Thanks to my children, Jeremy, Joanna (my coffee buddy), Matt, Jonathan, Paul, Karyn, and Andrea; my grandchildren, Josiah, Fisher, Ashlyn, London, Ethan, Avyn, Ella, Creed, Kendyl, and Owen; my brothers, Bill and Bob; and my cousin Barbara for the stories that helped me understand the book of John.

Thanks to family members who didn't get mentioned in this book; especially, Jennifer Poe, Kim Koenig, Laura Carrion, Shelby Martin, Dexter Martin, and Bruce Terry. God knows your stories and how they have impacted my life.

Thanks to Dr. Bruce Terry, who read over my material to make sure my theology is correct. Thanks also for the brilliant idea of using the Easy-to-Read version as the text for John. It's great to have a Greek, Hebrew, and Bible scholar in the family.

Thanks to Paul Gorsline, Mike Cope, Dr. Randy Harris, and Dr. Jeff Childress for the articles they wrote for my book on the Trinity, the

Kingdom of God, and the New Birth. It's great to go to church with preachers of the Gospel of Messiah Jesus and Bible Professors from Abilene Christian University.

Thanks to Susan McCabe and Larry Copeland, who helped in editing my book.

Thanks to my (wife) Annette, Terry St Pierre, Steve McDonald, Tim Wilson, and Larry Copeland for allowing me to use this book in a Thursday night Bible Study to see if it was understandable.

Thanks to my Tuesday morning prayer group—Terry, Larry, Pat, and Bob who prayed for this book as I was writing it. Thanks for your suggestions. And thanks to Bo Whitaker for praying for me and discussing my writing on Monday mornings.

Thanks to Ruth Jackson for the painting of the tree with the grandchildren's palm prints on our living room wall on the front of this book. You were also our Planting Saturday photographer.

Thanks to Freedom Fellowship and FaithWorks who gave me the idea to write to new believers or non-believers who may not come from a Bible background, by using family stories and the Easy-to-Read version of the Bible. Hopefully, these stories and this version of the Bible will help in making this gospel understandable.

Works Cited

Songs

Anonymous. *He Paid a Debt.* Date Unknown

Green, Steve. *Find Us Faithful.* 1988

Leeland. *Way Maker.* 2019

Wade, John Francis. *O Come All Ye Faithful.* 1744

Walker, Anna Louisa. *Work for the Night Is Coming* (poem). 1854

Private E-mail Responses

Childers, Jeff. *What Is Being Born Again?* 2022

Cope, Mike. *What Is the Kingdom of God?* 2022

Gorsline, Paul. *The Trinity in the Life of a Christian.* 2020

Harris Randy. *What Is Being Born Again?* 2022

Sermons

Faulkner, Paul. Marriage Seminar. Date Unknown

Hughes, Shane. From a Sermon at Highland Church of Christ. February 9, 2023

Storment, Jonathan. From a Sermon at Highland Church of Christ. Date Unknown

Books

Lewis, C. S. *Mere Christianity.* New York, NY: Harper Collins publishers. 1952

Lucado, Max. *Jesus—The God Who Knows Your Name.* Thomas Nelson. 2020

Wright, N. T. *John for Everyone.* Louisville, Kentucky: Westminster John Knox Press. 2004

Internet

Wikipedia Article. *Son of Man (Christianity).* No Date

Bible Footnotes

NIV Study Bible Notes. 1995

Easy-to-Read Footnotes. 2004

Bible Study Fellowship Lessons

BSF Lessons on Revelation. 2015

How to Contact the Author

Or Buy More Books

Feel free to contact Darell Martin at:

thatyoucanbelieve@gmail.com.

I welcome questions and comments about the book That You Can Believe.

I was given salvation freely by the grace of God through our Messiah Jesus. Therefore, I will not receive a commission on the books that are sold at any venue. The only charge is whatever cost there is to publish and mail books. The cost per book from the publisher, H V Chapman is $18.68, tax included. I can buy the books directly from the publisher for that price. A separate cost for shipping will be added.